CONTENTS

SOURCES

The following are the main historical sources for Dollar:

The Statistical Account of Scotland. Vol. 15 No. 10   Watson 1792
The New Statistical Account of Scotland. Vol. 8.   Mylne 1841
The Third Statistical Account.   Stirling and Clackmannanshire   1966
Reminiscences of Dollar, Tillicoultry etc. Gibson 1883/1885
Reminiscences of Dollar. Stewart c.1890
Reminiscences of Dollar, Church, and Sunday School. Lawson c.1900
Dollar Past and Present. Lecture by Sheriff John Tait. 1865   (1894)
Annals of the Parish. Ensign Peter Porteus c.1830
Reminiscences of Charlotte, Lady Wake. ed. Lucy Wake 1909
Alicella. (Alice and Ella Christie). Avril Stewart. Murray 1955
Articles and Reminiscences etc. from *The Dollar Magazine.* Various authors
   (Index Dollar Academy Library) 1st edition 1882-1884, 2nd edition 1902-
School Records Dollar Academy. (Catalogued to 1998)
Inscriptions, Dollar Cemetery. (Card Index to 1970 Dollar Academy Library)
A Dollar Chronicle. Early Times to 1800. Baillie 1987 (Dollar Academy Library)
Dollar Academy to 1851. Baillie 1988 (Dollar Academy Library)
Dollar Academy 1851-1918. Baillie. (Dollar Academy Library)
Clackmannan & the Ochils. Swan 1987 R.I.A.S.
Documents, Maps and Photographs held in The Dollar Museum
Statistical Accounts for Clackmannanshire and other Local History Publications
   by Clackmannanshire Library
Records held in the Clackmannanshire Archives, Alloa Library

Udney's Plan of Lower and Upper Mains 1793
Roy's Map of Clackmannanshire 1750
Stobie's Map of Clackmannanshire 1783
Drysdale's Plan of Dollar 1807 (Copy not found)
Clerke and Horne, Plan of Dollar 1836-38 (Copy not found)
Ordnance Survey Maps. Various Scales and Dates 1866-
Estate Maps of Harviestoun 1819-1861

Copies of most of these are available either in the Dollar Museum, the Academy Library, the local library, or the Reference Section at Alloa.

Photographs, unless otherwise stated, are from local collections: Dollar Magazine (DM + year), Dollar Academy Archives (DAA) and Dollar Museum (DMus).

HISTORY OF DOLLAR

BRUCE BAILLIE

Dollar Museum Trust
1998

© Dollar Museum Trust
1998

Cover photograph
© Allan Wright

Other photographs
© Dollar Museum
© Dollar Academy

Published by
Dollar Museum Trust
1 High Street
Dollar
Clackmannanshire
FK14 7AY

ISBN 0 9534542 0 7

Printed by
Burns Harris & Findlay Ltd
Dundee

FOREWORD

This *History* was originally produced in photocopy form for schools and those particularly interested in local history. I am indebted, therefore, to Dollar Museum for undertaking its general publication, in particular to the working committee of Jennifer Campbell, Janet Carolan, Richard Dunning and Hector Soga, without whose expertise publication would not have been possible.

I am also, of course, deeply indebted to all those individuals and publications mentioned in the list of sources, from the *Statistical Accounts* of 1792 by John Watson and 1841 by Andrew Mylne to the reminiscences of William Gibson, George Lawson and John Stewart describing life in the parish in the 19th century. Following these the establishment of a town and gown quarterly, *The Dollar Magazine*, in 1902 allowed such excellent local historians as Andrew Drysdale, Robert Paul and W B R Wilson to record their researches and for many others to reminisce or have their photographs reproduced.

Complementary with these have been documents, registers, photographs and minutes relating to the history of Dollar Academy from 1800 onwards which survived the disastrous 1961 fire by being stored under the roof of the technical hut.

The establishment also, ten years ago, of the Dollar Museum with its policy of staging both permanent and temporary exhibitions has led already to the donation and acquisition of an invaluable collection of maps, articles, photographs, paintings and sundry objects relating to the locality.

All mistakes and opinions are mine. In the case of the former, notification of them and additional information should be given to the Curator of the Museum, as all rights in this work are now the property of that body.

I enjoyed compiling this volume. I hope that some of that enjoyment transfers itself to the reader.

Bruce Baillie
1998

The Trustees of Dollar Museum wish to express their thanks to the Scottish Museums Council for their generous grant towards the publication of this book.

For Beverly

THE OCHILS

"Ochil" is a straight rendering of the Brythonic Gaelic "Uchel", high; hence these are the High Hills, the highest of which is Bencleugh at 2365 ft. Those close to Dollar are Kingseat 2125 ft, Whitewisp 2108 ft, Tarmangie 2116 ft, and the lower fore hills, Craiginnan or Saddle Hill 1712 ft, Dollar or Bank Hill 1128 ft, and Hillfoot Hill 1450 ft. From the southern flanks of the hills small streams flow to join the River Devon in its strath or valley below. Eastward from the Harviestoun or Ellistoun Burn the named ones are: the Whitehornduff and Blackhornduff Burns, running from the prominence named the Duff; the Kestrel or March Burn, forming the parish boundary between Ellistoun and Dollar Hills; the Quarrel or Quarry Burn; the Dollar Burn; and the Kellyburn, forming the boundary with Muckhart.

The largest of these is the Dollar Burn which is formed by the conjunction of two streams. The larger, the Burn of Sorrow, rises in a high moor in the middle of the range, known as the Maddy Moss, and flows southwards between Whitewisp and Kingseat in the valley marked on maps as the Glen of Sorrow although old charters refer to it as Glencairn or Glencarny. This name would appear to be derived from the alternate name given on old maps for Kingseat of "Inner Cairn". The name Outer Cairn is given for the northern flank of the hill and Cairnmorris is the name for another hill at the head of the glen. The cairn on Kingseat is, or was, of considerable size and was possibly a memorial of some form. The smaller stream, the Burn of Care, rises on the side of Whitewisp and flows west through its own little valley to join the larger at the base of the castle

Dollar around 1900 - D Mus

1

rock in the fault known as Dollar Glen where both become the Dollar Burn. Early this century there was an anti-romantic tendency to term them the Bank and Turnpike Burns but the antiquity of the romantic names is vouched for by the traveller Pennant in 1769 referring to the "glens of Care" and the "birns of Sorrow" while Scott speaks of "Dolour" and the "burn of Grieff".

The hills are formed mainly of igneous rock from a volcano that existed in the far distant past to the south-west of Stirling, the nearest vent being Bencleugh from which the lava tended to flow in an easterly direction. This basaltic lava was later broken by further intrusions from below of quartz dolerite, the most obvious example occurring at Gloomhill where the south face formed of this rock was quarried during this century for road metal, the quarry ceasing production in 1947. Almond-shaped craters also formed in the lava from bubbles which were later filled with minerals. One such crater on top of White Wisp proved a particularly rich source of "Ochil Eyes" or agates.

During the ice ages glaciers helped round off the top of the hills and deposited the debris in the form of sands and gravels in the valleys. Such a glacial river formed the ridges or moraines on the Burn of Sorrow and the alluvial fan of gravel which forms the site of the old town of Dollar and the hazards of the golf course. The ice also carried down boulders from elsewhere and dropped them as it melted. One of these, a large boulder of Peterhead granite, was found at Thornbank, and a companion existed at the mouth of Glen Quey for several thousand years until it was discovered by an enthusiastic group of Dollar curlers. The best known of these erratics is the boulder of white quartz, some three feet by two and a half, which lies high on the south flank of Kingseat between the Dollar and Harviestoun Hills known as "The White Stone of Tam Baird". The name has possibly been derived from the Gaelic Tam a Bhaird "the knoll of the enclosure". A large five-sided enclosure – the original purpose of which is not at all clear – does lie on the flank of Dollar Hill but it is a ridge away. Possibly the name refers to the enclosure of the hills themselves. The other curious, and

unexplained, name here is that of the tappietourie on the top of Dollar Hill, rebuilt both after World War II and on the Jubilee of 1977, which is known as The Pirrick. The name may be a local pronunciation of "parrock" again a Scots word for an enclosure – a large rectangular two-sectioned one very visible on air photographs existing by the path to the west at the top of the hill – the name being possibly transferred to the cairn after the use of the enclosure was forgotten. Turf and drystane walls abound on the hills. Of no defensive value these presumably form old estate boundaries, the most noticeable one being that which runs the length of Dollar Hill and which probably formed the boundary between the grazing belonging to the small farms on the Banks and the common grazing land to the north. Easier to decipher are those that lie in the shallow ground between White Wisp and Hillfoot Hill where the sheepfold marks the site of Craiginnan Farm of which the enclosures were the fields. The farm must have functioned originally as an adjunct to the castle and was still in being in the early 1800s, *Gibson* recollecting that in a famine of 1800 the tenants, the Guilds, provided food for callers at the farm door. Part of it is also said to have been the residence of that literary curiosity, mentioned with pride in the *Statistical Accounts* of 1792 and 1841, the shepherd, James Christie, born in 1712, who accrued a valuable library of 370 volumes and whose books were sold off at the north bridge after his death. One of the gable ends at Craiginnan stood until the 1950s and its outline may still be found lying where it fell. The names Bearsden and

Tam Baird's Stone - DM 1905

Bearsknowe – exact locations unknown – are associated with this area. The little cottage of Brewlands, on the brow of the hill, after lying derelict for many years, was rented and restored as an outdoor centre by the local Scout Association. It is now a private house.

The valley here leads into the narrow defile of Glen Quey providing a short cut to Glendevon. In the defile a pool by the fence to the right is known as "The Maiden's Well" and, being spring fed, provides, even in the height of summer, cool refreshment. A story associated with it states that it is haunted by the spirit of a beautiful maiden which only appears at night and, should any male attempt to kiss her, coronary thrombosis immediately occurs. The path here winds round a knoll before proceeding down to the reservoir, constructed in 1910, and thence to Glen Devon. Blanket afforestation on both sides will shortly change the nature of the area as it has on Hillfoot. This knoll is also associated with her ladyship, being known as ... but let Andrew Clerk, Fellow of All Souls, Oxford, and former inhabitant of Lower Mains, relate the story to Professor Ernest Rhys, the folklorist, as young Andrew heard it from the sexton or "bethrel" who had it, in turn, from the bethrel's father:

Glendevon is a parish in the Ochils about five miles from the town of Dollar as you come up from Glen Quaich and down by Gloom Hill. Glen Quaich is a narrowish glen between two grassy hills. At the top of that glen is a round hill of no great height, but of a very neat shape, the grass of which is always short and trim, and the ferns of the shoulder of a very marked green. This hill seems entirely to block the way. It is called "The Maiden Castle". Only when you come quite close to this hill do you recognise the path winding round its foot. A little further on there is a fine spring bordered with flat stones in the middle of a neat turfy spot, which is called "The Maiden's Well". The hill road here described, until the new toll road was made on the south side of the hill over which it passes on the way to Dollar, was the thoroughfare between Dollar and Glendevon.

The following is the story as told by what was known as the "bethrel":

A piper, carrying his pipes, was crossing from Glendevon to Dollar in the grey of the evening. He crossed the Garchil, (a little stream running into the Quaich), and looked at the Maiden Castle and saw only the grey hillside and heard only the wind soughing through the bent. But when he had passed beyond it, he suddenly heard a burst of lively music and turned round to look at what was causing it. And there, instead of the dark knoll which he had seen a few moments before, he beheld a great castle, with lights blaring from the windows, and heard the noise of dancing issuing from the open door. He went back somewhat incautiously to get a closer view, and a procession issuing at the moment from the Castle's open door, he was caught up and taken into a great hall ablaze with lights, while people were dancing on the floor. He was at once asked to pipe to them and was forced to do so, but agreed to do so only for a day or two. At last getting anxious, because he knew his people would be wondering why he had not come back in the morning, as he had promised to do, he asked permission to return home. The fairies seemed to sympathise with his anxiety and promised to let him go if he played a favourite tune of his, which they seemed fond of, to their satisfaction. He played his very best. The dance went fast and furious, and at its close he was greeted with loud applause. On his release he found himself alone in the grey of the evening, beside the dark hillock, and no sound was heard save the purr of the burn and the soughing of the wind through the bent. Instead of completing his journey to Dollar, he walked hastily back to Glendevon in order to relieve his folk's anxiety. He entered his father's house and found no kent face there. On his protesting that he had gone away only a day or two before, and waxing loud in his bewildered talk, a grey old man was aroused from a doze beside the fire, and told how he heard when a boy from his father that a piper had gone away to Dollar on a quiet evening, but had never been seen or heard since, nor any trace of him found. It turned out the piper had been in the "Castle" for a hundred years.

Glen Quey is obviously no place to be on a dark night.

Glen Quey with Maiden Castle on right - DM 1936

The place name "Maiden Castle" is associated with a hillfort on the Lomond Hills, the huge hillfort in Dorset and, in plural form, with the Castra Puellarum of Edinburgh. Alas for such eminent company, no defence works are to be seen on the Glen Quey hill even from the air, nor is there any evident indication of the burial mound to which this form of fairy story is usually appended. Large-scale maps indicate a spot opposite on Hillfoot Hill as Greig's Grave. There would seem to be something ancient here but of what nature it is, at the moment, impossible to say.

The hope of finding a fortune in these hills goes back a long way. The Lord Treasurer's Accounts for 1540 include a payment of £12 4s Scots for "Item. Gevin to Balstart Howsfar, Ducheman, and Richard Wardlaw to pas to campbel to serche the metallis and ore of silver". Their hope was possibly inspired by such reports as that by Robert Seton a few years earlier that "Gold is found at the following places ... at James Crawfords in Muckhart Millen unelto, not far from Culros, three or four miles above Torrieburn." A Colonel Borthwick, in charge of some of the Scottish mines in 1683, noted that

"At Castle Campbell there is a great quantity of sulphur" – he possibly means coal, it being regarded as a rock somehow impregnated with sulphur – and the Rev John Watson noted in 1792: "Silver ore in considerable quantities is likewise said to have been found in the Glen of Care, or rather Cairn, on the west of Castle Campbell, but it did not answer the expense of working it" – a statement which has led to the theory that the burn names, Sorrow and Care, have been transposed but Watson, in fact, is referring to Glencairn and not the burns. "The expense of working it" did, of course, prove luckier at Alva around 1715 when some £50,000 of silver – minus what his workmen stole – was mined in the Silver Glen there for Sir John Erskine in fourteen weeks.

Around Dollar it was the more prosaic minerals which proved most lucrative. The south side of the Ochils forms a geological fault line, the ground having subsided several thousand feet. Small tremors still occasionally occur. The sunken part here has been covered with layers of gravel and coal, sometimes separated by layers of limestone laid down under the sea as the land rose and sank, and these deposits have been exploited for generations. Sandstone has been found and worked on both sides of the valley, principally at the quarries on Sheardale which were reopened in 1818 to provide stone for the building of the Academy. A small quarry existed at the start of the Glen path, and another on the Quarrel Burn from which stone was excavated for possible use in building the Parish Church in 1841. Mylne mentions two quarries in operation at this date. Coal has also been worked for many years. Two main coalfields exist in the parish, both oval and running west to east, one under Dollar itself and the other on the Sheardale Ridge.

The Dollar coalfield is about a mile long and half a mile broad, lying under the town and extending into Middleton and Westerton of Pitgober in Muckhart parish. The earliest mining, by means of simple vertical pits, seems to have taken place along the valley of the Kelly Burn. Later this was extended to horizontal shafts at the dry day level, then deeper into wet levels where the ground water had to be pumped out. This was done, at first, by means of a water-wheel, then by a steam engine, at Kellybank. Mining here, however, had to be abandoned in 1832 after a long legal dispute between Tait of Harviestoun, owner of the coal, and the owner of Westerton of Pitgober, who objected to the polluted water being pumped back into the burn on the farm land, was decided in favour of Westerton. Coal mining, however, continued at Middleton of Pitgober, managed by a Mr Snowdowne for the owner Mr Maxton, into the twentieth century, a pit there being known as "The Klondyke" after the gold rush of 1896. W.K. Holmes recollected not only being taken down it as a boy but also being allowed to work the machinery. A chimney for the pumping engine was a feature there till recent times. Cottages were built at Middleton for the miners and also at a street in Dollar running parallel to Sorley's Brae called Carbo "coal", which was demolished in 1935 and replaced with Council houses. A pit at Kellybank was called "The Appleyard" while the "Stair Pit" lay in the area of The Ness housing scheme, the name presumably indicating the type of pit in which descent and ascent was made by means of a series of ladders and landings, the coal, being carried on the backs of women and children, often weeping with the strain to the surface. *Gibson* states:

> This system of carrying the coals was still in existence at Dollar in my young days, for I recollect well of watching the poor women toiling up the long stairs with their heavy loads. The creels were placed on their backs, and were supported by a belt put round their foreheads, and in this way they laboured up the long stairs of 108 feet (18 fathoms) with their grievous loads of two and three hundredweights.

The usual bag of coal delivered by a coalman weighs around one hundredweight.

The other main coalfield on the Sheardale Ridge was worked in a small way for many years, while another little community appears to have existed down the ridge at Mellochfoot, working a mine owned by the Duke of Argyll. The miners here went on strike in 1766 for better pay in what must have been one of the earliest cases of industrial action in the industry.

All these coal sources have received attention in more recent times. A new Dollar Mine – although actually in Muckhart at Westerton – was in production from 1951 to 1973. Its spoil

Dollar Mine at Westerton of Pitgober - DMus

heap and workings have been so well reclaimed that it is difficult now to believe it existed. A small private mine also operated on the Harviestoun estate in recent years from the quarry in which stone was extracted for the porch and tower of the castle. This closed in 1989, the site still being evident. Opencast techniques are at present ripping the coal out of the coalfield on the Sheardale ridge so laboriously toiled for in past days and at nearby Blairingone, "the field of the smith", a village built for his miners by the Duke of Atholl in days gone by.

Iron ore was mined at Vicar's Bridge, towards the end of the 18th century and after, by the Devon Ironworks, the ore being conveyed to their furnaces on the Devon near Sauchie for smelting. At the same period an attempt was made to bottle the "iron" or chalybeate water, still seen dripping down the rocks there, as "Dollar Mineral Water" though the venture was not a great success. Iron ore was also mined at other places in the vicinity.

Clay was mined and fired in kilns at several places – on the Kellyburn near the main road, on the Sheardale Ridge and, principally, at the clay pits to the west of Lower Mains, filled in in recent years with refuse. The demand for bricks and tiles in the 19th century was prodigious, tiles including not only roofing tiles but the types produced in their millions for inserting as field drains in the gradual improvement of the land.

Lime also seems to have been extracted at Kellyburn, lime kilns and a brickworks, owned by a Mr Penny, existing near the present Drum bridge.

A copper and lead mine was worked sometime around 1800 half way up the Burn of Sorrow in Glencairn (near the Glenfauld burn on the right), the site being easily identified by the barren gravel in the bed of the Sorrow. An elderly lady in the 19th Century remembered it being worked by miners from Devon under the foremanship of a John Robinson, whose daughter, Belle, collected the village post by walking to Alloa daily. The ore was dragged along the side of Kingseat in small horsedrawn sledges and then down the Slunk Road that cuts across the front of Dollar Hill to Dollarbank Farm where it was loaded onto wagons and, apparently,

Copper Mine on the Burn of Sorrow - DM 1916

shipped from Alloa to Holland for smelting. The usual meaning for "slunk" is marsh or a rut in a road but it may be a local word for sledge. The remains of a small house lie near the road, and a small farm at the top of the Golf Course appears to have borne the name of "The Slunk".

The Ochil Hills from the railway line at Tillicoultry showing Castle Craig before it and its hillfort were quarried away - DMus

6

EARLY DOLLAR

The old village of Dollar, lying in the north-west of the present township, like the majority of its neighbouring Hillfoot towns was sited on the cone formed by the debris carried down by one of the streams that flowed off the Ochil range at the end of the ice ages. This ensured proximity to a supply of fresh water for the earliest inhabitants and a relatively dry site above the woods and marshes of the Devon Valley. An added asset in Dollar's case would be the closeness of a good defensive site. These advantages would be later exploited for water power and for the building of a castle, leading in turn to the village providing for the needs of the castle and its garrison. Although not evident today the village also lay on a crossroads, lying as it did on the main road running west to east from Stirling to Fife, coinciding with fords across the Devon to the south and convenient passes for foot and horse travellers through the hills to Strathallan and Glen Devon to the north.

The Devon Valley, like the rest of Lowland Scotland, would have been heavily forested in ancient times; the low-lying parts covered with a thick layer of peat bog. Inhabiting this would be, besides the animals we know, others such as bears, elks, wolves, wild pigs, beavers and, said to be the most dangerous of all, the Caledonian wild bull. Gradually as time passed the woods would be cleared, the dangerous animals destroyed, and such moss as could be cleared removed to get at the fertile soil underneath until by the 17th century the greater part of the Lowlands consisted of bare hills, bare moors, and, in winter, bare fields, there being very few trees.

The derivation of the name "Dollar" has been variously ascribed to the Brythonic Gaelic "dol" (a field) + "ar" (arable, ploughed) or "ard" (high) or, to "doilleir" (sombre or gloomy). It is first referred to in connection with a battle in A.D. 877.

Two of the earliest traces of man known in the near vicinity are the little burial mounds mentioned by the Rev. John Watson in the first *Statistical Account* of 1792. These he placed in the Old Town a quarter-of-a-mile apart, one of them having been opened and two urns with bones removed. The mounds are also mentioned by the Rev. Andrew Mylne in the second *Account* of 1841, one lying in the N.E. corner of the Old Town and the other half-a-mile west bordering the old turnpike road. The latter had also been excavated and more urns with bones removed, the urns from both mounds being at one time in the manse but since lost. Mylne mentions these tumuli as still in existence in 1841, adding to the perplexity expressed by William Gibson in his *Reminiscences* of 1885 on being told, late in life, of a "great pyramid" from which a thousand cartloads of stones were taken as bottoming for the new turnpike road – Bridge Street – in 1806. The field known as Cairn Park must, presumably, have been the site of this cairn or one of the others.

Outwith the actual parish boundary a stone cist or coffin with bones was unearthed in the construction of the west drive to Harviestoun Castle. An urn found therein (donated to the Royal Scottish Museum) has been dated to around 1500 B.C. Further west at the Cunninghar (Rabbit Warren) on the outskirts of

The Harviestoun Urn - DM

Tillicoultry opposite the present church a stone circle existed, the stones – five to six feet in height – being removed last century to cover drains at Tillicoultry House. Some appear to have resurfaced with the building of the housing scheme. Another urn was unearthed there in 1894 during sand quarrying and, at some date, another stone coffin as well, this one having a decorated stone cover which is now in the old graveyard. A hill fort of some considerable size also existed on Castle Craig, the picturesque prominence demolished in the development of Tillicoultry quarry. To the east of Dollar a standing stone still survives on the back road to Cowden, a polished stone axe was found in the grounds of Hillfoot House and a "celt", presumably another axe, at Gloomhill quarry in 1939. A burial urn was also found in a garden at Kellyburn Park in 1958.

Despite the tendency to attribute anything ancient to the Romans, no Roman remains have been found in the parish. Roman sources, however, name the area around the head of the River

Standing Stone – DMus

Forth as Manau Guotodini, the Guotodini or Votadini – their capital was at Traprain in East Lothian – being the main tribe in the area. They also make mention of four stones used as rallying points for the Caledonian tribes, of which the Clach Mannan or Stone of Mannan may be one. This stone, placed on top of a larger one, may be seen in the village to which it gave its name, Mannan either being the name of the Celtic god of the sea, credited not only with an

island but with three legs, or that of a local lesser tribe. Another local tribe may have been the Maetae, commemorated in Myot Hill and Dumyat, the Roman historian, Dio Cassius, mentioning bribes being paid to them and the Caledones in A.D. 197 to persuade them to remain docile. The coin hoard found at Rumbling Bridge may be part of the bribe, the latest coin being dated 184. Mentioned along with the legendary Arthur, a leader from Manau Guotidini, Cunedda, is said to have led his family and followers to Wales at the end of the Roman occupation and to have founded one of the Welsh royal families. It was undoubtedly a wise move for not much later the area must have been less than salubrious with the Irish (under their nom-de-guerre of Scots) hacking their way eastwards, and the Saxons (under their alternate name of Angles) hacking their way northwards as the poor original inhabitants played Pict in the middle. Their peace was further disturbed after A.D. 700 by a religious fanatic named St Servanus (under his alternate name of Serf) creating mayhem with the established religion using the unfair means of working miracles. These included reconstituting a chopped up ram at Airthrey, doing the same for a similarly deconstructed pig at Alva, bestowing an insatiable appetite on some poor soul who had offended him in Tullibody, and, nearer home:

> *In Tulycultry til a wife*
> *Twa sunnys he raisit fra ded to lyf*

Accordingly most of the churches along the Hillfoots are dedicated to him, as well as the island in Loch Leven which bears both his name and a little cell, all that remains of the Culdee monastery, one of the priors of which, Wyntoun, told the story of the saint in his *Orygynale Cronykill of Scotland*.

The Dollar Pict, fortunately or unfortunately, seems to have been spared this particular saint's attentions, possibly because, if the ascription of the parish church is correct, he may already have been converted by St Columba or his followers a hundred years before.

A change of faith did not, however, bring lasting comfort for another disturber of the peace arrived in the form of the Vikings, turning up for a fixture, not with the locals, but the national team around A.D. 877. It is in references to this, the Battle of Dollar, that the name first occurs. The account given in *The Pictish Chronicle* is as follows:

Constantine, Kenneth's son, reigned for sixteen years. In his first year Maelsechlaind, King of the Irish, died and Aid, Neill's son, held the kingdom. And after two years, Olaf, with his Gentiles wasted Pictland and dwelt in it from the kalends of January to the feast of St Patrick. Again in his third year Olaf, drawing a hundred ships (or tribute?) was slain by Constantine. A little afterwards a battle was fought by him in his fourteenth year at Dolair between Danes and Scots, and the Scots were slain and driven to Achcochlam (or Coachcochlam).

Elsewhere in *The Wars of the Irish with the Foreigners* we are told that "that was the occasion when the earth gave way under the men of Scotland and that Constantine was slain then", while *The Annals of Ulster* date the battle to 875 stating that: "At Fifeness there is a cave called Constantine's in which he is said to have been killed by the Danes". *The Chronicle of St Andrews* adds that in his sixteenth year he was killed by the Danes at "Inverdovofacta" and was buried at Iona, while *The Chronicle of Melrose* asserts that: "fighting in battle he fell by the arms of the Danes. The place where the battle was fought was called Nigra Specus (The Black Cave)". Achcochlam is usually identified with Newport in Fife although it may be Cocklaw near Dunfermline. Yet another source dates the battle to 881 and gives the place of death as Merdo Fatha or Werdo (possibly Perth). This battle, previously considered of little account, is beginning to be considered strategically important to the subsequent history of the Scots.

This Constantine was Constantine II, one of the sons of Kenneth Macalpine, King of the Scots, who, in 844, had won ascendancy over the Picts at the Battle of Tullibody, an event for which a successor, David I, apparently founded a church there as well as an abbey at the "bend of Kenneth", Cambuskenneth.

An English sword, dating roughly from the 9th or 10th centuries A.D. and donated by the Academy to the Royal Scottish Museum, was dug up during the construction of the water garden at Harviestoun in 1802 and may be a relic of the Battle of Dollar. A mound to the west of the farmhouse might also merit inspection.

The first mention of a building connected with the church is recorded in 1336 when some English "pirates" stole a newly completed rood screen from the church but consequently suffered

The Harviestoun Sword
(Drawing by Jennifer Campbell)

drowning for their temerity, while the first mention of a castle occurs in a Papal Bull of 1466 in connection with the dinging down of the tower of Castle Gloum by an uncle of Isobel Stewart, wife of Colin Campbell, the Earl of Argyll, in a dispute over the will of her father, Sir John Stewart of Innermeath. The quarrel seems to have been resolved, for the castle was repaired and the name changed in 1490 to Castle Campbell.

The church was further in the news in 1539/40 with the arrest and consequent execution in Edinburgh of its vicar, Thomas Forret or Forrest, on a charge of heresy. Such are the turns of history that a few years later in 1556 the arch-heretic, John Knox, was dispensing the sacrament to the old Earl and his household in the castle and only a few years after that, in 1563, his particular abomination, Mary Queen of Scots, was attending the wedding of the late Earl's daughter.

Details of these events are given in the chapters on the history of the church and castle.

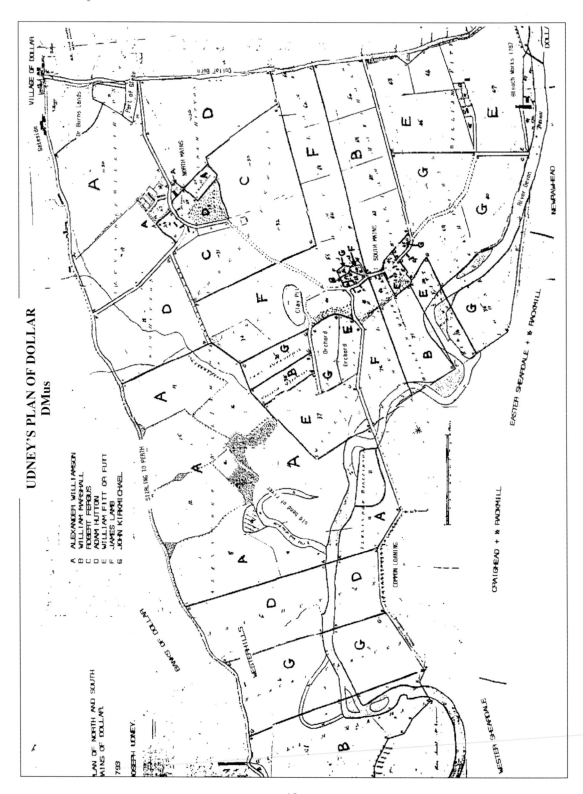

UDNEY'S PLAN OF DOLLAR
DMus

A ALEXANDER WILLIAMSON
B WILLIAM MARSHALL
C ROBERT FERGUS
D ADAM HUTTON
E WILLIAM FITT OR FUTT
F JAMES LAMB
G JOHN KIRKMICHAEL

THE LANDS OF DOLLAR
UDNEY'S PLAN 1793

The plan was drawn before the existence of the present main road, the road shown to the north being the Lower Back Road. The bend at North Mains is that of the present Manor House Road.

The southern boundaries probably represent the course of the river as it was in 1605. Thus Haig's straightening of the river to the west of the Rackmill in 1820 would appear to have diverted it back onto its old course. The old loop shown at Williamson's Haugh is on the site of the skating pond.

Relation between 1605 Feuars and those on Udney's Plan

Taking an 1/8 as being approximately 40 acres, Alexander Williamson would, in 1793, appear to have possessed two 1/8s. How he came by them is not clear, possibly one at least through his wife. Hutton would also seem to have increased his holdings from 1/16. Marshall in 1784 had bought Westerhills, a mansion house and field from a Brown who had it from a Campbell in 1753.

1605 Feuars

							Plus
?	Gavin Merschel	John Jameson	William Hutton	Thomas Drysdaill	John Drysdaill	James Fergus	William Harrower 1/8
	1/8	1/8	1/16	1/8	1/8	1/8	Thomas Kirk 1/16
				½ Orch		½ Orch	John Drysdaill Gregorson 1/16
						Kirkmichael 1766	James Scott 1/16
		Robert Fergus				Tod 1781	John Lambert 1/16
A 89 acres	B 40 acres	C 41 acres	D 47 acres	E 41 acres	F 33 acres	G 31 acres	
Alexander Williamson	William Marshall	John Izat	Adam Hutton	William Futt	James Lamb	John Roebuck	

Owners of Sheardale and Dollarbeg

West Sheardale	Craighead	East Sheardale	Newrawhead	Easter Dollarbeg	Wester Dollarbeg
Argyll	Crown land	Argyll	Crown land	Dunfermline	
W Drysdale 1605 Orr 1861?	Reid Drummond Gray 1690	Burn 1605 Stewart Schaw 1739	Drysdale (part)	R Mason 1456 R Dury 1544 Earl of Dunfermline	
	Schaw L Cathcart	L Cathcart Tait 1800	Erskine Haig 1810	J Scotland Drysdale (Hillfoot) J Gray 1704 Richie 1713 J Scotland 1767 J Tweedie	T Scotland
				D. of Atholl 1784 W Fergus 1792 J Macnab C Tait 1806 Campbell Clark Murray 1843 Dobie 1887 W.T.A.	

In a feudal society land was granted by the sovereign, for payment or services rendered, to his main followers who, in turn, granted it to theirs. The land was sometimes granted free or "carte blanche", possibly with a token payment such as a rose. Large areas were granted to religious houses for their upkeep, sometimes being worked by the monks, sometimes feued out to other large landowners for payment. The ownership of land, even in a tiny parish such as Dollar, could prove extremely complicated after the passage of years. The lands of the parish seem to divide, somewhat arbitrarily, into five main divisions:

1. Those known as "The Kirklands" or "Ten pund land of Dolor".
2. The lands of Over and Nether Mains.
3. The Banks of Dollar Hill, Gateside, and Glencairn.
4. The four quarters of Sheardale and the "milne of Dolarbeg".
5. Easter and Wester Dollarbeg

1. THE KIRKLANDS

These lay between the Dollar and Kelly Burns and included the castle, the village, Mill Green, and the church. They were granted by the king to the Bishop of Dunkeld but the date of granting is not known as no cartulary of charters for Dunkeld has survived. A charter in the charter chest of the chief of the Campbells, the Duke of Argyll, at Inveraray Castle contains, however, reference to three sasines, dated the 9th April 1465, by the deceased Sir John Stewart, second Lord Lorne and Innermeath, granting a third part of the lands of Dollar or Gloum to each of two daughters and the son of a third – the last daughter presumably having died. (A sasine is both the act of giving property and its recording.) These lands were held by him from the Bishop of Dunkeld for the annual feu duty of 16 marks or £10 13s 4d, hence the "ten pund land". The sasines were made out to:

The son of Margaret (or Janet) who had màrried Sir Colin Campbell of Glenorchy.

Isobel who had married Colin Campbell, First Earl of Argyll.

Marion (or Marista) who had married Sir Archibald or Arthur Campbell of Otter.

Thus three Stewart heiresses had, in the course of time, married three of the Campbell clan. Their father left them other lands as well.

Some process of land-swapping then appears to have taken place between the Campbells so that Argyll, on behalf of his wife, took possession of the Dollar lands. He also made an agreement with the girls' uncle, Sir Walter Stewart, that he would help him to gain the title of Lord Innermeath if Sir Walter would relinquish any claim to Lorn and its title. Somewhere during the process, however, Sir Walter took umbrage and, in the words of a Papal Bull to the Dean of Lismore instructing that worthy to resolve the matter, Sir Walter had: "demolished a certain dwelling with a tower of the place of Glowm situate in the territory of Dolar, diocese of Dunkeld". The Dean appears to have brought the parties to agreement for the castle was repaired but at whose cost is not recorded. Sir Walter received his title and Argyll the land he wanted plus the title of Lorn for his eldest son and its ship – usually the sign of a Viking connection – for his coat of arms to quarter with the gyrony or division of eight, supposedly representing the hacked shield of an early Campbell hero. The Papal Bull is the first record of a castle at Dollar. The land here, then, belonged to the Bishop of Dunkeld and was granted by him firstly to the Stewart family, possibly as early as 1361, and then to the Campbells.

In 1491 all Muckhartshire was also granted in feu to this first Earl of Argyll by Archbishop Shevez of St Andrews, probably as a bribe for his support in a dispute about precedence with the Archbishop of Glasgow.

2. THE OVER AND NETHER MAINS

These lands extended west from the Dollar Burn to Tillicoultry parish and probably originally south to the Devon although later sometimes across it, possibly due to its change of course over two hundred years. They included: an area known as the "Westerhills" to the west, lying between the Devon and the Back Road; the Banks of Dollar Hill; and the two farmtouns of Upper and Lower Mains – the term "mains" being applied to farms, the chief duty of which was to provide for the maintenance of the landlord and his family. These appear, with other parts of Dollar, to be included in the grant of "all our land of Dolar, in the fief of Clackmannan" made by King Alexander II to the monks of Dunfermline in 1237. When the Abbey of Dunfermline feued the land to the Argyll family is not known but it was presumably after the Campbells acquired the castle.

Each "farmtoun" contained the dwellings of a number of families who shared the land and, where necessary, would work it together.

In 1561 the Register of Dunfermline recorded the following yearly cash rent in addition to those of Upper and Lower Mains:

Doloure in penny meall be zeire

	li	s	d
The horhart		xxvj	viij
Dolour beig	iij	xiii	iiij
The myllne of Doloure		xxvj	viij
Schirdaill	xiij	vj	viij
The mylne of Dolour beig	iij	vj	viij
The bank in anno	xL		

Summa of penny meall of Doloure with the bank Lxiiij li.

As the Mill Green mill was on Dunkeld lands and the Dollarbeg mill on the Devon is listed, there would appear to have been a third Dollar Mill at this time. Not all these lands were feued to Argyll. The riddle of the peculiar "horhart" is solved in 1563 when Queen Mary confirmed to her Treasurer, Robert Richardson, a charter from her step-brother, James, now installed as the Commendator or lay-Abbot of Dunfermline – a racket by which the gangsters of the Reformation grabbed the former church lands – for the lands of Orchart, Brewland (probably Gateside), 3/4 of Sheardale, Banks of Dollar, and Over Kineddar (the last at Saline).

The Orchard, recorded separately no doubt because of its special importance, lay to the north of the "common loaning" a path part of which still exists leading west from Lower Mains to the Devon. A semicircular field halfway along is still named "Orchard" in early maps long after the trees it contained must have ceased to exist.

Gateside seems, for an unknown reason, to have had a separate little history of its own.

In 1579 Colin, the Earl of Argyll and Dame Agnes Keith, his spouse, were granted or regranted the lands of "Over et Nether Manis de Dolour and Glencarny lying behind the Bank de Dolour on a reddendo (feu) of £36 8s" by Robert, Commendator of Dunfermline. Around the same date he also seems to have been granted "the Bank de Dolour, Oirchaird, half the milne of Dolourbeg, and two quarters of Schyrisdaill plus Ovir Kineddar in Fyff", some of the lands given to Richardson.

The superiority of these "Dunfermline" lands now seems to have been taken over by the Crown for we find James VI bestowing them as his "morning gift" to Queen Anne on their marriage in 1589, and in 1641 Charles I bestowed them in life rent on Charles Seton, the second Earl of Dunfermline, though in practical terms they still belonged to Argyll.

In 1605, probably in need for currency due to the court's move to London, the Earl feued out the Mains and Bank lands to his "kyndly" – related or long resident – tenants, the terms of which are given in detail. Listed in the Mains are: Gavin Merschell, James Fergus, John Drysdaill elder, John Jameson, John Lambert, William Hutton, Thomas Drysdaill, William Harrower, Thomas Kirk, John Drysdaill alias Gregorsoune, James Scott, and on the Banks: Gavin Merschell, Thomas Kirk, Robert Lambert, John Drysdaill Yr, William Lambert, Edward Vannand, John Moreis, and John Cunynghame.

The Upper Mains, Dollar - DM 1912

The details of the feus were:

Notes on charter to his lands held from Dunfermline Abbey granted by the VII Earl of Argyll and his countess to his tenants on 8th November 1605.
From the copy of the vernacular version belonging to Colonel Haig of Dollarfield.
(These lands lie west of the Dollar Burn and across the Devon – part of the lands west of the Rackmill.)

(a) Gavin Merschell, James Fergus, Johne Dryisdaill elder, John Jameson, John Lambert, Wm. Hutton, Thomas Dryisdaill, Wm. Harrower, Thomas Kirk, John Dryisdaill alias Gregoursone, James Scott
Rentallaris & kyndlie & native tennents ilk ane of theme of thair owin pairtis & portions of the Maynes of Dollor, Ovir & Nethir, with ye Orchard of the said Maynis extending in the haill to sextene oxingang of land.

and also

(b) Gavin Merschell, Thomas Kirk, Robert Lambart, Johne Dryisdaill Yr, Wm. Lambart, Edward Vannand, Johne Moreis, Johne Cunynghame
rentallaris, kyndlie tennents & occupyairs ilke ane of thame of thair awin prtis & portiones of the Bankis of Dollor which extend to sext pairt of landis.

(c) John Burne, rentaller & occupr. of ane quartar landis of the landis of Scherisdaill & of the half mylne of Dollorbeg.
Williame Dryisdaill rentaller & portioner of ane uther quartar of the saidis landis of Scherisdaill.

For the above lands plus Glencairne the Earl paid annually £90 17s 4d money of North Britain to the Commendator and convent of Dunfermline, his immediate superiors.

(a) Each tenant in (a) paid for the Mains 4 chalders 8 bolls oatmeal (= 72 bolls), 1 chalder of beir (barley), 8 dozen poultry, carriage of 8 score loads of coal from Sauchie (at furthest) to

the place of Campbell and also £20 gressum every five years (now to be £4 yearly), (gressum was the charge on the granting of or the renewal of the lease of land) and for the Orchard £4, and 10 marks gressum every five years (now to be 2 marks yearly), plus a firlot of pears, or failing these, a firlot of apples if grown.

(1 chalder = 16 bolls = 64 firlots. 1 boll = 6 imperial bushels. 1 bushel = 80 lbs)

(b) The total for (b) was £80 silver maills (rent in cash); 72 poultry; carriage of 120 loads of coal from Sauchie at furthest to the place of Campbell with 20 carriages yearly from Castle Campbell to Striveling or Sauling at furthest plus £40 gressum every five years (now to be £8 yearly)

(c) For each quarter of Sheardale £18 13s 4d, 24 poultry, 40 loads of coal with 10 other carriages, £13 6s 8d gressum each five years (now to be £2 13s 4d yearly).

For the half mill of Dollarbeg £6 13s 4d, 12 poultry, £6 13s 4d gressum each five years (now to be £1 6s 8d yearly)

In order to satisfy the feu duty of £90 17s 4d in cash to be paid to Dunfermline the above gressums were to be paid one-fifth each year. This cash came from:

(a)   £9 6s 8d (half yearly Whitsunday and Martinmas)
(b)   £56 18s 8d silver maills
      £8 0s 0d gressum
(c)   £12 2s 0d silver maills
      £4 0s 0d gressum + 18 poultry

This to be paid direct to the Earl's immediate superiors:

and ilk ane of thame bindis & obligis thame & their foirsaidis to utheris to warrand freith releve & skaithles keep the said nobill Lord his airis & successouris And everie ane of theme to fesith and fra all dammage & lois keip utheris & thair foursaidis anent the yeirlie payment

The tenants to obtain due receipts from the said

superiors or their chamberlains & to be answer-
able for them & show them when required.

and the said Nobill Lord considering the
Statutes & Acts of Parliament maid
condescendit & aggreit upoun be oure
Sovera Lord the Kingis Majestie maist
excellent predecessouris with avyse &
consent of the thre Estates in Parliament be
the qlkis. It is Licentiatet & permittet to all
Bishopis Abbotis Priouris utheris prelatis
Earllis Lordis Barroneis & persones
quhatsumevir for planting of treis for
decoratioun & policie of the Realm, to sett
in feu ferme & heritage thair landis &
heritage to thair native & kyndlie tennentis;
As also the said Nobillis Lordis tennentis
above written ilk ane of thame for their
awin pairt haffing untile advanceit payit &
delyverit to the said Mychtie Lord & Lady
Spouss. All haill the soume of Elleven
thousand & five hundreit merkis money
current within North Britan for outredding
their effairs & honbl advis tending to their
honors weill & comoditie . . . For the quhilk
soume the said Nobill Lord hes gevin
grantit dimittit sett & in few ferme laittit &
perpetually confermit. . . . to the saidis
tennentis their airs quhatsomever &
assignayis the above lands.

(There is no mention of Glencairn although its
feu duty was payable by the feuars of the other
lands.)

For example, Gavin Merschell, the Constable,
had to pay yearly for 1/12 of the mains + 1/3 of
1/12 acquired from Jame Scott = 2 oxingang,
otherwise 1/8 part of the Maynis to:

. . . the said Nobill Lordis airis &
successors their Chalmerlains & factors in
thair name nyne bollis ait meill twa bollis
beir guid & sufficent stuff measour & met
of the Burgh of Sterling yairly betwixt the
feists of yuill & Candilmas with ane
dussine of pultrie and the carrage of twentie
laidis of coillis from the heuche of Saulchie
or ony uther Coilheuch narrest & maistewist

to the place & fortalice of Campbell thairin
to be delyverit yeirly quhen thay salbe
requyrit. And answerand yeirlie to thre heid
Courtis of the Barony of Dollour quhenvir
tho same sal be haldin within the boundis
thairof be the said Lord his successors or
thair deputtis …

Altogether he paid:

> 10s gressum (payable half yearly Whits &
> Marts to Dunfermline duty)
> 9 bolls oatmeal ⎫
> 2 bolls barley ⎬ between Yule
> 12 poultrie ⎭ and Candlemas
> Carriage of 20 loads of coal from Sauchie to
> Castle Campbell
> 3 attendances at the barony court of Dollar
> £5 on entry of every heir
> £5 as herezeld (on death – the best animal or
> composition for)

Although the west of the Glen was part of the
Banks of Dollar, Argyll reserved it with its
timber, giving the tenants in exchange "the Lands
callit Berribank presently possessed & occupied
by them".

***The Road to the Upper Mains with Daniel Macbeth
- DMus***

If the feuars were at any time not called on to cart
their agreed numbers of loads they were not to pay
for this exemption. (The lord paid for the coals.)

Provision was made for the division of land a,
b & c (Orchard excepted) between the respective
feuars. If not satisfied with their division they

could have another division of their mucked land, infield & outfield, with their pertinents (their houses, biggings and plantings excepted) by four discreet persons and two skilled measurers and the marches to be fixed for ever.

Should the burn or the Devon erode and cast and join a feuar's ground to another person's land the former shall "seik crave & follow thair ground & land that sal be tane away" since the water cannot be accounted a permanent march.

Feuars were to remain thirled to the Rack Mill, paying the usual dues, and keeping it in repair or rebuilding elsewhere if destroyed by the Devon floods.

The Lower Mains of Dollar - DM 1912

Summary of Feu Duties by Feuars of the Mains

Land held	Feuar	Meal bolls	Barley	Poultry	Grassum	Orchard maills	Loads Coal	Entry & herezeld
1/8	G Merschell	9	2	12	10s		20	£5 £5
1/8	T Dryisdaill	9	2	12	10s		20	£6 £6
$\frac{1}{2}$ Orch		$\frac{1}{2}$ firlot	App/prs		13/4	£2		
1/8	J Fergus	9	2	12	10s		20	£6 £6
$\frac{1}{2}$ Orch		$\frac{1}{2}$ firlot	App/prs		13/4	£2		
1/8	W Harrower	9	2	12	10s		20	£5 £5
1/8	J Dryisdaill	9	2	12	10s		20	£5 £5
$\frac{3}{4}$ x 1/16	T Kirk	3b1f2p	0b3f	4 $\frac{1}{2}$	3/9		7 $\frac{1}{2}$	£1$^7/_8$ £1$^7/_8$
$\frac{1}{4}$ x 1/16	W Hutton	1 0 2	1	1 $\frac{1}{2}$	1/3		2 $\frac{1}{2}$	12/6 12/6
1/8	J Jameson	9	2	12	10s		20	£5 £5
1/16	J Dryisdaill alias Gregorsoun	4 $\frac{1}{2}$	1	6	5s		10	50s 50s
1/16	J Lambert	4 $\frac{1}{2}$	1	6	5s		10	50s 50s
1/16	J Scott	4 $\frac{1}{2}$	1	6	5s		10	50s 50s
		72	16	96	£5 6s 8d	£4	160	£42 £42

To Dunfermline

The "ferme meal and bear" to be delivered at Castle Campbell or Stirling or the Pow at Alloa or intermediate distance as requested.

The relationship of the heritors shown in Udney's Map of 1793, almost two hundred years later, is not altogether clear but they would seem to be:

Gavin Marshall's 1/8 would be inherited by William Marshall.

William Hutton's 1/8 would be inherited by Adam Hutton.

T. Drysdaill's land was sold or passed down to Futt, Fitt, or Foot of Glensherup.

Jameson's 1/8, including Upper Mains and part in the Westerhills, was bought in 1748 by Robert Fergus, a wright in Dollar, whose daughter, Helen, married John Izatt, a shipmaster in Kincardine, hence the later "Laird" Izatt of Upper Mains. The lintel of a cottage there, where the council houses now stand at the corner of

Thornbank Road, bore the inscription: 17 RF CD 58 for Robert Fergus and Christian Dickie. This 1/8 was later bought by Tait.

J. Fergus sold his 1/8 and 1/2 Orchard to Kirkmichael in 1766 who sold it to Tod in 1781, who sold it to Dr Roebuck of the Devon Iron Company in 1792. Haig bought it in 1798.

(Roebuck is an interesting character. Born in England he took a medical degree then turned his talents to industry rendering the production of the then expensive sulphuric acid easier and cheaper by using lead chambers instead of glass retorts. Coming to Scotland he set up a factory at Prestonpans for this purpose and, later, a pottery there as well. He then helped found the Carron Iron Works and, later, the Devon Iron Works before going bankrupt. He lived at Kinneil House near Bo'ness and employed James Watt in his ventures, Watt stating later that his career would not have prospered without Roebuck's help. Why Roebuck bought land in Dollar is not clear, possibly he was involved with the setting up of the bleach works as the land he bought was by the Devon.)

An 1/8 sold by John Drysdale of Hillfoot to James Lamb in 1771. It included the clayfield, the land around the railway station, the Laird's Took, and Arnsbrae, south of the brickworks. Older residents can still remember Lower Mains being occasionally called "Lambstown".

An 1/8 plus 1/8. Around 1750 apparently inherited by Christian Robertson, the wife of Alexander Williamson of Balgray near Lockerbie. This included the Manor House of Upper Mains. With twice as much acreage Williamson also appears to have bought land from some of the other smaller feuars of 1605. Around 1805 it was sold to Tait of Harviestoun.

A word perhaps about the Drysdales. Although there were members of the family here before 1500 – Drisdales occupied Eliotsdawac and Hervyisdawac in 1480 – some, according to their own account, arrived later:

On the twentieth day of May, one thousand five hundred and three years, we, Thomas, William, and James Douglas, sons of the departed Thomas Douglas of Brushwood Haugh in the parish of Drysdale and shire of Dumfries, left our native place for the reason here assigned, viz. defending our just and lawful rights against our unjust neighbour, Johnstone of Greenstonehill, who, being determined to bring water to his mill through our property, and having obtained leave of his friend, the King, began his operations on Monday 16th May. We prevented him by force. The next day he brought twenty of his vassals to carry on the work. We, with two friends and three servants (eight in all) attacked Johnstone with his twenty, and in the contest fourteen of his men were killed along with their base leader. A report of these proceedings was carried to the King, and we were obliged to fly (the tocsin being sounded). We took shelter under the shadow of the Ochil hills, in a lonely valley on the river Devon. After having lived there full two years, we returned home in disguise, but found all our property in possession of Johnstone's friends, and a great reward offered for our lives. We, having purchased a small spot, called the Haugh of Dollar, and changed our names to the name of our native parish, were clearly in mind to spend the residue of our days under the ope of the Ochils, and wish the name of Drysdale to flourish in the lonely valley. The King passed through this with his court on the 12th of June 1506, going from Stirling to Falkland; dined on Haliday's green (an eastern neighbour); but we were not recognised.

Despite the names of Brushwood Haugh and Greenstonehills no longer being known in Drysdale (or Dryfesdale) in Annan, and the Halliday's not taking possession of Tullibole Castle till a century later (the proprietor in 1506 being Andrew Hering of Glasclune), there seems no reason to doubt the basic truth of the story. The version given here, taken from the Rev. Robert Paul's discussion of the subject in *The Dollar Magazine* for March 1909, had a note appended to it that it was first "copied" by Simon Drysdale in the Haugh of Dollar in 1620 and by subsequent members of the family after that.

3. THE BANKS OF DOLLAR HILL, GATESIDE, AND GLENCAIRN

The Banks of Dollar Hill would seem to be the slopes between the head dyke and the lower Back Road, roughly the territory of the present Dollarbank farm and Golf Course continuing westward to the parish boundary at the March or Kestrel Burn and eastward to Dollar Glen. Divided into sixths, two of these were subdivided so that in 1605 when they were feued out there were eight feuars in all, two of whom Merschell and Kirk were also feuars in the Mains. Some of the dwellings are marked on Stobie's Map. Westbank lay on the Belmont Burn above the dyke; Middlebank is now Dollarbank; Knowehead lay at the Roundel on the golf course with the Slunk in the northwest corner; Eastbank would, presumably lie in the same area; Heughhead lay near the Quarrel Burn; and Whitehillhead is still there. They would also appear to have had grazing rights on Dollar Hill and possibly in Glencairn but the turf wall running along the crest of Dollar Hill may be an attempt to separate the two. In 1801 the Duke of Argyll bought out the feuars to form one large farm, Dollarbank, and then sold the land to the Harviestoun estate. Separate from these at the south-east of the Banks was the little estate of Gateside, dealt with separately in the estates section.

The Burn of Sorrow, Glencairn - DM 1918

Summary of Feus for the Banks of Dollar

		Dunfermline		Argyll					
		Gressum	Silver mailles	Silver mailles	Pou ltry	Loads coal	Other loads	Entry	Herezeld
1/12	G Merschell	13/4	£6 13 4	-	6	10	2	£2 10s	£2 10
1/6	T Kirk	£1 6 8	£10	£3 6 8	12	20	4	£5	£5
1/6	J Dryisdaill	£1 6 8	£10	£3 6 8	12	20	4	£5	£5
1/6	R Lambart	£1 6 8	£10	£3 6 8	12	20	4	£5	£5
1/6	W Lambart	£1 6 8	£10	£3 6 8	12	20	4	£5	£5
1/12	E Vannand	13/4	£3	£3 13 4	6	10	2	£2 10	£2 10
$\frac{2}{3}$ x 1/6	J Moreis	17/9 $\frac{1}{2}$	£5	£3 17 9 $\frac{1}{2}$	8	13 $\frac{1}{2}$	2+	£3 6 8	£3 6 8
$\frac{1}{3}$ x 1/6	J Cunynghame	8/10 $\frac{1}{2}$	£2 5 4	£2 3 6 $\frac{1}{2}$	4	6 $\frac{1}{2}$	1+	£1 13 4	£1 13 4
		£8	£56 18s 8d	£ 23 1 4	72	120	24	£30	£30

4. THE FOUR QUARTERS OF SHEARDALE

Sheardale was divided into four: From east to west – Newrawhead or Loanhead, Easter Sheardale, Craighead, and Wester Sheardale. Only Easter and Wester belonged to Argyll. Although farmed in common each quarter contained its own particular dwelling. These descriptions of them were given by the Rev. Paul around 1900:

Newrawhead or Loanhead was held by Erskine of Aberdona from the Crown and stretched from the Dollarbeg bounds to the Rackmill Burn, and did not, strangely, include the present Loanhead Farm, the dwelling being by a sycamore tree behind the present (1900) cottage. Eastside and Stonehall, however, belonged to William Drysdale in Wester Sheardale, Stonehall lying at a sycamore near the Stey Brae where that steep road straightens above the wood. The quarter was eventually bought by the Haig family in 1810, and later sold to Harviestoun.

Easter Sheardale was held by Argyll from Dunfermline. It included 1/2 of the Rackmill and lay from the Rackmill Burn to the next burn westward, Byles Cleuch. In 1605 it was feued under similar terms to those of the Mains to John Burn. Later the quarter was acquired by Schaw of Sauchie passing to his heir, Lord Cathcart. In 1800 Haig of Dollarfield and Tait of Harviestoun bought the property between them and later divided it, Tait receiving most of the land and Haig the whole of the Rackmill. East Sheardale House was opposite the present Rosehall by two plane trees.

Craighead, which included the other half of the Rackmill, was held of the Crown by the Commendator of Dunfermline who granted charter to a Henry Reid in 1557. It was sold to a Duncan Drummond of Balhaldie in 1662, his son, Alexander, selling it in 1690 to the Rev. John

The Rackmill with its rack or ford - DM 1904

Gray of Dollar who, in turn, sold it to Sir John Schaw of Sauchie, whose heir was Lord Cathcart. The house and block were above East Sheardale quarry. Drummond was actually one of the proscribed Macgregors, whose very name was outlawed, and the son, Alexander, was afterwards recognised as the chief of the Clan. Lord Cathcart eventually sold the land to Harviestoun.

Wester Sheardale, held of Dunfermline by Argyll, was feued in 1605 to William Drysdale and eventually sold to the Duncanson family of Alloa in the nineteenth century. The son-in-law of Dr Duncanson was Andrew Bell, the first

Summary of Feus for Two Quarters of Sheardale and Half Rackmill

		Dunfermline			Argyll				
		Gressum	Addition mails	Poultry	Mails	Loads coal	Other loads	Poultry	Entry
1/4 Shdle	W Dryisdaill	£1 6 8	£4 13 4	6	£4 13 4	20	8	6	£5 £5
1/4 Shdle	J Burne	£1 6 8	£4 13 4	6	£4 13 4	20	8	6	£5 £5
1/2 Rackm	J Burne	£1 6 8	£3 5 4	6	£3 8 0			6	£2 £2
		£4	£12 12 0	18	12 14 8	40	16	18	

Mathematics teacher at the Academy, and it is in the old house here that he worked out the Mathematical Tables. Later this quarter too was acquired by Harviestoun. Its dwelling – recognisable by its skewputts – lies below the brae and has had harling and an extension added. Its ruined carriage block and walled garden still exist alongside.

5. DOLLARBEG

Dollarbeg seems to have been one of the most often purchased properties in Scotland. The chief portion of "little Dollar" belonged to the Abbey of Dunfermline and was, possibly with other Dollar lands, feued by the Abbot to William Mason of Clackmannan in 1456. In 1544 a later Abbot granted Dolorbeg to Robert Dury and Katherine Lundy, his wife. Around 1640 Dollarbeg appears to have been acquired by Thomas Scotland of Glenheid of Gleneigies, one of the covenanting members of the "Drunken Parliament" of 1662, and the property became divided into Easter – the sunny half – and Wester – the shadow half.

Half of Easter Dollarbeg was sold to John Drysdale of Townhead (later the laird of Hillfoot) in 1683, who sold it to the Rev John Gray in 1709, it passing on to James Bruce who had acquired the other half in 1704. His grandson then sold a half to John Kynneir and Alexander Richie, shipmasters in Burntisland, it being conveyed to Capt. John Scotland by trustees and then again by trustees being sold to John and James Tweedie in 1766. From them it was acquired by the Duke of Atholl, the owner of Blairingone, in 1784.

Dollarbeg - DM 1905

Wester Dollarbeg remained longer with the Scotland family. In 1706 the wedding banns of "Thomas Scotland of Wester Dollarbig, who is seventy-two years of age, and Elizabeth Reid, relict of Andrew Drysdal, miller at the Rack Milne" were proclaimed. Two years later the poor relict "was guilty of the sin of Sabbath breaking by having a web dreiying on the trees in her yeard upon the last Sabbath of February in view of all the people yt went to church that way." On the appointed day of her punishment "the minister in name of the session held out to her the danger of prophaning the Sabbath and rebuked her for it, and she seeming to be grieved and promising amendment yt she should never do the like again, was absolved from the scandal". In 1782 Wester Dollarbeg too was purchased by the Duke of Atholl.

The whole estate was then sold in 1792 to Walter Fergus, merchant in Kirkcaldy, then to John Macnab W.S., whose daughter, Anne, sold it in 1806 to Craufurd Tait of Harviestoun. Tait disposed of it to a Lt Col Campbell, who sold it in 1818 to William Clerk W.S., who drew up the rules for Dollar Institution and became Sheriff substitute for the county in 1832. The house was again sold in 1843 to Robert Murray, then of Winterfield House, West Lothian. After Murray's death in 1861 the property was conveyed to his nephew and nieces who lived there till 1887 when it was sold to William Henry Dobie of the tobacco firm. Dobie replaced the old house with the present castellated mansion, buying also the neighbouring lands of Pitfar and Lambhill. His wife was an American and his mother a sister of Jane Welsh Carlyle. The Dobies sold it to the Workers' Travel Association in the 1920s which ran it for many years as an hotel till the 1970s. The house and grounds have been sold separately since, but the house remains largely derelict seeking a suitable use although planning permission has been granted for its conversion into flats with attendant housing.

Basically then, although feued by Argyll, up to the Reformation the superiors of the Dollar Lands were:

1. Those known as "The Kirklands" or "Ten pund land of Dolor": Dunkeld.

2. The lands of Over and Nether Mains: Dunfermline.

3. The Banks of Dollar Hill, Gateside, and Glencairn: mainly Dunfermline (Gateside possibly the Crown).

4. The four quarters of Sheardale and the "milne of Dolarbeg": Dunfermline and the Crown.

5. Easter and Wester Dollarbeg: mainly Dunfermline.

6. Muckhartshire: St Andrews

Two minor hiccoughs disturbed the Argyll holding of all their Dollar lands. The eighth Earl and first Marquis was arrested and tried after the Restoration in 1660 for his part with the Covenanting forces and executed, his estates being forfeited to the Crown. They were, however, rapidly regranted to his son. The son in 1686 came out in support of the abortive attempt by Charles II's son, the Duke of Monmouth, to seize the throne from James II, and was captured and executed in his turn. This time the estates were granted to James' sycophantic Chancellor, the Earl of Perth. The grant forms the most complete list of the Argyll holdings which comprised: "the lands of Burnsyd of Dollar and Kirklands thereof extending to ane ten pound land . . . the lands of Overmaynes of Dollar and neather maynes thereof . . . the lands of Bancks of Dollar and Glencairn with half of the milne of Dolarbeg and the two fourth pairts of the lands of Sherdaill. The lands of Craighead, Wester Dollarbeg, Easter Dollarbeg, and the lands of Gatesyd with the lands of Glumhill . . . little Salin, Bordland of Salin and lands of Over Kinedder . . . the muire commonly called the muire of Dollarbeg . . . the lands of Easter Dollarbeg on the west, the lands of Solsgirth and the coatter land of Dollarbeg . . . pairts upon the south side of the water of Dovan" with all "the biggings, castles, towrs, woods, fishing etc". The grant was to cost the Earl the annual payment of 3 pennies Scots. In 1686 an Act of Parliament granted him two fairs yearly in the town of Dollar, on the second Tuesday in June and the second Tuesday of October plus a weekly market on Wednesday.

Alas his good fortune did not last. James II was deposed, Perth fled with him to France and the tenth Earl and future first Duke of Argyll returned in triumph in the wake of William and Mary to reclaim his estates, being in his turn in 1701 granted the tremendous honour of having two fairs yearly at the Kirktoun of Dollar on the 8th of June and the 8th of October.

In 1702 according to the Marquis of Bute in *The Arms of Scottish Burghs,* Dollar was created head burgh of the regality of Campbell. This seems to have been taken to mean that Dollar became a burgh of barony at this date with certain trading privileges. Gavin Marshall, however, in 1605 was instructed to "answerand yeirlie to three heid Courtis of the Barony of Dollar" so it must to have been a barony long before 1702. Marshall, in fact, seems to have been in charge of the barony. In 1623 a "Thomas Jamesoun in the Maynis of Dolour, a common and notorious thief" being apprehended "with a fang of stollin in sheep and now in custody of Gawane Merschell, chamberlane of Campbell" was put on trial. Later another such, William Wilsoun in the Hill of Mukkart having had his house "rypit by the said Gawane their was fund thairintill certane stollin muttoun and sheiptauch (tallow)", Marshall here being described as "constable of Campbell".

Towards the end of the 18th century the Argylls began to sell their Dollar and Muckhart lands, finally disposing of the last "the ten pound land of Dolor" in 1807 to Tait of Harviestoun.

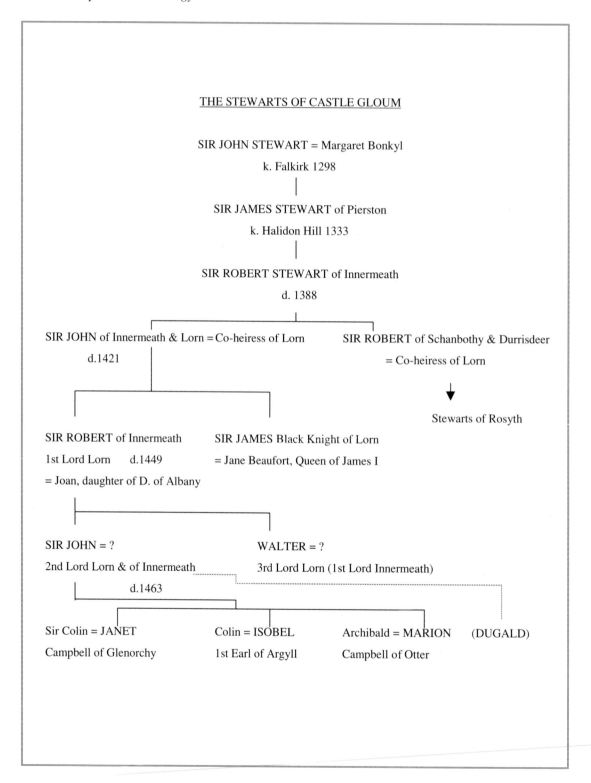

THE STEWARTS OF CASTLE GLOUM

SIR JOHN STEWART = Margaret Bonkyl

k. Falkirk 1298

SIR JAMES STEWART of Pierston

k. Halidon Hill 1333

SIR ROBERT STEWART of Innermeath

d. 1388

SIR JOHN of Innermeath & Lorn = Co-heiress of Lorn   SIR ROBERT of Schanbothy & Durrisdeer

d.1421   = Co-heiress of Lorn

Stewarts of Rosyth

SIR ROBERT of Innermeath   SIR JAMES Black Knight of Lorn

1st Lord Lorn   d.1449   = Jane Beaufort, Queen of James I

= Joan, daughter of D. of Albany

SIR JOHN = ?   WALTER = ?

2nd Lord Lorn & of Innermeath   3rd Lord Lorn (1st Lord Innermeath)

d.1463

Sir Colin = JANET   Colin = ISOBEL   Archibald = MARION   (DUGALD)

Campbell of Glenorchy   1st Earl of Argyll   Campbell of Otter

CASTLE CAMPBELL AND THE ARGYLLS

Castle Campbell in Snow - DM 1951

Although it seems likely that the ancient inhabitants of the district made defensive use of the site of the castle, any traces of their occupation have long been buried under later development. The raised mound on which the tower stands appears to be artificial to some extent and suggests that it may once have been crowned by a Norman type motte castle, tradition holding that Malcolm Canmore had a hunting seat here. Foundations of what would appear to have been a drawbridge spanning a deep ditch, now filled in, have been found at the present entrance to the castle grounds.

As noted the castle at first belonged to the Stewarts, passing to the Campbells by marriage in 1465. The site appears to have been included in the grant, by Dunkeld, of the lands of Schanbothy, Durrisdeer and Innermeath to a Sir James Stewart in 1361. His grandsons, John and Robert, both married Macdougall heiresses and acquired Lorn. By family agreement John inherited Innermeath and Lorn and Robert the

other lands. (Robert was the ancestor of the Stewarts of Rosyth, their castle still standing there.) Thereafter Innermeath and the Dollar lands passed down to John's son, Robert, and then to his son, another John.

This John had three daughters all of whom married Campbells, one of them, Isobel, marrying the young Colin Campbell, 1st Earl of Argyll. Again by family arrangement Isobel received the Dollar lands and the tower of Gloume. However her uncle Walter, lord of Lorn, disputed the division and attacked and demolished the tower. The Church intervened to settle the dispute, Argyll thereupon backing Walter in his claim for the lordship of Innermeath and receiving Lorn in exchange, giving him both a title for his eldest son and the Macdougall ship for his coat of arms.

In 1489/90 by an Act of Parliament James IV changed at the behest of:

his cousing and traist consalor Coline erle

of Ergile lord campbele and lorne … the Name of the castell and place quhilk wes callit the gloume ... the samy castell to be callit in tyme to cum Campbele.

**The Arms of the Argyll Family
with the Galley of Lorne
quartered with the Gyrony of Eight**

The original peel tower with its bailey had its accommodation improved by the building of the South Range or "pailace" with its "allour" or wall walk on top around 1500. The windows were barred – the bailie of Campbell being falsely accused of selling the iron for personal gain in 1760 – and presumably the defences to the south and east were stronger than they are today.

The first Earl died in 1493 and the second was killed with his sovereign at Flodden in 1513. The third died in 1529. The fourth, Archibald, was presumably involved to some extent when the vicar of Dollar, Thomas Foret or Forrest, was accused of heresy and burnt at the Castlehill in Edinburgh in 1539 or 1540 during the reign of James V. He was also involved in besieging St Andrews Castle after the killing of Cardinal Beaton there in 1546 by early reformers, many of these surrendering only to be sent to serve on the rowing benches of French galleys, among them John Knox. The Earl took part in the Battle of Pinkie in 1547 and then, either out of conviction or cupidity, joined the reformers. His son, Lord Lorne, welcomed Knox home on his return to Scotland in 1555, while the old man himself

entertained him at Castle Campbell in July 1556. Knox relates of himself in the third person:

> He himself by procurement and labouris of Robert Campbell of Kingzancleuch, remaned behind in Scotland, & passed to the old Erle of Ergyle, who was then in the Castell of Campbell, where he tawght certane dawis. The Lard of Glenquhare (which yit liveth) being one of his auditouris, willed the said Erle of Ergyle to reateane him still, but he purposed upoun his jorney, wold not att that tyme stay for no requeast ... and so in the moneth of Julij he left this realme & past to France, & so to Geneva.

Knox returned to Scotland in May 1559. Although the tradition that he administered the Sacrament of the Lord's Supper at Castle Campbell is probably correct, it is more likely to have been done in the hall rather than on the knoll known as "Knox's Pulpit", it not being the custom at that date to dispense ordinances in the open air. The fourth Earl died in 1558 and it was his son, Archibald, who joined the Lords of the Congregation and established Protestantism as the main form of worship, much church property passing into the hands of the lords.

On the return of Mary, Queen of Scots, from France, Argyll became one of her councillors and in 1563 she visited Dollar to attend the wedding of Argyll's half sister, Margaret, to James Stewart, Lord of Doune and Commendator (lay abbot) of Inchcolm. Their future son was eventually to marry the daughter of Mary's brother, the Earl of Moray, and to become the "Bonnie Earl o' Moray" killed at Donibristle in 1592 by the Earl of Huntly. His mother had a painting, still in existence, made of his body and its wounds in an attempt to demand justice. The visit to the marriage took its toll of Mary as reported by Randolph, the English agent, to Cecil, Elizabeth's Chief Minister:

> 31 January 1563. I received your letter of 14th instant with one from the Queen's Majesty to this Queen which I presented on her recovery from sickness, which we conjecture was nothing but a will to keep

her bed for five or six days after her evil journey at Castle Cammell.

The consequences rather resemble those which she was to suffer later at Jedburgh after an equally evil journey to Hermitage Castle when she came close to death. It is conjectured that she suffered from a hereditary disease called porphyria which also affected her descendants, particularly George III.

Relations between Mary and her half-brother, Moray, now became strained, Randolph again reporting in February 1564:

> There has been unkindness for a good space between the Queen and Murray ... He got leave to Fife for 8 days, but tarried 21, and returned not unsent for. Meanwhile he met Argyll at Castle Cammell

Relations between Argyll and his wife, Lady Jean Stewart (yet another illegitimate child like Moray of the "Guid Man o Ballengeich", James V) were also strained. Her half-sister, Queen Mary, somewhat strangely, persuaded Knox to act as conciliator who "brought them to concord" but it did not last. After the announcement of the betrothal of Mary to Darnley, Argyll and Moray supposedly plotted to intercept them near Kinross on a journey from Perth and to take Darnley to Castle Campbell and later to hand him and his father, the Earl of Lennox, over to England. A local laird, however, warned the Queen's party of troops in the vicinity and the plot was foiled. Later, after the marriage, the two Earls rose in revolt in the Chaseabout Raid and after its failure Argyll sought refuge in the Highlands, Moray fleeing to England. The successful Mary and her King Henry "returned to Stirling and from thence to Fife, and in their passage caused to take in Castle Campbell which was delivered without impediment to the lord of Sanquhar". Lady Argyll was present at Holyrood when the nobles murdered Rizzio and also held the future James VI in the Chapel Royal at Stirling as proxy for Queen Elizabeth in what was seen by the reformers as a Popish christening ceremony.

After the murder of Darnley at Kirk o' Field

Argyll was one of the nobles who subscribed to the bond in favour of Bothwell marrying Mary and on the marriage taking place he promptly subscribed to another bond for the defence of her infant son, James, against Bothwell. In the abdication document Mary signed at Loch Leven on the 24th July 1567, he was named as one of the Governors of the Kingdom. After her escape, however, on the 2nd May 1568 he joined her forces and commanded them at the Battle of Langside on the 13th against the opposing lords but at the commencement of the engagement was seized with a fit which delayed the advance of her troops, an illness which may have contributed to her defeat and subsequent flight to

Three Campbell Lords
from the Book of Taymouth:
Duncan of Lochawe; his son, Colin of Glenorchy;
and his grandson, Colin (not Archibald),
First Earl of Argyll -
DAA

England. Soon afterwards he made peace with his old associate Moray.

In 1573 the redoubtable Lady Argyll found herself in Edinburgh Castle when two of the exiled Queen Mary's former opponents, Maitland of Lethington and Kirkcaldy of Grange, rose on Mary's behalf and were besieged there. In negotiating terms for surrender Kirkcaldy requested that the Countess be not delivered into her husband's hands. She had already been the recipient of a "sencure of excommunication against zow for non adhering to my lorde zour husband". The Earl subsequently obtained a divorce on the grounds of desertion and married Jean Cunningham, the daughter of the Earl of Glencairn, Argyll life-renting her Castle Campbell, Muckhart and Menstrie as he had previously done to Jean Stewart. A month later, on 12th September 1573, he died at the age of 43.

There being no heir by either marriage the title passed to his stepbrother, Colin, whereupon a dispute broke out about the rights to the proceeds of the lands gifted to the wives. Eventually Jean Cunningham received the main proceeds but Jean Stewart the teinds. Among the Dollar tenants mentioned in the proceedings were John Campbell in the town of Cambell, Peter Fergus in the Nethyr Mains and Andrew Drysdaill, tenant in the Smythland of Dollar. Lady Jean Cunningham lost her rights on remarriage in 1579 to Colquhoun of Luss. Lady Jean Stewart, no doubt, claimed her dues until 1587, dying a few months after the execution of Queen Mary in England, and was buried at Holyrood. She features in the well-known painting by Sir David Wilkie, *Knox Preaching Before the Lords of the Congregation*, being often mistaken for her half-sister, the Queen. In 1582 Colin himself made provision for his wife, Dame Annabel Keith, by granting her in liferent the ten pound land of Dollar with the fortalice of Campbell as well as Muckhart and Menstrie. He died in 1584 after a long illness and was succeeded by his son, Archibald, then eight years old.

Archibald's first notable action was to appear at court in full armour, aged twelve, on the day appointed for mourning the execution of the king's mother. In 1587 the Earl's Captain in Castle Campbell, Alexander Menteith, is noted as having trouble with a family of Peirsons from Borland, Clow, Quhytehill and Eirynside in Fossoway and two years later Menteith is having trouble with the king and government himself "touching the release of Henry Mersair convicted of treasounable fyre-raising, murthour, slaughter, and utheris odious crymes" who was supposed to have been executed "to the deid eftir the said convictioun".

The Earl is said to have narrowly escaped death by poisoning at his wedding feast in Stirling, his bride being a daughter of the Earl of Morton who, as Sir William Douglas, had been Queen Mary's jailer at Loch Leven. Partly out of revenge for the killing of his relation, the Bonny Earl o' Moray, the eighteen-year-old Argyll, as the King's Lieutenant, warred against the "Popish earls" Huntly, Errol and Angus, and was defeated by their use of cannon at the Battle of Glenlivet, being led weeping off the field. James VI, however, was not displeased at the come-down of an over-weening retainer being heard to exclaim "Fair fa' thee, Geordie (Huntly), for sending him hame like a subjeck!"

In February 1596 the Earl ordered an inventory to be made of the contents of Castle Campbell entrusting the task to "william menteth of powmawth milne, jon patoun of hilfutt, william cunnigham in ye (blank), jon patoun in middiltoun, alexander kirk in blairhill, william nutoune (hutton?) in mains of dowlar, john smyth in dowlar, duncan drysdaill, thomas allexander." The document is important historically as it gives a comprehensive account of the furnishings of such a castle at the time. It is dealt with fully in *The Dollar Magazine* Nos 128 and 129.

Four years later a complaint was made by a Thomas Alexander of Balruidy through his procurator, James Stirling, about his illegal imprisonment in the Castle of Campbell, the captain of the castle, John Archibald, contesting this on the grounds that Alexander had been discovered with the "fang" or loot of the sheep he had stolen and his trial had been delayed because of the weakness and disease of the bailie of the lordship and barony of Campbell. Again we have evidence that Dollar was a barony before the received date of 1702 and that, in this case, the captain and the bailie were two distinct officers.

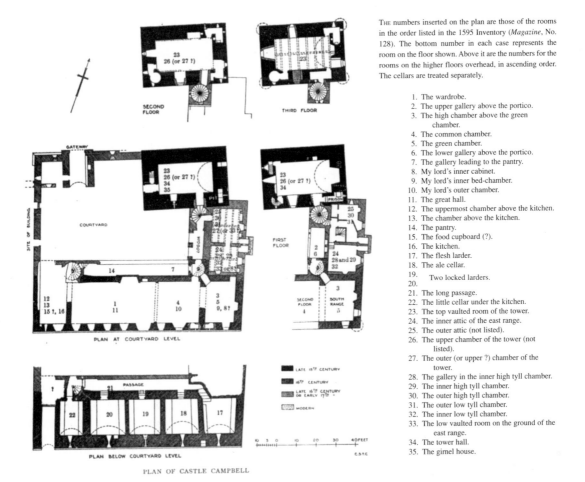

PLAN OF CASTLE CAMPBELL

Plans of Castle Campbell with identification of rooms - DM 1934

Around 1600 the castle was again improved by the addition of the East Range with its fine stone walls and unusual arched loggia.

On 29 July 1602 there was a further complaint, this time from Johne Campbell, Williame Hutton, John Drysdaill in Dollar, and Johne Patoune in Hilfute that they had been put to the horn – declared outlaws – for not paying the Bishop of Dunkeld £16 feu when they held no lands off him and that the horning had been done in Perth and not in Clackmannan.

In 1603 Argyll accompanied James VI south in his journey to claim the English throne but was back in 1605 arranging to feu out all his Dollar and Muckhart lands with the exception of the Castle and two farms. This gave the tenants perpetual tenure on their ground on the payment of an annual feu duty though they still farmed the lands in common.

From 1609 each parish had to appoint two constables and in 1617 James Brek, one of the Dollar constables, supplied fifteen horses for his Majesty's luggage between Stirling and Falkland. After this royal visit Argyll went to the Netherlands. There and, later, in Spain where he served under the Spanish king, he consorted with banished British rebels and was accordingly declared a traitor and rebel at Edinburgh Market Cross in February 1619. The sentence was, however, reversed within two years. The constables of Dollar and Muckhart – Johne Drysdaill, Johne Kirk, James Patoune, and Johne

Alexander – had to supply 80 horses for Charles I's luggage on his visit in 1633. Having handed over much of his estates to his son, the seventh earl died in retirement in 1638.

Archibald, the eighth earl, born in 1598, apparently had an unhappy upbringing, being at variance with his father. He inherited heavily encumbered estates, some on his father resigning them before his death, these including Dollar in 1627. In that year he crushed the Macdonalds of Ardnamurchan and in 1635 brought to book the freebooter, Gilderoy. In 1638 on his father's death and having cleared his debts, he began to play his part in politics, the same year undergoing a massive spiritual conversion and

Highland Refugees - DM 1952

becoming fanatical in the cause of the Covenant – although he does not seem to have been present at the initial signing in Greyfriars Church, as was Montrose – binding the signers to uphold the Presbyterian form of religion against the attempts of the King and government to make the Episcopalian form, with its bishops, compulsory.

Quarrels broke out between King and Parliament in England and in 1641 Charles revisited Scotland in an attempt to bring the leaders onto his side, Argyll being created a Marquis. Despite the honour Argyll, however, remained true to the Covenant. When war broke out in England, the English Parliament signed a treaty with the Scots, *The Solemn League and Covenant*, promising to introduce Presbyterianism into the English church although they had little intention of doing so. A Scots army was duly assembled and sent south to aid the Roundheads which they did, principally at the Battle of Marston Moor near York. Meanwhile, Montrose, now also created a Marquis, alarmed at the increased religious fanaticism of the Covenanters and the possibility of their doing away with kingship, a concept he was equally fanatical about, broke with them and threw his lot in with the king's party. He travelled north, bearing the king's commission, with only one companion to try and raise an army and to join with a force of Irish and Islanders, sent over by the Earl of Antrim, under the leadership of the giant Sir Alasdair Macdonald, known after his father as "Colkitto". With them, the men of Atholl, and other supporters, Montrose in the next twelve months waged an incredible campaign against the large Covenanting forces, resulting in outstanding victories such as those at Tippermuir, Aberdeen, and Fyvie, before undertaking a winter march through the mountains – led by an inhabitant of Glencoe – to ravage the Campbell heartland of Argyll itself, waging there the battles of Inveraray and Inverlochy, from both of which Argyll escaped in his galley, leaving his clansmen to suffer. He was no coward, however, having two horses killed under him at the later battle of Alford. In July Montrose's army unexpectedly appeared near Perth, where the Parliament was sitting due to the plague in Edinburgh, crossed the Earn, and came down into Fife. Argyll heard the news at Berwick where he was on his way down to England and immediately returned to Castle Campbell, bringing with him a young boy, Evan Dhu Cameron of Lochiel, son of the chief of the Clan Cameron and a Campbell mother, whom, in the Highland custom of fostering, Argyll was rearing. Cameron later told what happened to his grandson or great-grandson, Drummond of Balhaldie.

(*Memoirs of Locheill*. Abbotsford Club. 1842):

Montrose, in the meantime, haveing recruited his army, formed a designe of invadeing Fife, in order to suppress that rebellious country; which, obligeing argyll to return to Scotland, he left Berwick, and touching at edinburgh, went straight to Castle Campbell, a strong house of his own, where he placed a garrison, in order to protect a considerable estate which he had on the borders of Fife called the parishes of Muchard and Dollars. While he stayed there he had the mortifications to see all that country ravaged, and the villages laid in ashes, by the Macleans, his neighbours, whom he had used in like manner while they were absent in service of the crown.

This happned in Montrose his march from Kinross towards Stirling. His hatered to Argyle, as well on account of the cause he was engadged in, as of injuries he had done him, prevailed with him to permitt the Macleans to step aside, and to committ that outrage: and these people were so incensed against the Marquess for the burning of their chief's estate, and other mischiefs which he had done to that family, that, to make quick work of it, they divided themselves into small partys, and so spreading themselves over the countrey, they spaired nothing that came in their way. One of these partys had the boldness to march up to the very walls of the castle, and to insult the garrison, which, though six times their number, had not the courage so much to fire a gun at them, or even to look them in the face. Locheill, who always attended his guardian, having attentively observed what passed, told the governour, that he and his garrison deserved to he hanged for their cowardice, and then, addressing himself to Argyle: "For what purpose, my lord, said he, are these people kept here? Your Lordship sees the countrey destroyed; that they may be easily cutt to pieces, one by one, without their being able to unite and assist one another; but your fellows ar so unfitt for the bussines for

which they were brought here, that they have not courage so much as to look over the walls." Argyle made little answer at that time; but when the Macleans were gone after satisfieing their revenge to the full, he chid the governour and turning him out of office putt another in his place. This he thought necessarey to cover the reproach that was brought upon himself, by being eye witnes of the desolation of his own lands, without attempting to relieve them, and he inclined that the blame should fall upon the governour.

Lochiel was, obviously, no respecter of his

The Maiden Tree - DM 1907

foster-father. After a tough life in the Royalist cause during which he bit the throat out of a large English officer declaring it "The sweetest morsel I ever tasted"; killed the last(?) wolf in Scotland; kicked a snowball from under a sleeping clansman's head saying: "Are you so luxurious you cannot sleep without a pillow?"; and in 1716 at the age of 87 having a grip so powerful that it squeezed the blood out of Drummond's fingertips, the doughty old horror died peacefully in his bed in 1719. The Drummonds we have met before as at one time the tenants of the Craighead quarter of Sheardale and Macgregors to boot.

Argyll put himself at the head of the Covenanting army, joined by 1,200 of his own Highlanders and 3,000 Fife men out for revenge, and pursued Montrose to Kilsyth only to be defeated once more on the 15th of August. Montrose, however, received his come-uppance a few weeks later at Philiphaugh near Selkirk on his way into England from the Scots army under Leslie coming up from the south, Colkitto and most of his men having already stravaiged off north to roast more Campbells in their castles. Those Highlanders staying with Montrose surrendered on being given quarter and, on the behest of the Covenanting ministers present, were promptly slaughtered, the same happening to their women and children near Falkirk as they were attempting to make their way to safety. "The work," as one minister famously remarked rubbing his hands, "gangs bonnily on."

Montrose went back to the Highlands to recruit more troops but was ordered into exile when Charles unavailingly attempted to placate Parliament. Later Charles II sent him back to the north of Scotland where his landing with a small body of untried Orkney men was promptly defeated. He again escaped but was betrayed and brought to Edinburgh for trial where he was found guilty and hung as quickly as possible. Argyll refused to take part in the trial declaring himself too prejudiced.

When Charles I surrendered to the Scots army at Newark they handed him over to the English Parliament on condition he should come to no harm. On his execution and the rejection of the conditions of the Solemn League, the Scots indignantly proclaimed Charles II king and Argyll placed the crown on his head on the 1st January 1651, Charles having sworn to uphold Presbyterianism. Cromwell consequently invaded Scotland. After his victory over the Scots at Dunbar and the "crowning mercy" of Worcester, Argyll was captured at Inveraray, promising to live peacefully under the Protectorate and even expressing some zeal for

the government. Consequently when the Earl of Glencairn headed a rising in 1653, a Colonel Lilburne wrote to Cromwell: "Hee promises to use his endeavour to his utmost power to preserve peace, & uppon his return from Castle Camell, which will be shortly, he will send for some of these new engagers & try if he can convince them of their follie". Argyll does not seem to have been very successful in his convincing, his eldest son, Lord Lorn, afterwards the ninth earl, joining Glencairn in 1654 with 1000 men and being among the last to submit to Cromwell.

Towards the end of 1653 the castle seems to have been garrisoned by government troops placed there by General Monk, Cromwell's Commander in Scotland, the poor burghers of Culross being requisitioned for "22 fether beddis with 22 fether bolsteris" and other bedding for the garrison, a councillor making four trips before they agreed to deduct the articles from the "cess" or tribute money laid upon the burgh, settlement costing him fifteen shillings of "smart money" (bribery?) on behalf of the garrison. Argyll seems to have been in debt at this time, the Keepers granting to "Thomas Harrisone of South Myrnes in the County of Middlesex . . . the lands of Doller called Castle Campbell . . . in payment of £300 sterling", it being customary to apprise or distrain the whole lands regardless of the value of the unpaid debt. There is no indication when the debt was repaid and the lands were still possibly in Harrison's grant when General Monk reported to Cromwell on the 29th July 1654:

> Some small parties of the enemy are abroad in the country, & on Monday & Tuesday last burn't Castle Campbell, an house belonging to the Marquesse of Argyll, & Dumblainn, a garrison kept by us last winter, & say they have orders from Middleton to burne all the strong Houses neere the Hills.

The destruction is celebrated in a local version of the ballad of "Edom o' Gordon" containing the verses:

I think we'll go o'er to Castle Campbell
The good lord's far awa:
I think we'll go o'er to Castle Campbell
And ye my merry men a'.

Lady Campbell looked o'er her window
All in a dress of black etc. . . .

Oh Johnnie the Mason ye'll gang up
That kens the key o' the stane:
Oh Johnnie the Mason, ye'll gang up
And ken'le the flames on them.

The last verse supposedly refers to a local mason who prised a stone out of the wall and allowed the besiegers to draw back the bar securing the gate. The full version is given in *The Dollar Magazine* No. 13. The attackers were possibly those under the Earl of Glencairn.

Argyll lived unmolested until the Restoration in 1660. Going unsuspectingly to London to greet Charles II, he was arrested, committed to the Tower, and then sent by sea to Edinburgh for trial on the grounds of compliance with Cromwell's usurpation. He was about to be discharged when a packet of letters arrived, sent by Monk, which contained references to his compliance. On being condemned he exclaimed, in an example of hope springing eternal: "This reminds me that I had the honour to set the crown upon the King's head, and now he hastens me to a better crown than his own." He died by "The Maiden", that female precursor of the guillotine, now preserved in the Royal Scottish Museum. His memorial ironically lies across the aisle from that of Montrose in the High Kirk of St Giles.

After the Civil War the Argylls purchased the newly built Argyll Lodging in Stirling and resided there.

The ninth earl, Archibald, fought at Dunbar, joined the Glencairn rising, submitted to Cromwell on the King's instructions but refused to renounce the Stewarts. Imprisoned in Edinburgh Castle he was injured by a thrown bullet and had to have his skull trepanned.

After the Restoration he was again imprisoned for condemning his father's execution and Charles II had to intervene on his behalf. In 1663 the forfeited lands were restored to him. In 1681 on being asked to swear to the Test Act against Roman Catholics he added "as far as it was consistent with itself and the Protestant Religion", enough for him to be again condemned to death for treason. Escaping from Edinburgh Castle under the guise of a page to his daughter, Lady Sophia Lindsay, he fled to Holland only to return in 1685 in support of the Duke of Monmouth. On the attempt failing he was recaptured and beheaded, having "The Maiden" levelled to his satisfaction before embracing "the sweetest maiden he had ever kissed".

His lands were bestowed on the Duke of Perth who held them till the Glorious Revolution and the accession of William and Mary when they were returned to the tenth Earl and first Duke of Argyll.

Henceforth little historical mention is made of the Castle. A party of Mar's troops passed by shortly before the Battle of Sheriffmuir in 1715 apparently, according to Sir Walter Scott, "to insult the garrison by marching in their view". Two Muckhart dissenters, objecting to the installation there of the Rev. Rennie, were imprisoned in 1733. Thereafter the Castle fell into decay and was sold to Tait of Harviestoun around 1806. About 1848 it was occupied by a shepherd and his family and, later, by a local poet and cobbler named Boyd who tried to sell beverages there to locals picknicking on the then flat top of the tower, a favourite venue also for the annual visit of the Oakley Town Band. Around 1874 James Orr of Harviestoun carried out repairs, Knox's pulpit being almost completely rebuilt. The date 1875 and the initials JR and JS on the fireplaces in the south range may be those of the masons. The Castle and Glen were donated to the National Trust in 1950 by J. Ernest Kerr of Harviestoun and the Castle is now in the care of Historic Scotland.

Watson mentions two legends associated with the Castle: one of a princess imprisoned by her father there who said, "It was a gloomy prison to her. Hence, says tradition, it came to be called the Castle of Gloum". A more exciting explanation of "Kemp's Score or Cutt", other than the usual "ceum scoir", the staircase in the rock, relates to a somewhat oversized outlaw by the name of Willy Kemp (Kemp being a common Scottish soubriquet for a giant):

WILLY KEMP

Willy Kemp was a reiver bold,
And he bigged in Castle Gloom,
A strappin lad, he was eight feet tall
Frae his heels tae his cranium.

He vexed sore old King Canmore
Wi sic cruel depredations
As doin in his next-a-kin
An other near relations.

"This canna go an!" the auld king cried.
"We're runnin oot o princes,
Far I'm no sae blate as I was o late
At keepin up the production rate.
No, I'm no sae guid in the clinches!"

So he caad his knichts tae Dunfermline toon,
An offered tae gie his daughter
Tae ony yin whae was braw enough
Tae pit an end tae the slaughter.

But whiles they was batin among themsels
As tae which was the yin tae win her,
Big Willy sneaked in the back door
An made aff wi the roasted boar
The king was tae hae for his dinner.

When they telt the King he near blew up
Wi spontaneous combustion
"Is there no a clot amang you lot
That I can pit some trust in?"

Then up there spak a poor wee knight
Whae sat at the foot o the table,
"I'll hae a bash at doin his hash
If you'll lend me a nag frae your stable."

They grabbed him afore he could change his mind
Or onyin raise an objection
An pit him upon the king's best nag
Wi its heid in the right direction.

The King gied it a dunt on the rump
An it took aff like a rocket
"Och weel", said he, "It could be worse
If it comes tae the bit he's no much loss
But I'm beginnin tae regret the lane o that horse
We should hae made him walk it!"

The poor wee knight rade on and on
Till he cam tae the castle wa.
An he parked his nag in the parking place
An went doon tae pay a ca.

Big Willy Kemp's a feardy knight!
He canna fight for toffee!
His heid is made o ginger breid!
An his feet smell somethin awfy!

Big Willy cam oot the castle yett
Wi a glour as black as thunder!
"Whae's that oot there takkin the mick?
I'll pit him six feet under!"

The twa hae met upon the green
The big yin and the wee yin
An sic a battle there was seen
As you'd never hope tae be in!

They hackit high, they hackit low,
They hackit doon the middle
Till the poor wee knight was fair worn oot
Wi hoppin, skippin, and jumpin aboot,
Like a herrin on a griddle.

He kent the pace he couldna last
So he essayed one stroke bolder,
An wi a giant leap and a mighty sweep
Hacked Willy's heid frae his shoulder.

"Och michty me!" Big Willy cried
"I'll never mak tomorrow.
The dirty wee blighter's blinded me!
Wi oot ma heid I canna see!"
An he staggered that way and staggered this
Till at last he fell ower a precipice,
An drooned in the Burn o Sorrow.

The braw wee knight picked up the heid
An back tae the King did canter:
"I've done ma bit. Big Wully's deid.
Noo your daughter, I hope you'll grant her."

"Tush! Tush!", said the King. "Is it no sad?
I trust you'll no mistake it?
But we mairrit her off on an English lad,
Cos we didna think you'd make it."

A saut tear dripped frae the wee knicht's eye,
At this blow tae his ambition.
"Noo, noo," said the King. "Man, dinna fret!
There's mony a fish in the sea left yet
For a knicht sae strang an able."
An he patted his heid and sent him back -

Doon tae the foot o the table!

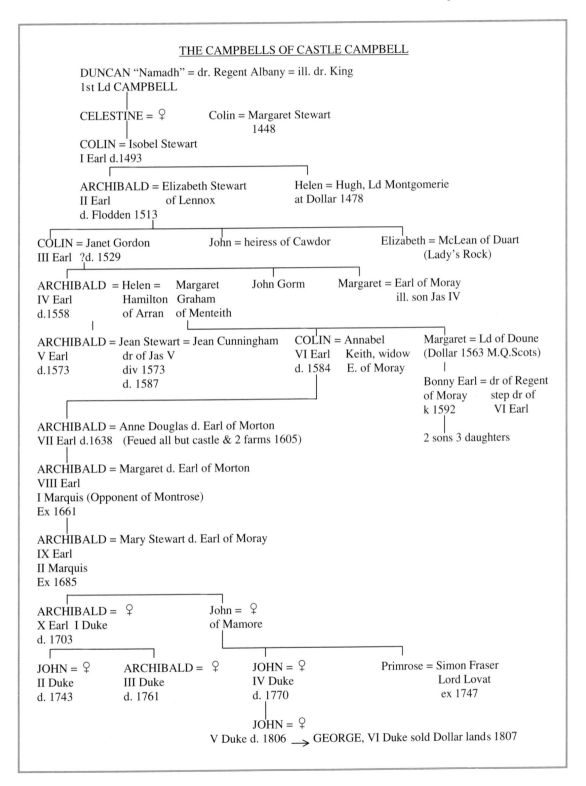

THE CAMPBELLS OF CASTLE CAMPBELL

DUNCAN "Namadh" = dr. Regent Albany = ill. dr. King
1st Ld CAMPBELL

CELESTINE = ♀   Colin = Margaret Stewart
                                1448
COLIN = Isobel Stewart
I Earl d.1493

ARCHIBALD = Elizabeth Stewart   Helen = Hugh, Ld Montgomerie
II Earl   of Lennox   at Dollar 1478
d. Flodden 1513

COLIN = Janet Gordon   John = heiress of Cawdor   Elizabeth = McLean of Duart
III Earl ?d. 1529   (Lady's Rock)

ARCHIBALD = Helen = Margaret   John Gorm   Margaret = Earl of Moray
IV Earl   Hamilton Graham   ill. son Jas IV
d.1558   of Arran of Menteith

ARCHIBALD = Jean Stewart = Jean Cunningham   COLIN = Annabel   Margaret = Ld of Doune
V Earl   dr of Jas V   VI Earl Keith, widow   (Dollar 1563 M.Q.Scots)
d.1573   div 1573   d. 1584 E. of Moray
             d. 1587   Bonny Earl = dr of Regent
                                                                      of Moray   step dr of
                                                                      k 1592   VI Earl
ARCHIBALD = Anne Douglas d. Earl of Morton
VII Earl d.1638   (Feued all but castle & 2 farms 1605)   2 sons 3 daughters

ARCHIBALD = Margaret d. Earl of Morton
VIII Earl
I Marquis (Opponent of Montrose)
Ex 1661

ARCHIBALD = Mary Stewart d. Earl of Moray
IX Earl
II Marquis
Ex 1685

ARCHIBALD = ♀   John = ♀
X Earl I Duke   of Mamore
d. 1703

JOHN = ♀   ARCHIBALD = ♀   JOHN = ♀   Primrose = Simon Fraser
II Duke   III Duke   IV Duke   Lord Lovat
d. 1743   d. 1761   d. 1770   ex 1747

                                 JOHN = ♀
                      V Duke d. 1806 ⟶ GEORGE, VI Duke sold Dollar lands 1807

THE EARLY CHURCH

The conversion of the Hillfoot pagans is mainly ascribed to St Serf (St Servanus) and his followers. St Serf was possibly born at Culross around 700 AD. The ascription of the parish church in Dollar is, however, to St Columba, who died in 597, suggesting that he or his followers had founded a mission here a good deal earlier although some authorities consider this unlikely and believe there may be a confusion with one of several, later, St Colmes.

The Columban ascription is given some authority, however, in that during the reign of David I (1124-53) when sub-division was made of the bishopric of Dunkeld – Dunkeld having become the centre of the Scottish church in 818 due to the Viking attacks on Iona – Dollar was one of the parishes deliberately retained by Dunkeld and not granted to a nearer diocese, such as Dunfermline or Cambuskenneth, because they were specifically connected with Columba. This Columban connection with both the Dollar church and Inchcolm is pointed out in the first historical event mentioning the church in Dollar, an English raid recorded both in *The Book of Pluscarden* and in Bower's continuation of Fordoun's *Scotichronicon*. The Pluscarden account runs:

During the period of Baliol's attempt to regain his ascendancy in Scotland, the English army in 1336 which had reached Scotland both by sea and by land, ravaged the north of Scotland. Meanwhile, those who remained in the fleet in the Firth of Forth overran the whole land of Fife and Forthreve, and laid it utterly waste as far as the Ochil mountains. Coming to the church of Dollar, which is acknowledged to belong directly to St Columba, they found there the church just beginning to be rebuilt, with carpenters at work upon it with choice and marvellous woodwork, and these limbs of the devil carried away with them in their carts to the fleet the whole of the logs so fashioned, and stowed them in the aforesaid ships in order to take them over to England for the sake of the wonderful and curious workmanships thereof, so everything prospered with the said sailors, until they came near the place of the said St Columba, which is called the island of Emonia (Inchcolm), when suddenly, in the twinkling of an eye, they sank in the raging waters at a very deep spot in the front of the said monastery, so that nothing was ever afterwards heard of any of those who were in that boat in which these beams and logs from the church had been put. This was noised abroad throughout England by the preachers as being a miraculous retribution.

The moral being, presumably, that it did not pay to monkey with a monk. "Forthriff" or "Forthreve" or "Forthrenn" was the area including the upper part of Fife with Kinross, Muckhart, and Dollar. Bower, born 1385, was an abbot of Inchcolm. In his account he calls the hills the "Hochel mountains", mentions that the work was being carried out by the abbot of Inchcolm, and that the English thereafter named Columba "Saint Quhalme".

A century later, on the

21st April 1478, in the presence of Colin Earl of Argyll, Lord Campbell and Lorne, Gilbert, Lord Kennedy, and the notary, and witnesses, Hugh, Lord of Montgomerie, on the one part, and Elen Campbel, one of the daughters of the said Earl, on the other part. Passing to the door of the parish church of Dolar, sir Patrick Makclery chaplain, asked them if they wished to be joined in marriage, who answered they did. Then the said Patrick asked them if they knew any impediment, or if either had made any contract before with any other person, or if they were constrained by force or fear thereto, who answered there was no impediment, but it was done of their own free will and gave their corporal oath thereupon. Wherupon the said sir Patrick placed the said Hugh's hand in the said "Elen's", and per verba matrimonio de presenti united them in marriage. And Hugh and Elen kissed each other in the name of matrimonie. Done in the church of Dolar the tenth hour before noon or thereby.

S ir Patrick Makclery is one of the only three Dollar clerics known before the Reformation. The others are sir Symon Greig, and the martyred

"Vicar of Dollar", Thomas Foret or Forrest. The "sir" here is purely an honorary title equivalent of "Father" and denotes a cleric who was not a university graduate and one who, in fact, was near the bottom of the religious hierarchy. Forrest would be a graduate and entitled to be called "Master" and probably be expected to pay someone to do the actual work of being parish priest.

Thomas Forrest was the son of the master of the royal stables, probably those at Falkland Palace, in the reign of James IV. Having studied at Cologne, Forrest returned to Scotland and became a canon regular at Inchcolm. Later he was appointed vicar of Dollar, a church of which at that time Inchcolm seems to have held the patronage. In later accounts he began to carry out his duties in a manner which annoyed his fellow priests, refusing such usual perquisites as the best cow, the best suit of clothes, or the bed coverlet due on the death of a person. He also preached in the common tongue and denounced the sale of indulgences and other such abuses. Being summoned before Bishop Crichton of Dunkeld he was told to conform and on protesting that he but taught the Old and New Testaments received the reply: "I thank God that I never knew what the Old or the New Testament was. Therefore, Dean Thomas, I will know nothing but my breviary and my pontifical, and yet thou seest I have come on indifferently well." Forrest was thereafter summoned several times but on refusing to comply was condemned to death for heresy, being strangled and burnt with other heretics on the Castlehill in Edinburgh on the 28th February 1539. He is remembered locally in the name of "Vicar's Bridge" at Pitgober which he is said to have had constructed to replace stepping stones so that parishioners would find it easier to attend mass in bad weather.

The church of this time, and earlier, lay in the old graveyard south of the present ruin built with the reused stone though some walls may have been used for grave surrounds.

At the time of the Reformation in 1569 the priest was sir Henry Balfour but he did not join the Reformers. Accordingly, there being a great shortage of suitable ministers, Dollar, in common with many parishes, had a Reader appointed temporarily, this being in Dollar's case the curate, Robert Burn. Poor Burn after having served faithfully for 40 years was dismissed in 1586 for

Vicar's Bridge - DMus

failing to read distinctly, allowing discipline to lapse and "being giffen to drunkines and intemperance". He denied the last two charges but excused the first "be ressoun off his gret aige and other infirmities". The parson and vicar, however, seems to have been a Master James Paton for the King's Messenger-at-Arms, Thomas Murray, in 1572 delivered a copy of a charge against the parishioners of Dollar for refusing to pay a third of the parsonage and vicarage teinds to Paton, the charge being delivered to Patrick Kirk, officer to the Earl of Argyll, George Drysdale, and Thomas Scotland. He charged the parishioners of Muckhart similarly to pay Mr Paton's third.

The "teinds" were the tithes, supposedly a tenth part of one's income or produce, originally intended to support the parson and the parish service. In the course of the centuries these had been diverted to the upkeep of religious institutions, these (or individuals in them) becoming the legal "parson" who then paid the "vicar" to serve the "cure" of the parish. Even the Vicarage teinds were often removed to a non-resident vicar who paid a small salary to a deputy to act as parish priest. About half the Reformed clergy had been in orders pre-Reformation, and many of these, especially in the upper echelons, were members of the aristocracy. Such were the vested interests that the entire pre-Reformation ecclesiastical structure was left in being and an arrangement was made that the original holders of benefices were to retain two-thirds while the other third was to be divided between the crown and the new ministers. Hence Knox's caustic remark about two-thirds gone to the devil and the other third shared between God and the devil.

THE SEVENTEENTH AND EIGHTEENTH CENTURIES

In 1605 the Earl of Argyll, possibly in need of cash as a result of following the court to London, in addition to the goods and services required at home, began to feu out some of his Dollar lands to the sitting or "kyndly" tenants, details of the duties paid being given in the chapter on the ownership of the land. Much of the area would still be moor land and could still be treacherous as when nearby, in 1629:

> ane great and large moss of the thickness of ane spear has been driven by the force and violence of wind and water fra the firm ground and bounds where from all beginning it immoveably stood to the lands of Powis and Powmilne . . . and has overflowed and covered the saids whole lands and has tane ane solid firm and settled stand thereon, and has overturned the whole houses of the most part of the saids lands so that twenty families were constrained for life and deid, and with the extreme hazard of their lives, to flee and leave their houses and all within the same to the violence of the moss.

Not long after, in August 1645, the parishioners of Muckhart and Dollar were "fleeing and leaving all" not from the violence of the moss but from the violence of mankind as the soldiers of Montrose's Royalist army came sweeping through what came to be known as the "Montrose Yetts" (Gates) at Muckhart deliberately pillaging and burning as they came the lands belonging to the main leader of the enemy Covenanting forces, the Marquis of Argyll. Thomas Hope, the Lord Advocate, reported to Erskine of Alva:

> The public bussines here gois very crocely for the Irische crosit Ern on 7 August, and oferit to join battell with our army lyand thair, quhilk thai wyselie schonit (shunned) til the country wer gatherit to their supplie. But in the mean tyme the enemy went toward Burley (Burleigh Castle, Milnathort) and herryit Kinroschyr and his lands, and thair fra wan to Castel Campbel and the uther landis lyand about it

perteyning to the Marquis of Ergyll and heryit them. And this last nycht they were at Alloway quhair as I hear Montrose was resett (entertained) by your brother (The Earl of Mar), quhilk I will not believe. And this day he has past Forth at a ford near the Keir, and quhair they go non knowis.

While Henry Guthry, minister at Stirling, recorded in his *Memoirs*:

> Montrose marched away first to Kinross and then Westward towards Sterlin, where on the way Maclane and his People burn'd the Parishes of Muckhart and Doller belonging to the Marquise of Argile, in requital of the like formerly done by him in Maclane's country, as they alleged.

The Macleans were apparently seeking reparation for the burning of their own lands and the Ogilvy's Bonnie House of Airlie. Montrose was making for Kilsyth, where he again defeated the Covenanting forces, before heading south, minus most of his Irish, in an attempt to link up with the English forces of Charles I. He was, however, defeated by Leslie at Philiphaugh near Selkirk and, although he escaped to the Highlands and began to reform his army, was ordered by Charles to the Continent. Later he returned at the behest of Charles II only to be betrayed and hanged in Edinburgh.

The Castle, with Argyll inside, remained unharmed at this time but the surrounding countryside was devastated. One house in each parish is said to have been spared, the Dollar one being Boghall across the river (actually outwith the present parish) which was believed to belong to the Earl of Dunfermline, and may also have been Montrose's temporary headquarters and rest place. The damage to the two parishes was estimated at £80,000 Scots or a twelfth of that in sterling. The inhabitants petitioned Parliament for assistance craving "present mantenance for manuring the ground and interteining the lives of them, their wyfes, children and families, in respect their whole houses were burnt, their cornis destroyed, their bestaill and plenishing taken away". In December Parliament issued a warrant allowing them to "appryse the wood of Hairshaw (a mile east of Kennet) belonging to the Laird of Rossith, presently incarcerit as ane delinquent, that the timber thereof may be cuttit for the use of supplicants, and reparacioun of their houses and buildings". A year later Parliament also relieved them of the necessity of paying taxes or quartering soldiers and awarded them 20,000 marks to be distributed among them by the Marquis of Argyll. A warrant for the payment of this out of the £50,000 sterling to be paid by the English Parliament for Scottish military services rendered was granted in 1647 but the inhabitants were still petitioning for it in 1649 and again in 1651. Whether they ever received it is doubtful.

The actual burning of their houses may have been the least of their woes as these would mostly be of drystone and turf walling with roofs of straw and turf, akin to those known as "black houses". The main loss would be in the wood "couples" – the A-shaped vertical supports – and "pans" – the horizontals – for the roof, hence the permission to cut timber. The thatch was normally removed every few years anyway when outworn and burnt for manure, having been allowed to become richly coated on the underside with soot from the central fire. The corn would be oats and barley, the latter taking the form of "bere" and requiring manure, this being followed by two years of unmanured oats. The bestial (small by our standards) would be oxen and horses, milk cows, sheep, and pigs. Little meat would be eaten by the majority of people although hens were a monotonous feature of the diet, and an old ox might be killed and salted at Martinmas to last over the winter. The only greens would be one of the forms of kale such as cabbage. Brose – hot water poured over oatmeal, kale broth, kale greens, pease and barley bread, butter and cheese, with buttermilk, beer, or barley ale to drink would be the basic diet. Towards the end of the 18th century potatoes and turnips were becoming common and some wheat was being introduced. The Devon would provide fish, the *Statistical Account* of 1792 mentioning fresh-water trouts, sparr, in great numbers, with sea-trout of 2 to 4 lbs and salmon of 5 to 20 lbs, the latter, alas, greatly decreased from the "illegal and murderous manner of killing them with

spears at an improper season". "Sparr" would presumably be parr, young salmon, possibly not recognised as such at the time, and, alas, not in great numbers today.

The method of farming was the old medieval form of run-rig, the tenants usually living in farm-touns, each with his own house and yard, as in the Lower and Upper Mains, but farming the land in common. The land immediately around the toun was the "in-field", kept manured with cut turf, old thatch, compost middens, and sometimes lime, where lime and coal together were available as they were at the Kelly Burn. "Fields" were ploughed with the Old Scots Plough – a heavy wooden swing plough without wheels but with iron share, coulter, and strengthening band pulled by an average team of 8 oxen. (A "ploughgate" was the land such a team could plough in one year, an "oxengate", the land one ox could theoretically plough.) The method was to slice the soil inward from both sides to form a ridge from 18 to 36 feet in width with a shallow ditch on either side between one ridge and the next. The size of the team and the method of holding the plough caused serpentine ridges or riggs over the years up to three feet in height at centre and with curved ends where the large team turned round. Hill riggs were less broad and traces of them are still visible on the golf course and at the Ramshorn. The riggs were suited in breadth to hand sowing (or "broadcasting") and reaping with sickles, and the often unjustly maligned plough did its job efficiently. Riggs in each field were often reallocated yearly to try to ensure a just distribution of land. The "outfield" remained mostly unmanured, though sometimes stock would be quartered in a section which would after be sown with oats. The outfield also provided turf, cut from it with a "flauchter", for roofing and manuring the infield. It also provided close at hand grazing early in the year, stock being moved out to the common land in summer, presumably that beyond the "heid dyke" on Dollar Hill. There is no reason to think that the "sheiling" system, transhumance of whole families to temporary accommodation in the hills, was necessary here but herdboys may well have spent time there. The *Alva Account* 1792 mentions horses being sent to the hills for five months. Sheep were grazed but, apparently, not reared on the hills, year-old sheep being bought at market in Linton and shorn "twice white" before being sent to the butchers as were any lambs produced.

Such farming was labour intensive and required cooperation both in labour and the loan of draught animals between the relatively wealthy tenant farmers resplendent in their two-roomed but-and-bens, additional labour coming from the cottar or farm labourer in his one-roomer, and at harvest from the village dwellers. Corn would be stooked, stacked and, later, threshed, possibly by the "barnman", with a flail on the "chaps", a threshing floor of wood or clay. Winnowing was done on a "shilling hill" or between open barn doors, and the grain dried in pots or kilns. Bere was dried in nets above a low fire. Finally the grain was ground, usually compulsorily at a local mill, or (possibly illegally) by hand in a stone quern, the mills in Dollar being those on the Mill Green and at the Rack Mill. Early mills were breastshot or undershot, the water hitting the wheel midheight or flowing underneath; not until the 19th century bucket wheel were they overshot from above. Those "thirled" to a mill paid an often resented proportion or "multure" of their grain to the miller or the landowner. They were also responsible for the repair of the mill and the fetching of millstones – a dangerous job accomplished by rolling them vertically with a beam through the centre hole – from the nearest suitable quarry. The *Logie Account* of 1841 states that millstones had to be bought from France until the French Wars made them impossible or expensive to obtain. A James Brownhill found that the stone from the Abbey Craig, Stirling was suitable and won a prize offered by the Society for the Encouragement of the Arts in London for a substitute. Presumably Dollar stones would have to be obtained from these sources. The district thirled to a mill was known as the "sucken".

The actual village of Dollar lay where the main road from the west crossed the Dollar burn and then ascended to split into the North or Back street and the South or Front street later to be gentrified as Hillfoot Road and High Street. At the fork another road, the Drum Road (now

Holeburn - DM 1915

Argyle Street) took off south to meander its way through Wester, Middle, and Easter Pitgober, Holeburn, and the Leys to Muckhart, much of it now making a pleasant afternoon walk, although the little settlement at Holeburn has disappeared leaving only its legend of a kindly dweller named Crawford whom, in time of dearth, the fairies of the nearby Gowan Dell rewarded with gold for his generosity to his neighbours.

The junction of the roads in the Old Town was named the Cross Keys after a public house which stood at the Drum Road corner until it was demolished in the 1930s. The name, from the keys of St Peter, was an old medieval one for pubs. The main inn, however, stood at the side of the gate or road west of the village and was named appropriately "Gateside", the road from it to the town across the bridge being known as the "Nappy Gate" after the name for ale.

The first comprehensive account of the village and villagers occurs in the *1792 Account* by the Rev. John Watson, by which time conditions in both town and country were in the process of improvement. Previous to that the houses in the village would be much the same as those in the countryside. None, in their present form, are likely to predate 1775. Slates and pantiles, for example, were not in general use until after 1800. The population of the whole parish was 517 in 1755 and 510 in 1792, with the number of families in the town in 1792 being 51, and in the country 71. Watson's breakdown of livelihoods gives:

Proprietors 19	Ministers 1	Schoolmasters 1
Merchants 2	Musicians 4	Cornmillers 2
Miners 18	Smiths 3	Masons 2
Joiners 2	Weavers 5	Tailors 4
Shoemakers 2	Dyers 2	Coopers 1
Bakers 1	Butchers 2	Carters 1
Excisemen 1	Publicans 2	
Male Servants 3	Female Servants 29	
Bleachfield Workers 30		

Some of these occupations may overlap. Bleachfield work depended on the season and the musicians were possibly Blackwoods from a weaving family. Servants presumably includes farm labourers. The list is basically one of tradesmen providing services for the local population and travellers along the road, only the miners and bleachworkers betraying any main difference from a typical farming parish. The population of Tillicoultry parish at this date was 853 (34 farmers, 21 weavers), Alva 612 (no details), Clackmannan and Sauchie 2528 (116 colliers), Muckhart 526 (23 weavers). Strangely only Muckhart mentions a surgeon, and no one mentions a saddler, a trade apparently not then invented.

The average yearly wage of a farm servant, fed in the farm kitchen as was the custom, was for men £6 Scots (£1 Scots = 1s 8d Sterling) and women £2 10s. Men labourers received from 10d to 1s per day, women 6d. Slightly more was paid at harvest. These furnished their own provisions. A mason earned from 1/8d to 2/- a day, a slater 2/-, a joiner 1/6d to 1/8d, and a tailor only 8d.

A collier with wife and daughter earned 12 shillings Scots for a five-day week with free house, cheap meal and other perks. Agricultural labourers worked a six-day week for less, yet no agricultural labourer would permit a daughter to marry a miner, so low was the miner's social standing. Indeed, so isolated were they that they are said to have conformed to a distinct physical type. Miners were, at least theoretically, freed by the Act of 1799 but women and children were not banned from underground until 1843.

The price of grain was regulated by the prices (fiars) in Clackmannan town. Butcher meat cost 3d to 4^1/2d per lb Dutch weight; a hen 1/-; chickens 4d to 6d; eggs 3d to 4d per dozen; butter 1/6d per lb; cheese 3^1/2d.

Old Parish Church and Schoolhouse - DM 1904

THE CHURCH & EDUCATION

The Church

Little is known about the early ministers:

Robert Menteith (1587) officiated in Alva, Tillicoultry, Tullibody, and Dollar, but was removed for lack of knowledge of religion. There followed Gavin Donaldson (1589); Alexander Grieve (1603-16); Archibald Moncreife (1619-34); Thomas Strahan (1634-43); James Edmonstone (1644-45); Robert Geddes (1646-56) dismissed for the uncivilised offence of fighting; John Craigengelt (1656-59); Robert Forrest (1659-64); Humphrey Galbraith (1664-84); and George Monro (1684-98), an Episcopalian who clung to both cure and stipend after the Glorious Revolution of 1688. There was no resident minister or elders for ten years and in 1698 the Presbytery appointed Simon Drysdale, Thomas Drysdale, John Fergus, John Blackwood, James Gib, William Hutton, James Kirk, and Andrew Harrower as Elders. The later well-known evangelist Thomas Boston was called to preach and did so on the 19th February and 30th March 1699 but was not appointed due to opposition from the Presbytery and Dollar was spared his particular brand of hell-fire and damnation.

John Gray, age 20, was appointed and did duty from 1700 to 1745. He was known as "The Baron" because of his land dealings, purchasing the baronies of Fossoway in Perth and Teasses in Fife for £5,000. He also at one time purchased a quarter of Sheardale. This seems to have been achieved by running a banking business among his parishioners and investing some of the money from the Kirk Session, not an uncommon practice at the time. The *1841 Account* relates the story of how when there was a run on his money he filled pint stoups with sand, placing coins on top, and fooled callers into believing their deposits were safely banked. He was also of the Evangelistic persuasion, or regarded as such, and on August 4th 1736 the Session Minutes record "Being our fast day before the Communion in this place and August 7th being our preparation day and August 8th being our high Communion Sabbath Day and August 9th being the Thanksgiving Day, there was collected in whole for these days £63.9.6d", the contributions here being almost as much as was usually collected for a year. What was happening here was a "Great Work" when ministers and people flocked in from all parts to listen to several days of sermons and exhortations. Communion was not then a quietly taken monthly event but a highly charged "Occasion" involving weeks of preparation spent visiting and preparing the local congregation. On the weekend of the Communion a "tent", a wooden pulpit with a roof, was put up and ministers took turns in preaching. Hell-fire sermons detailing the gruesome tortures that most of the congregation, not being of the "chosen few", would suffer were the most popular, listeners deserting the more boring theological lectures for the ale barrels. Between emotion and alcohol the atmosphere became highly charged, communion eventually being celebrated at long tables on the Sabbath. Huge congregations could assemble – Ebenezer Erskine at little Portmoak on Loch Leven could attract a thousand worshippers, few of whom could have heard the sermons – and the expense on the local parish of providing food, drink and shelter for those that came was considerable; hence such an event would only take place every few years or, if unaffordable or the congregation felt to be too sinful, not at all. Burns satirised its excesses in the "Holy Fair" of his poem. It gradually died out but we find the Institution being given a holiday for such an occasion in the mid-nineteenth century.

Through its depletion by death it became necessary to elect a new Kirk Session in 1742 not long before Mr Gray himself died. It consisted of James Burn of Gateside, John Christie of Craiginnan, John Hutton in Kirkstyle, William Henderson in Upper Mains, William Harrower, weaver, of Whitemire, and Robert Drysdale, weaver, at the Rackmylne. They immediately had to deal with two cases of fornication, one recorded as a "Trilapse", and a case of child abandonment: "Likewise taking into yr serious consideration yt ye young child yt was barborously and inhumanly laid down by its unnatural parents about ye beginning of May last by past unto Clerk Burn's malt-kilnlogie, and seeing no way how it can be nursed or brought up, they agree upon, yt be nursed out of ye poor box by giving a woman eight pounds Scots (13/4d English) and a furlot of meal each quarter, untill they think proper to alter ye wages". This is the baby mentioned in the account of the Gateside estate, John Sorley being sponsor at its baptism as "(John) Dollar". On examining the Kirk Box they found £22 Scots of bad copper, a bond by the Rev. Gray for £1000 Scots from 1731 and no carents (interest) paid since that date, and also a bill by Mr Gray for 105 merks (mark = 13/4d) from 1732 and no carents paid, several papers relating to the security they had on Westertoun of Muckhart with 400 merks of it, 40 merks mortified of old for the use of the schoolmaster, and a bond granted by the deceased Jenat Glass for 100 merks with four years carent owing. Two bills owing carents were also found, one for £12.12s Scots for John Burn of Sherdale, and for £12 Scots to James Christie, and in "ye minutes of ye old session book that Simon Drysdaill, portioner, Nether Sherdale is resting eighteen pounds Scots of ye Price of ye Pew posest by him, in ye sayd loft of ye kirk". This pew was bought by Drysdale in a reconstruction of 1716 when two balconies were built so popular was Mr Gray's preaching, the construction being paid for by the Duke of Argyll; his uncle, John Campbell of Mamore, proprietor at this date of Craiginnan; Thomas Scotland of Wester Dollarbeg; James Bruce of Easter Dollarbeg; John Blackwood of Wester Gateside; and James Burn of Easter Gateside. Pews were bought by

Drysdale of Wester Sheardale; Janet Glass, merchant in Dollar; James Lambert of Upper Mains; James Gib of Burnside; and John Scotland of Easter Dollarbeg.

On Mr Gray's death in 1744 no minister was appointed for twenty months and the Session enquired into the cases of Ann Forrester, who attempted to abandon a child in Alloa and was later discovered sheltering in a glen below the Rackmill; Ann Drysdale who accused John Scotland of being the father of her child – he was debarred from all Church privileges; and Christian Clark's similar complaint against a landed proprietor but she was reported to have left the parish. Such cases took up much of the Session's time, the main objective being to find the father and make him contribute to the child's maintenance. A much more sensational case, however, occurred after the new minister, William Walker, age 50, was appointed. By this time the Session had again shrunk to only two elders, John Christie and James Burn. On Burn's death two more were appointed: John Hamilton, dyster, and Thomas Hall, weaver. Then John Christie of Craiginnan, the Session Clerk and Elder, was accused of scandalous behaviour which he vehemently denied. After a year of investigation by Session and Presbytery he was found guilty of having got a young girl with child and removed from office. This would seem to be the same John Christie author of *A Collection of Sermons delivered by Sundry Ministers at Different Occasions. Taken from the mouth by John Chrysty and Others. John Chrysty his book.* Price £1 10s. Begun July 30th 1733, a handwritten copy of which, and there seem to have been several for sale, is among the Academy muniments. His "scandalous behaviour" seems to have been later forgotten for he appears also to be the "Literary Shepherd" mentioned with amazement in the *1792 Account* who had a valuable library of 370 volumes. It states he was born in 1712 and lived with his brother William, and sister Margaret, all three unmarried. His books were auctioned at the North Bridge after his death. The new minister also enquired into the finances and two mort cloths – black coffin covers – were bought for hiring out at 4 shillings (5 for outsiders) for the larger, and 6d (2/-) for the smaller.

The Rev. Robert Findlay, age 41, was appointed in 1757 and served till 1792. Again an efficient minister, he was involved in the case of the strike for pay already mentioned at Mellochfoot in 1766 which must be one of the earliest among miners, the Session learning on the 4th of May that "the colliers of Mellick had recently entered into an combination among themselves and sworn unlawful oaths". John Duncan, Charles Forrester – the "first movers", James Roy "administrator of the oath", and seven others were interrogated. The matter went to the Presbytery and a month later they were given a sessional rebuke by Mr Findlay with "serious exhortations. And they seeming to be sorry for what they did, were absolved". He also undertook the unpopular induction of a Mr Thomson to St Ninians on the order of the General Assembly but made it in such a blunt manner that he was called to the bar of the Assembly and rebuked. In February a meeting of the whole parish was held and the minutes proudly make record as "witness to after ages of the noble stand the whole inhabitants of this parish made to the said Bill passing into law", the Bill so nobly withstood being that which attempted to repeal the laws against Roman Catholics.

The Session minutes, strangely, make no mention of the erection of a new church in 1775 but full details are given in the minutes of Stirling Presbytery. An inspection revealing the old church to be in a parlous condition, the Presbytery resolved to build a new church on a different site as the old church was closely surrounded by burials. The site chosen was on part of the minister's glebe to the west and he was compensated by a grant of land to the east. The church was to seat 500 and the cost was £115 9 5d plus £33 expenses this being met by some eighteen heritors, large and small. The erection required the removal of the "Jug Tree", possibly one either connected with the iron collar called "the jougs" or with folk-lore, and the building of a small session house as well for £18 5s plus an extra shilling for the traditional "drink with the masons".

On Findlay's death the next minister, the Rev. John Watson, was appointed at the age of 56. A native of Lanark he graduated in Glasgow in

41

1763 and had been a probationer for sixteen years before being appointed as assistant at Bonhill. The church possessions listed on his taking over were: a chest, two communion flagons, two large pewter plates, two servitors, one dimity table cloth, one long table cloth, two silver cups, a bag of tokens, two bibles, three volumes of the Acts of the Assembly, a box for the poor money, four mort cloths, two pewter collection plates, two stools to set them on, a "tent" for preaching from on sacramental occasions, and a basin and dimity towel for baptisms. There were thirteen different bonds and bills amounting to £435 12 6d Scots. The collection plates were set outside the church and an elder kept an eye on the congregation as they filed past on the way out, it being related of one of the McArthur Moirs that he tended to bawl out on his spell of duty: "Never mind me. Mind the plate!". Within a year of his appointment Mr Watson was to complete that invaluable aid to the understanding of the time, the first *Statistical Account*, no doubt very much helped by his efficient Session Clerk, the parish schoolmaster, John McArbrea.

Living conditions began to deteriorate at the turn of the century, famine becoming commonplace. In 1796 the minutes state: "owing to the present scarcity and the high price of meal, the labouring classes were not able to supply their families by their earnings." £20 was advanced to James Gibson, merchant in Dollar, to purchase meal at 1s 6d a peck to be sold at 1s a peck, bere or barley meal to be purchased at a 1s and sold at 9d. The clerk was asked to write to another Mr Gibson, the minister at Muckhart, pointing out that their Kirk Session ought to support the families of John Alice and Alexander Sinclair who had come from there, and the Rev. Watson and Mr Fuill were to speak to Mr Fishwick and Henry Scotland about supporting their own colliers as "the Session did not look upon them as parishioners". In 1800 the Session "moved by the clamantly necessitous condition of the industrious and labouring poor in this season of great scarcity and dearth of every necessary of life" voted another £50 from the poor fund. It was the period when Gibson recollects the Guilds in Craiginnan Farm giving out meal to villagers.

The Session records also contain details of the purely numerical census of 1801 which Mr McArbrea carried out, the population being 693, compared with the 510 of 1792, the increase being due to the enlargement of the bleachfields. He also pointed out that the Duke of Argyll had begun to feu land adjoining the old village on which a good number of substantial houses could be built and that seven farmsteadings had been demolished to build park dykes, the farms themselves being let to one tenant – a reference to the creation of Dollar Bank farm.

Education

There are no references to education being provided for the children of the parish before 1640. Around 1650 an enquiry was made into the state of education in the presbytery and all those present, including Mr Geddies, the Dollar parish minister, signified they had a schoolmaster. The first mention of an actual schoolhouse is in 1693.

The earliest schoolmaster to have his name mentioned is John Gib who was really a divinity student in Edinburgh making ends meet by teaching until he could qualify as a minister. The position seems to have been one sought after, for a quarrel occurred at the beginning of the 18th century over the holding of the post and the Duke of Argyll himself at one stage had to remove the right to draw the master's salary from a Mr Ritchie. The schoolhouse seems to have been used for meetings such as those of the Kirk Session – the schoolmaster was usually the Clerk – and the Heritors, those possessing landed property over a certain amount, who had responsibilities for the upkeep of the church and the school as well as ultimate provision for the poor. In 1791 according to the *Account* the schoolmaster was John McArbrea who taught English, Latin, writing, arithmetic, etc. and was much respected. His fixed salary was only £100 Scotch, but he drew the interest of 560 merks Scotch of sunk money, besides perquisites, as precentor, session clerk, etc. The 560 merks consisted of 500 gifted by an Archibald Paterson, merchant in Edinburgh in 1652, and 60 merks by one Kirk in Dollar. The school was originally erected in 1640 for 100 merks Scotch. Mr Watson states that "The schoolmasters, established in this parish, have, from time immemorial, been men of a liberal education, and several men of eminence have been taught in this school. Many of Mr McArbrea's scholars fill respectable places in the church, both in the establishment and the secession." Unfortunately he gives no names. (£1 Scots = one-twelfth of a £1 Sterling. Mark = 13/4d.) The *Alva Account* states that the schoolmaster there received 200 merks or £11 2 3d sterling, the maximum appointed by the law for the salary of a parish school. The Tillicoultry schoolmaster received £100 Scots.

In 1799 Mr McArbrea asked for a meeting to consider the state of the school. It then consisted of a schoolroom 16 feet square, the schoolmaster's house adjoining consisting of one room and a kitchen. On consideration the Heritors decided to combine the schoolroom and schoolhouse and build another storey on top for the schoolmaster, the existing roof to be taken off and replaced. The cost was £160.

Stobie's Map 1783 - DAA

43

THE NINETEENTH CENTURY

AGRICULTURE

In 1801 the schoolmaster John McArbrea carried out the first census of the parish, counting: 137 inhabited houses, 4 uninhabited; 157 families; 693 persons consisting of 310 males and 383 females, 43 of these in husbandry, 56 in trade, and 594 not in either category. The increase from the 1792 figure of 510 was put down to the further feuing of land by the Duke of Argyll and the development of the bleachworks.

The Duke of Argyll was most certainly feuing off the land, for by 1801 only the castle land and the hill farms remained in the actual possession of the Campbells. With fortunes being made in industry, the old order was selling off to the new, surplus elite muck being turned into needed brass and surplus brass being turned (hopefully) into elite muck. When the assessment was made of heritors to be taxed for the building of a new church in 1775, some eighteen proprietors, large and small, are listed, the smaller being mostly the heirs of the "kyndly tenants" of 1605. In a petition of 1808 both Argyll and some of the smaller tenants seem to have been bought out, only eight heritors being listed. These new owners had both the will and the money to embrace the latest ideas of the time as regards the management and care of their estates. It was the age of improvements and enclosures.

Enclosing began in South East Scotland in the late 17th century with regard to animals. Grazing parks were enclosed first, then mains farms, and finally tenants' fields by the end of the 18th century. The first enclosures locally seem to have been in Alva House grounds around 1720. Clearances led to the making of stone dykes, hedges, banks and drainage channels, and there was much draining of marshes and lochs by means of pows or ditches, open, boxed with flat stones, or filled with round stones. Drainage tiles – at first horseshoe shaped and laid on a flat tile – came in after 1826 and three tile works – Lower Mains, Kellybank, and Sheardale were producing drainage tiles and bricks, as well as pantiles for roofing. Trees, regarded as somewhat delicate plants, were first planted close to the main house then out to hedgerows, shelter belts and woods. "Improved farms" took the form of a square with a stone and mortar farmhouse of 2 to 3 rooms, a barn with stables opposite, and a midden in the middle. The farmhouse was improved first, then the farm buildings and, finally, the labourers' cottages. Later the farm house became separated from the farm buildings. The Devon Valley with its fields, woods, trees and hedges, as we know it, or have known it, derives from this period.

According to *Watson* the old "run-rig" system of farming in Dollar – he is, probably, chiefly referring to the Upper and Lower Mains – was given up in 1774:

> different proprietors got their respective proportions of ground laid together, each by itself. This has been productive of several very desirable consequences: such as, cutting off endless quarrels and disputes, that were continually taking place between the different proprietors, or their tenants, about their encroaching or trespassing upon one another; and so establishing peace and harmony amongst neighbours, instead of strife and variance.

The division of the Mains Lands is shown in Udney's Plan of 1793, the proprietors then being Alexander Williamson, William Marshall, Robert Fergus, William Fitt or Foot, Adam Hutton, James Lamb, and John Kirkmichael (later Dr Roebuck). Their relationship to the 1605 feuars is given in the section on the Lands of Dollar. Strangely, run-rig seems to have persisted at Sheardale till later although each quarter had the advantage of having its own separate dwelling.

The enclosure of land would not have been possible without technical improvements in farming methods. Proper crop rotation was now understood and the cultivation of wheat, turnips and potatoes became common. In Clackmannanshire in particular it became customary to let patches of land out to tradesmen for growing potatoes. Potatoes eventually provided 25% of the Lowland diet and 75% of the Highland, an imbalance which was to lead in the middle years of the century to famine conditions. A potato plough was invented in 1855 and spinner lifters in 1896.

The Old Scots Plough was replaced by improved versions. By 1790 "English" ploughs, drawn by up to 10 horses were in use, but these also were being replaced by the plough invented by James Small of Berwick with its triangular frame and curved mouldboard. This was being fully cast in iron by the Carron Iron Works in 1780, and was followed by further developments by Gray and Wilson at Uddingston, and by the Oliver from America. Such ploughs suited the ploughing out of the old ridges and were operated by two horses and a man. The local smiths adapted them for local conditions.

The sickle with a toothed cutting edge used by women was replaced by the smooth-bladed scythe-hook which took a man's strength to use, leading to Highland women being replaced by Irish men, some 40,000 being estimated as coming over for the season in 1840.

The scythe-hook, in its turn, was replaced by the scythe with a triangular or curved frame also requiring to be used by men. The preferred method with both the smooth sickle and scythe was to cut across the ridges as long as they were owned in one block, the cutters working in echelon followed by a male strapmaker, women lifters, and a male bandster who tied and stooked. The first attempt at a reaping machine was made in 1805 by Gladstone at Castle Douglas but machines were not successful until the introduction of the McCormick reaper from America in 1840. The labour force was not reduced even then as 16 people were required to keep up with it. Only after 1878 with the introduction of the binder mechanism and other improvements was less labour required.

The first successful threshing machine was made by Andrew Meikle of Knowe Mill in East Lothian who built it for Stein of Kilbagie at Kincardine. Meikle's father had built the first winnowing machine and his son erected the huge waterwheel that drained Blair Drummond moss. The motive power was by wind, water or the open or closed horsewalk for 1 to 6 horses. Old maps disclose lades and dams at Kellybank, Dollarbank, and Middleton for water, and Hillfoot Farm and Westerton had the little circular buildings for horses. What happened at the Mains Farms and Sheardale is not known.

Horse-gangs were replaced by steam engines in the 1830s – the first portable mill was in 1864.

Such improvements made many farm workers' old jobs redundant and they turned to other skills. The tasker with the flail dropped out but with the establishment of hill farms shepherds became important. The new skills of hedgers, ditchers, and dykers came into being. The farm grieve or foreman appeared about 1750. The change from ox to horse brought in the new class of horsemen and ploughing matches were organised. Grades of horsemen were created as well as the horsemen's secret society with its "horseman's word" that made any horse obey the initiated. Saddlers also seem to have appeared to make proper harness. Farm servants became moveable and their work saleable. Hirings were made every six months for the unmarried and every year for the married. The hind and half-hind were replaced by the married couple. Farmworkers began to assert themselves and ministers fulminated about fashions in dress, tea drinking and the alcoholic dram.

Gradually the smaller proprietors were bought out until the parish became divided into a number of larger estates. The largest of these was Harviestoun with much of its land also in Tillicoultry parish. It was owned by the Tait family until 1832, then by Globe Insurance till 1859 when it was bought by the Orr family and subsequently enlarged. Dollarfield, owned by the Haig family, remained smaller with its focus on the bleachworks. Hillfoot was improved but not enlarged, the McArthur Moirs also owning land at Dunoon. West Sheardale was owned by the Duncansons and then, later in the century, by a Mr Miller, finally being acquired by Harviestoun. Sheardale belonged to Lord Cathcart but was later bought by Harviestoun, and Dollarbeg, as was its wont, went through several hands.

HARVIESTOUN

Harviestoun was originally the eastern half of a village that lay athwart the Harviestoun Burn, the other half being known as Ellistoun, the whole sometimes being referred to as Ellertown. It is named Easter Tillicoultrie on Stobie's map of 1783 to distinguish it from the then smaller

Wester Tillicoultrie also known as Colerstone, Collintown, Coaltown and Cairntown. *Gibson*

Harviestoun Castle - DMus

states there were seventeen houses in the Harviestoun half of the village alone (Dollar village had 51 families in 1792). The earliest reference appears in the Exchequer Rolls for 1480-7 when Robert Drisdale is listed as living in Eliotsdawac and Andrew Drisdale as in Hervyisdawac, presumably the davoch – an ancient measure of land of up to 416 acres – belonging respectively to early owners Harvey and Elliot (or Ellis). Names cited as being portioners of the hamlet around 1800 are Henderson, Meiklejohn, Patoune, Duncanson, May, and Huitcheone. Easter Tillicoultry contained a small mansion house which, sometime around 1780, was purchased, apparently, from a John Drysdale by John Tait, an Edinburgh lawyer, who commenced to improve both the mansion and the estate, tasks undertaken even more enthusiastically by his son after his father's death.

John Tait was born in 1727, being the son of a mason in the parish of Longside near Peterhead. He was sent down to Edinburgh in 1750 to join the law firm of Ronald Craufurd, W.S. Tait became a Writer to the Signet himself in 1763, and later inherited the firm, Craufurd's only child, a daughter, marrying the Earl of Dumfries. John Tait married a Charles Murdoch, daughter of a staunch Jacobite who had had his land confiscated, and they had one son, Craufurd. Tait also bought an estate on Loch Fyne which he named Cumlodden after his wife's father's former lands. Harviestoun was for summer use,

the family home being at 2 Park Place, Edinburgh, off George Square, a site now occupied by the University Medical College. Charles died when Craufurd was in his teens and it was arranged that her sister, a Mrs Hamilton, also a widow, should come north from Dumfriesshire with the younger members of her own family to keep house. She was the stepmother of Robert Burns' friend, Gavin Hamilton, and as such occasioned the visit to Harviestoun of the poet in 1787 when he was nobly entertained and conducted to all the local points of scenic interest for inspiration. The sights that inspired him turned out to be Miss Charlotte Hamilton to whom he paid tribute in "The Banks of the Devon" and her cousin, Peggy Chalmers, remembered in the last poem he wrote "Fairest Maid on Devon Banks".

Craufurd followed his father into the law firm, falling in love with the girl next door at 1 Park Place, who, fortunately, turned out to be Susan, the daughter of Sir Ilay Campbell, Lord President of the Court of Session, and his wife the Edinburgh beauty, Susan Murray. John Tait died in 1800 and was buried in the newly created family burial ground on the banks of the River Devon, having had himself immortalised in a portrait by Raeburn now at Hill of Tarvit House. Craufurd now indulged in energetic improvement, concentrating first on building cottages for his tenants at Loch Fyne and reforming their ancient ways. Alas, due to Gaelic suspicion, the cottages remained unoccupied and the ways ancient. The Cumlodden estate was sold in 1825 to Craufurd Tait's brother-in-law, Archibald Campbell, part of it now being Crarae Gardens. He then turned his enthusiasm on the Harviestoun estate. Gradually buying out or rehousing the portioners he demolished their primitive cottages and replaced them with a palatial farm steading, coach house, and walled garden. The mansion house was rebuilt in the latest Italianate style, the main road moved half-a-mile south with numerous bends incorporated so that travellers could admire the vistas, park trees were planted, and shelter belts formed. The construction of the West Drive in 1796 unearthed a prehistoric burial, and the formation of a Water Garden and Grotto in 1802 an ancient sword. He also introduced and invented a range of machines for processing cattle food, a kitchen spit powered by water power, and a much admired three-tiered poultry house with a series of ladders by which the hens ascended to the top floor, and the turkeys to the second, leaving the ducks and geese to grovel in the basement. He led the Clackmannanshire Yeomanry in exercises which, no doubt, terrified the local peasantry while keeping a caravan in readiness to evacuate his family should the dreaded Frenchies ever have the effrontery to float themselves up the Forth.

Craufurd continued to expand the estate by buying land when it became available and around 1807 acquired the first and last of the Campbell lands, the "ten-pound land" that included the castle, the glen, the Kellyburn coalpits, and the right to appoint the minister. This last was by no means the least for he disapproved of the plans drawn up by the then minister and Kirk Session for the bequest left by John McNabb and led the parish opposition to it until the minister died and he was able to appoint a successor. No doubt he hoped to make money from the coalpits but this ran into trouble when the owner of Westerton went to law about the drainage of these and won, causing the pits to be abandoned. By 1822 he was in financial difficulty and, after Harviestoun was advertised for sale but not sold, he was forced to seek sanctuary for a time from his creditors in the apartment of a friend, the Duke of Hamilton, at Holyrood House. Broken in health he died in 1832 and was buried in the family graveyard. His wife, Susan, had long predeceased him, dying on Handsel Monday, the 3rd of January 1814, an hour after giving her children the customary New Year presents.

They had had nine of a family. The oldest daughter, Susan Murray, fell in love with an English cousin and they were married in 1818 at the house of Sir Ilay Campbell at Garscube, such frivolous ceremonies not being permitted in church – the groom even had to slip the ring discreetly on her finger after the ceremony. He was George Sitwell of Renishaw and they were destined to be the great grandparents of that terrible trio of the early twentieth century, Edith, Osbert, and Sacheverell. Her elder brother, John, had been brought home for the wedding from

Craufurd Tait - DM 1909

Geneva where he had been sent to cool off after falling in love with Sir George's sister, Mary Sitwell. He married his Mary, however, and became Sheriff of Clackmannan for thirty years, followed by nine as Sheriff of Perth and Kinross. He died in 1877. The second son, James, remained a bachelor and carried on the Edinburgh law firm of Tait & Young. A sister, Charlotte, married into the ancient English family of Wake and became Lady Wake, while another sister, Marion, married a Mr Wildman M.P., Recorder of Nottingham. The third son, Thomas, disappeared off to India for twenty-six years to become a Colonel in the 3rd Bengal Irregular Cavalry, Tait's Horse, which distinguished itself in the 1842 Afghan Campaign. Another son, Crawford followed him out to India but was almost immediately invalided home, dying at sea at the age of 21. Thomas, himself, was eventually also invalided home in 1857 dying two years later aged 54.

The two youngest sons, Campbell and Archie, were both crippled, Archie being born with club feet and Campbell contracting paralysis of the left leg due, said the medical profession, to the cutting of his teeth. At an early age, on the suggestion of Sir George Sitwell, they were sent down to Whitworth in Lancashire with their nurse, Betty Morton, for the attention of two bone doctors by the name of Taylor, who put them into tin boots fitted with screws which were adjusted early every morning, early because by ten o'clock both doctors were drunk and incapable. Nine months later they returned home, apparently cured. Archie by 1821, age 10, was coping with life at the High School and Campbell, a year older, was preparing to join a training ship at Portsmouth. Archie contracted scarlet fever but was well enough to attend a farewell party for his brother at the end of which Camie complained of a sore throat. Three days later he was dead.

Archie transferred from the High School to the new Edinburgh Academy in 1825, being dux in 1827. From there he went to Glasgow University and won a Snell Scholarship to Oxford, this being accomplished by the simple expedient of a rich Glasgow uncle inviting all the relevant awarding professors to dinner. From Oxford he spent a few years as a vicar and tutor at Balden nearby before, on the death of Dr Arnold in 1842, he was appointed headmaster of Rugby, marrying Catherine, the aunt of the well-known inventor of a linguistic lapse, Archdeacon Spooner of Coventry. Bad health forced Archie to give up Rugby in 1858 and, on recovery, he was appointed Dean of Carlisle. On the birth of their seventh child, scarlet fever struck again and five little girls died within three weeks, leaving only the baby and a seven year old son. The tragedy aroused immense sympathy, the Queen being much affected, and Archie was moved to the Bishopric of London when it became vacant. In 1862 he turned down the Archbishopric of York but in 1868 accepted that of Canterbury. He died in 1881, age 77, and is buried at Addinstone, Surrey. A bust of him is set into the wall of the University Music Building at Bristo Square, Edinburgh, commemorating his birth place. A daughter married Randall Davidson, a later Archbishop. Osbert Sitwell reckoned the Reverend Archie was the cause of his eccentric father, George, becoming a rampant atheist and blamed him for depleting the family wine cellars as he gargled with port for his health every morning and the butler considered that only the very best port was good enough for an Archbishop.

On the death of Craufurd Tait, Harviestoun was surrendered to the Globe Insurance

Tait's Tomb - DAA

Company which ran it for many years before selling it to the Glasgow merchant and ex-Lord Provost Sir Andrew Orr, in 1859. He added the porch and the tower and further enlarged and improved the estate by adding the estates of Aberdona in 1860 and the remainder of Sheardale in 1861 to the property. On his death in 1874 it passed to his brother, James, who added Gateside, Pitgober, and Lambton. He, in turn, was succeeded by a nephew, John H. Kerr, who was succeeded by his son, J. Ernest Kerr in 1904. The latter became well known as an agriculturalist and breeder of cattle, the Harviestoun Aberdeen-Angus being world renowned as was their breed of Shetland ponies. On his death the estate passed to his daughter, Mrs Margaret Grant, and thence to her daughter, Mrs Lucy Poett. The family moved to Aberdona House, and Harviestoun remained empty for some years until it was pressed into use as a Preparatory School for the Academy after the fire of 1961. After that it was unroofed and then finally demolished when it became dangerous.

All that remains is the graveyard, Taits' Tomb, now standing somewhat forlornly in the middle of a field. Originally an open horse-shoe shape it stood in a grove of trees by the side of the river. The railway, in 1869, cut off the river bend leaving it in a stagnant pool in a field and open to vandalism. It was accordingly walled across. The trees have since been felled and the field drained. Sheriff John Tait left the interest on £100 to be given annually to the Academy garden boys for looking after it; and the lease of a cottage, which the Archbishop owned and which was used for family gatherings, contained the condition that the future owner looked after the graveyard as well. The cottage is now Blairlogie Hotel. The tomb remains a sad memorial to the dreams of a man who, according to his daughter Lady Wake, had planned his estate following the description of the Garden of Eden in "Paradise Lost".

DOLLARFIELD

In 1786 a William Haig took a 38-year lease of the Bridgehaugh and Damhead, presumably on the north bank of the Devon at the Rackmill, the former meal mill of Dollarbeg. A year later he took a similar lease of the Rackmill itself and established a bleaching works. He seems to have been a descendant of a James Haig of the Orchard, Tullibody, who married Elisabeth Burn of Easter Sheardale, a relation of the Burns of Gateside. Haig was the grandson of an earlier James Haig who had come from Bemersyde on the Borders to Stirling in 1623 and who was also ancestor of Field Marshal Haig of the Fife family. Easter Sheardale was no longer owned by the Haigs but presumably he knew the district.

Early bleaching was done by the use of sour milk, exposure to sunlight, mechanical beating, boiling, and rinsing with water, hence the requirements of being close to Dollarfield farm for milk, having large areas of flat ground for exposure on the haughs of the Devon, a river diverted into lades for power, coal – a mine is marked at Dollarfield – and clean water from the Dollar Burn. Haig was soon into the newer methods of chemical bleaching, first by sulphuric acid and then by chlorine, which dramatically reduced the time required, and he won awards for developing the process. Presumably he was connected in some way with Roebuck of the Carron and Devon Iron Works who was connected with the production of sulphuric acid and who bought, at one time, adjacent land. The linen came in swathes of from 40 to 100 yards – Scots linen was notoriously dirty being, in early times, woven in smoke infested cottages. Latches were sewn on at two-yard intervals so that it could be handled and hung from posts in the fields. Such rows of rippling cloth must have made the fields by the Devon an impressive sight. The linen

came mostly from Dunfermline and Kirkcaldy and also, at the beginning of this century, from Freuchie and Northern Ireland. Cotton was sent from Glasgow as well. In later times the mill was bleaching finished pieces in the form of sheets, tablecloths etc. Haig was also interested in actual farming and bought other sections of the Lower Mains as they became available. A grandson William James Haig in 1878 gave the following account of the family land deals.

In 1795 William Haig bought Peddie's Westerhills opposite Lower Sheardale steading on both sides of the Devon; in 1798 Roebuck's land to the west of Dollarfield. In 1800 he and Tait of Harviestoun bought Easter Sheardale from Lord Cathcart, Tait taking the land and Haig the Rackmill. Haig also purchased Marshall's Westerhills, which he sold along with Peddle's to Tait. In 1809 he built the West Mill, now a barn with bricked up windows, which lay in the West Haugh alongside the Devon. In 1805 he bought the East and West crofts along the Ochilton Road; in 1810 the Newrawhead quarter of Sheardale; and in 1818 Husband's Haugh. In 1820 he had a new Devon Channel cut through Skipper's Haugh and the old channel turned into a lade past the West Mill. In 1831 he bought a small piece of Lamb's at the Tail Lade and at the same time built Ochilton House in part of Izatt's land leaving three fields known as North Park, Boston, and Ochilton. He also seems to have owned Glensherup.

The estate descended to his son, John, and on his death in 1859 it passed to his brother, William J. Haig, a surgeon with the East India Company and an F.P. of Dollar and Edinburgh Academies, who had married a daughter of Peter Balfour, the minister of Clackmannan. W.J. became Chairman of the Parish Council, Member of the School Board and a Governor of the Academy. He was succeeded in 1905 by his eldest son, Col. Robert Haig. Educated like the rest of the boys at the Academy and Loretto, he had trained as a chemist. Like his father he served on the Parish Council and the School Board and took part in local Opera and Drama productions. A second son, Lt. Col. P.B. Haig, was a surgeon In the Indian Civil Service, later joining Edinburgh Royal Infirmary. He retired to

Nairn. A third son, J.B. Haig, became Procurator Fiscal for Clackmannan. He bought Kelly Cottage in 1905 and replaced it with the large house known as Kellyside. A daughter, Lilian, was much respected in the parish for her kindliness and started the Dollar Red Cross.

Col. Haig died in 1935 and the Bleach Works ceased production in 1937, the buildings later being used as a sawmill. Dollarfield House was occupied by the army during World War II and was burnt down in 1940. It was replaced when peace came. The steading was once the largest lofted steading in Scotland. The Haigs sold the estate after the war and it is now the property of

Col. Haig and servants at Dollarfield - DMus

Arndean, the old dairy at present being used for the small brewery producing Harviestoun Ale. The bleach works buildings were razed in 1963, and the ground turned into the present Caravan Park. The weir, the Rack Mill lade, the Rack Mill – now a house but before that converted by Colonel Robert Haig into an electricity generating station – and the West Mill and its lade are still to be seen.

The bridge at the Rackmill dates from 1929. It replaced a metal bridge capable of taking one-way traffic. Before that there was a series of wooden foot bridges constantly damaged by floods. *Watson* states, however, there was a stone bridge destroyed some years before 1792, the *Tillicoultry Account* confirming that "an uncommon flood happened in September 1785, which carried away a prodigious quantity of corn, broke down a stone bridge at the Rack mill in Dollar, and occasioned other very extraordinary damage". The surviving keystone

and other parts were at one time stored at Gateside. It bridged the river opposite to where a chimney was built in 1852, presumably across from where the Stey Brae comes down from Sheardale, there being no road down from Dollarbeg in 1785. *Watson* also states that before this bridge there was a custom of stilting over the river on suitably cut branches, these being left on either bank. Flooding must have been frequent,

The metal bridge at the Rackmill - DM 1909

the Academy running a school at Sheardale for many years to save the children crossing the Devon. Old photographs reveal cottages on the left hand side at the bend of the turn up the brae as well as the original "rack" or ford that gave the mill its alternative name to that of being the "milne of Dollarbeg".

THE MANOR HOUSE
UPPER MAINS

The Manor or Mansion House of Upper Mains stood on the site of the present Academy Dining Hall & Swimming Pool. A two-storeyed building with four apartments and another single-storey (possibly the original) building attached at the west end, it was part of the little hamlet of Upper Mains. The date of its building is not known but around the middle of the 18th century it became the property of an Alexander Williamson of Dumfriesshire, born in 1724, Secretary to the second Earl of Hopetoun, the proprietor of the silver and lead mines at Leadhills. Williamson in 1786 bought the estate of Balgray near Lockerbie, His wife, Christian Robertson, came from Brunton in Fife and it was supposedly through her that the Dollar property came into the possession of the Williamsons. Udney's plan shows them possessing some eighty acres as against the forty of the other main feuars so its seems likely that they also bought adjoining land. Alexander Williamson died in Edinburgh in 1805 and, together with his wife who predeceased him in 1762, is buried in Dollar churchyard. They had three sons:

The eldest son, Charles, had a remarkable career. Born in 1757, he joined the 25th Regiment of Foot, later the KOSBs, in 1775, and rose to the rank of captain. The 25th was sent to America and in 1778 Charles was posted to join them. The ship he was travelling on was, however, captured by a French privateer and after being wounded in the fighting he landed up, as a prisoner on parole, in the house of a Mr Newell in Boston. Here he fell ill and was nursed by his host's daughter, Abigail, with whom he fell in love. In 1781 an exchange of prisoners was arranged and he and Abigail were married in New London, Connecticut in December before he brought his bride home to Dollar. Here he remained for six years though he seems to have travelled on the continent. In 1787 he moved to Balgray and some three years later was offered the post of administrator of 3,500 square miles of land in the north western part of New York State which an English company had bought for £75,000. With a selected party of Scots he set out and landed in December 1791 at Norfolk in Virginia. Settling his family temporarily at Philadelphia he took the oath of allegiance and became a naturalised American citizen before venturing north to survey the land he was to administer. It extended from Pennsylvania in the south to Lake Ontario in the north and from Seneca Lake on the east to the Genesee River on

the west and became known as the Genesee tract, including what is now called Steuben County. It was completely wild and Williamson's first task was to open up a highway from south-east to north-west. This was completed in August 1793 and he selected the site for the chief town in the Conhocton Valley naming it Bath after the daughter, Baroness Bath, of one of his employers, William Pulteney. Here he lived for the next eight years with his wife and children in a log house encouraging the settlement of the country, although meeting personal and political opposition. He resigned his post in 1781, owing

The Manor House, Upper Mains - DM 1904

to financial differences with his employers, but remained two years. He returned to Britain but during the next few years made several journeys back to America. In 1806 he was offered a diplomatic post with the British Government and was sent to compile a report on Egypt. Later carrying out a mission in the West Indies he died of yellow fever aged 51 and was buried at sea. His wife and family after 1806 continued to reside in America at a town he founded in 1794 named Geneva where she died in 1824. Around 1800 Captain Williamson sold part of his Dollar holdings to Tait of Harviestoun and, later, his son, Charles Alexander, sold the rest. The son resided at Geneva until 1836 when he returned to Edinburgh but became smitten by gold fever and set out for California, contracting cholera on the way and dying at Fort Leavenworth. The Indians who nursed him sent his watch and last letter home to Scotland. His son, Colonel D.R.

Williamson, who gave this account of the family, was the owner of Lawers in Perthshire early in this century.

The second son, John Hope Williamson, was born in 1758 and he too rose to the rank of captain in the 25th Foot. While serving in Spain at the end of the century a nun fled for protection to the British officers and was befriended by him. He brought her home with him to Scotland and married her and they took up residence at the family home in Dollar where he died in 1796. His widow "the little Spanish nun" Madam Williamson continued to live in Dollar for many years.

The third son, David Robertson Williamson, became an advocate in 1783 and was appointed Sheriff of Stirling and Clackmannan in 1797. In 1807 Stirling became separate and Clackmannan joined with Kinross and he became Sheriff of Stirlingshire. In 1811 he was appointed a judge under the title of Lord Balgray. Although married to his cousin, Williamina Robertson, the heiress of Lawers, he died in 1837 without issue and his nephew, Colonel Lawers, succeeded. The Balgray estate had been sold in 1851 to a David Jardine of Calcutta of the firm of Jardine, Mathieson & Company.

The father, Alexander Williamson, had occasion while factor of the Earl of Hopetoun to institute court action over a matter of school discipline against the Rector of Moffat Grammar School, James Clarke. Short of money and influence, Clarke, a native of Dumfries, appealed to his friend, the poet Robert Burns, for help and Burns aided him not only with money and influence but arranged a job in England for him if the case went against him. Clarke, however, won but later removed to Forfar and then became headmaster of Cupar Grammar School. Burns, at the end of his life, wrote to Clarke asking repayment of the loan and Clarke, although still deeply in debt repaid what he could, the remainder being paid after the poet's death. Clarke became the father-in-law of Peter Steven, the first Writing Master at the Academy, and presumably ended his days at Stevens' house "Seberham", dying, according to his tombstone which stands outside the old kirk, in 1825. Alexander Williamson lies some fifty feet away to the west!

The Manor House was thereafter variously tenanted but gradually deteriorated. It was eventually bought by the Academy and demolished in 1966. A fine watercolour of it by Ian Campbell hangs in the Academy Entrance Hall.

LOWER MAINS

Stobie's map marks a Manor House at Lower Mains. This small two-storeyed house was apparently built by William Futt, one of the feuars of Lower Mains. Its main claim to fame was an ornamental porch which made it look like a face with two window eyes and a nose. It was occupied at one time by the Hon. Harry Ogilvie who had the eccentric habit of setting his pigs at large and pursuing them on horseback with his hounds, the house henceforth being known as "Tallyho House". It was also lived in later by the rural postman who delivered the mail in a horse and brake. It was demolished early in this century and a much admired combined sundial and moondial was crated and sent down to England. The porch was also much admired by one of the McArthur Moirs and a copy was erected as a little garden folly at Hillfoot House where it stood until demolished with the remains of that house in recent years.

"Tally-ho" House. Lower Mains - DM 1915

HILLFOOT HOUSE

According to the old records held at Hillfoot House in 1790 a small part of the estate was held blanch of the crown, the rest from the Duke of Argyll. At this time 100 acres were under culture and 400 in pasture. The duty due to Argyll was

£16 Scots money, 21 stone of cheese and six stone of butter delivered to Castle Campbell, or 5/- Scots for each stone of cheese and 10/- for each stone of butter not consumed. Two chalders of oats were also to be delivered at the castle. For Lochiefaulds, Bog and Drymie the payment was 33/4d with 1 boll 3 firlots of barley, the work and labour of the iron instruments of the plough by which the lands in the Lordship of Campbell were cultivated, and axes for slaughtering the Duke's marts – the proprietor to have the heads of all those slaughtered in the Castle or in Stirling. In 1782 a lease of the oats was obtained

Hillfoot House - DM 1914

from the Duke at £2 17 11d per boll equal to the average for the 17 preceding years.

The oldest known charter was granted to a John Paton in 1569. A John Drysdale was known as the Laird of Hillfoot in 1683 and a descendant, "Old Hillie", seems to have retired from Hillfoot to the Old Town in the late 1700s, probably on the estate being bought by a Captain Paul Needrick who is listed as a heritor there in 1795. Shortly after it seems to have been sold to John McArthur Moir, a Writer to the Signet, who also owned the estate of Milton in Dunoon. He was succeeded in 1871 by his brother, James, who started the Dollar Volunteers and bought the former U.P. Church on the Burnside in 1913, presenting it to the Parish Church as a Church Hall. He was succeeded in turn by his son John, who had taken up ranching in Wyoming and married an American, Mercedes Gever. They continued to farm Hillfoot and Lawhill until 1923 when they moved to Dunoon. John died in 1937. All the

Moirs attended the Academy for their early schooling and took a very active interest in town, church, and school affairs. The estate was later sold. Lawhill was bought by a farmer who, having cut down the hedgerow trees, then sold off much of the land for housing. Hillfoot House remained occupied for many years but after World War II was abandoned and later demolished. A new house has been built on the site. The Home Farm remains in good repair with its central farm house and range of farm buildings, including a horse mill, all now converted into housing. The Hill Farm seems to have been on the site of the cottages at Gloomhill, the hill itself having been leased off for quarrying to the Balmore Quarry Company a large crushing plant being erected in 1935. It was, later, sold with Hillfoot Hill, for blanket forestry. The best known occupants of the hill farm were the Cram family, one of whom, Robert, was dux of the Academy. He went out to South Africa but died there young. The Academy Archives contain a letter from him giving a full description of a visit to the famous American Confederate cruiser, the "Alabama". The immediate area near the main house was known as Lochyfaulds and was reputedly the haunt of witches. A large whinstone in a field is known as "The Wizard's Stone", having been set there by one of the Moirs to take the place of a rotting stake said to mark the spot where the last Dollar witch (and, naturally, the last Scots one), named Forrester, was burnt, though this is probably folk confusion with the vicar of Dollar, Thomas Forrest. Two flat stones in the valley of the Kelly Burn are also reputedly haunted, the largest, "The Deil's Cradle", being that on which the local witches rock Satan to sleep at Hallowe'en. In the house grounds the remains of a coach house and walled garden still exist while to the north there is a large open reservoir and to the west a curling pond, long known to children as the Paradise Pool, but of recent years much overgrown. A spring and stone marked on maps as Moir's Well were eliminated by the builders of that housing scheme.

WESTER OR NETHER SHEARDALE

In 1605 this quarter of Sheardale was feued to a William Drysdaill and in 1775 was still in

Sheardale House - DMus

possession of a Simon Drysdale. Shortly after that date it seems to have been sold to the Duncanson family, presumably related in some way to the owner of the dry dock at Alloa. The owner, a Dr Duncanson, seems to have played a large part in the cultural affairs of the county. A daughter married Andrew Bell, who had the honour to be the first mathematics master at the Academy and also the first to be dismissed after an altercation with the Principal, Dr Mylne, over boys playing football in the grounds. He then ran a private school at Helen Place before illness forced him to retire to his in-laws at Sheardale. There he devoted himself to the onerous task of working out the mathematical tables which so many of the older of us remember scanning in booklets at school, and which the young conjure up at the press of a button. He died in a riding accident. The original house, recognisable by its skew putts, seems to be still there though added to and harled over. A coach house and walled garden lie behind. The estate was sold to a John Miller, owner of a large china business in Edinburgh and supplier of such wares to no less a customer than Queen Victoria. Miller built a new house in mid-century, known as Sheardale House, on the rise above the old one. He was much involved in religion and also built a United Presbyterian church in Dollar old town. The estate was sold to Harviestoun and though the house was then rented, it seldom saw the sun and was eventually demolished.

GATESIDE

Gateside consisted – in its latter days at least – of a brewing house where the present Gateside house stands, stables at the present garage, and the two-storied inn itself in the front garden of the present Meadowbank. The road from it to the village across the bridge was known as the "Nappy Gate", nappy being ale though happy might be as appropriate. Land going with it included the Brewer's Knowe on the golf course and the prep school field opposite. Though sometimes mentioned with the Argyll lands – as in the grant to the Earl of Perth – for the most part it seems to have been a little estate on its own, possibly "carte blanche" at one time from the crown if the curious little story – unbacked by any documentary evidence – that its feu was the provision of five gallons of new ale, five gallons of old ale, and five gallons in the process of brewing to passing royalty, bears any truth. For most of its recorded history it belonged to the Burn or Burns family presumably of Easter Sheardale inherited by marriage when a William Burn in 1692 married a Margaret Reid – again presumably of the Craighead quarter of Sheardale – whose great great grandfather is stated to have held it. The Burn's son, James or "Clerk" Burn married Kathleen Mayne described in the *Dollar Register of Burials* as a "sister of William Mayne, Lord Newhaven". Their initials appeared on a stone inscribed "Repaired July 1718. I.B.C.M." built into an addition to Gateside while a worn adjoining stone had a W.B. or W.R. for William Burn or Reid dated 16??. Clerk Burn's son (1727 – 94) described himself in a tombstone in the churchyard erected to his parents as "many years senior clergyman in Calcutta". His son, James, was furth of Scotland when a law suit was brought by the Duke of Argyll in 1801 to clarify the grazing rights on the Banks of Dollar, the Court of Session confirming Gateside's right to pasture "six kine and their soums (weaned calves)" but only under a herder on untilled land below the dyke between Whitsunday and Martinmas and between sunrise and sunset. It was also given leave to take "feals", shaped turfs, and "divots", clods, for the repair of houses, and stone from the Quarrel Burn and Heughhead. The inn was then tenanted by Robert Wright, tenant in Gateside and Knowehead like his father who died in 1768. The inn reputedly had a stone recording that Mary, Queen of Scots, had slept there and an antique bed known as the "royal bed" which eventually dropped to pieces and on which one of the Dukes was supposed to have slept. A tree to the west was known as the Argyll Tree. Gateside was still separate and owned by a Dunfermline lawyer in 1665 but was shortly after purchased by Orr of Harviestoun.

In 1742 a well-clad baby boy was found in the malt-kiln of the brewery by "Clerk" Burns and a search for the parents proving unsuccessful was christened "Dollar" and brought up by a Mrs Sorley. This "Foundling of Gateside" disappeared on reaching manhood and nothing more was heard of him. Around 1890 a gentleman bearing the name of Dollar and resident in southern England appeared in the village making enquiries and other descendants, knowing the connection, have more recently done so. The child was lucky, a less fortunate one found in a less fortunate place was condemned to bear the name Jenny Rigghead. A possible descendant of the Burns was Robert Burns, not the poet but the head of painting at Edinburgh Art School, the loss of whose magnificent furbishment of Crawford's Edinburgh Tea Rooms in the 1930s has recently been recognised as another major artistic misfortune, similar to that of the Cranston Tearooms, Glasgow.

ABERDONA

The house was built by the Erskines of Alva, relations of the Mar family, and it and the relevant quarter of Sheardale were bought by Harviestoun about 1860. After the decision was taken to remove from Harviestoun Castle it became the principal house of the estate.

COWDEN

Cowden House occupied the site of what was once an ancient episcopal residence erected about 1320 by William Lamberton, Bishop of St Andrews, the intimate friend and counsellor of Robert the Bruce, and completer of the Cathedral. The site is supposedly that of an old Pictish fort. All that remains of Lamberton's house is an arched gateway and the ruined foundations of a tower. It was called Castleton to distinguish it from the nearby Kirkton round the church in Muckhart. In 1491 Muckhartshire was

gifted by the then Archbishop of St Andrews, William Shevez, to the first Earl of Argyll for his support in a struggle over precedence with Blacadder, the Archbishop of Glasgow. A deed of 1573 by the fifth Earl gave sasine to Dame Jean Cunynghame, his wife's niece and later the wife of Haldane of Gleneagles, of the lands of Castleton in life-rent. In 1620 it was part of the extensive estate of Tullibole to which William Halliday was served heir. It underwent the same fortunes as the rest of the Argyll estates during the Civil War and the tenth Earl received the lands of Castleton and Blairhill back with others after his father's forfeiture. Castleton seems to have passed out of Argyll hands around 1700. Over the entrance to a tower of more recent construction there is an old lintel, not in situ, bearing 17 WP MH 07, possibly the initials of those that acquired it. Soon after, the property came into the hands of James Gib, whose son Adam, born there in 1714, was ordained the first minister in Edinburgh of the Secession Church in 1738. He was left the estate but relinquished it in

Cowden House - DM 1905

favour of an elder brother. A small second house was erected near the original one but was demolished in the nineteenth century, its door lintel with 17 AG IT 97 on it for Adam Gib and his wife, being set into one of the garden gates.

In 1758 the neighbouring estate of Cowden was purchased by a Dr William Bruce, the heir of the ancient family of Bruce of Clackmannan. Originally part of the lands of Pitgober, it was sold in 1736 by George Paton of Middle Ballilisk (Middlehall) to John Paton, bookseller in Edinburgh, by whom it was sold to Bruce. This old Cowden House was the birthplace in 1816 of Margaret Bruce who, in 1838, married the ninth Earl of Airlie. On the death of her father her mother married a Church of England clergyman, a Mr Glen. She added considerably to the property, acquiring Easter Castleton in 1828 when it was sold on the bankruptcy of John Gib, surgeon in Dunfermline. She took up residence there and greatly enlarged and improved the property. Eventually a James Gib sold Wester Castleton to "Mrs Margaret Oliver or Glen in life-rent and the Rt. Hon. Margaret Bruce, Countess of Airlie in fee". The old house, home of the Gibs, was demolished and gardens made along the Holeburn. The Countess of Airlie died at Brighton in 1854, leaving four sons who were brought up at Castleton by Mrs Glen. In 1866 the oldest son, who succeeded to the property after her death, sold it to a Mr John Christie. He further improved both house and gardens, including planting specimens of all known pines that would grow in Scotland at the time.

John Christie was the son of Alexander Christie, an ironfounder of "Devon Alloa", and Isabella Robertson. He attended Glasgow University and was employed at Arniston Colliery in which his father was a partner. In 1823 he purchased an estate called Milnwood in Lanark for £23,000 and in 1859 married Alison, a daughter of Thomas Philp of Dalkeith. They had three children, John Coldwells, Isabella Robertson, and Alice Margaret. In 1866 the Christies purchased the Castleton estate changing the name to Cowden. The son, John, died in 1872, aged 12 and John Christie himself became seriously ill in 1877 but had recovered by 1880 to commence a series of travels, taking Ella to Italy and Sicily. In 1887 he again became ill with pernicious anaemia and was treated by Dr Strachan of Dollar with arsenic. He recovered but gradually seemed to undergo a character change. In 1889 he was travelling on the continent with Ella and in 1893 was in Scandinavia with Ella and Alice, besides going on travels himself. Mrs Christie died in 1895. While John and Ella were in Egypt, he took ill and had to return home. He died in 1902, having been one of the wealthiest coalowners in Scotland, leaving property in

Glenfarg, Milnwood, Carnbo, and Edinburgh, as well as Cowden. On his will being read it was found, besides a great number of small donations to various charities, he had left his fortune to the trustees of three female industrial homes at Inverey, Tenterfield, and Templedean, to which he had already transferred large amounts of money as well as silver and valuables from the home at Buckingham Terrace in Edinburgh. The will was, naturally, contested by the family and an agreement was come to by which the family received Cowden, Milnwood, Buckingham Terrace, and all furniture etc., the rest going to the orphanages which had places for six to seven hundred girls.

Ella Christie - DM 1907

His daughter, Alice, became the wife of Robert King Stewart of Murdostone, Lanarkshire and they had two children, John Christie Stewart and Alexander Coldwells Stewart. Ella remained single and occupied Cowden becoming an inveterate traveller, managing to explore on her own: Tangier, Algeria, Palestine, Egypt, Greece, Asia Minor, India, Kashmir, Ceylon, Burma, Malaya, Japan, and China. A local story exists that on being met on Dollar Station platform one morning she was greeted with: "Off to Alloa to do some shopping, Miss Christie?" "No, no," said the redoubtable Miss Christie, "Tibet." On her Eastern travels she conceived the idea of creating a Japanese garden at Cowden and with the help of Taki

*The Japanese Gardens
Hand-washing Basin - DM 1909*

Honda, a Japanese lady gardener, and the Head of the Soani School of Imperial design, Professor Susuki, she created from a marsh a garden with a lake, ornamental stones, trees, bridges, tea houses, and shrines, which Susuki considered the best Japanese garden in the western world. From 1925 a Japanese gardener, Mr Matsou, who had lost his complete family in an earthquake, tended it till he died in 1936. The writer, Andrew Lang, known mostly now for his series of fairy tale books, was a great friend and visited the garden often. Queen Mary also visited it and the house in 1932; a story – no doubt apocryphal – going the rounds was that Miss Christie wisely hid all her choicest possessions knowing that if Her Majesty stopped to admire an object it was expected that it would be discreetly wrapped up and handed to one of her minions as she left. Ella Christie died in 1949, the house was demolished and the site developed for modern housing. The gardens still

*The Japanese Gardens
Snow-Scene Lantern - DM 1909*

existed but fell into decay and were vandalised. The story of the two remarkable sisters has been told by Alice's daughter-in-law, Averil Stewart, in her book *Alicella*. The estate passed to Alice's grandson, Colonel Robert Stewart whose residence is Arndean. Arndean itself was occupied around the 1860s by Thomas Archer and his family, one of the sons being William Archer, who became an outstanding London Drama critic, translating Ibsen and championing the work of Shaw, and then later by a family called Ogilvy, passing to the Archibalds who sold it to Cowden in the 1920s.

THE CHURCH

In 1801 as Session clerk, the parish schoolmaster, John McArbrea, carried out the purely numerical census of 1801, the population numbering 693, compared with the 510 of 1792, the increase being partly credited to the enlargement of the bleachfields. He also pointed out that the Duke of Argyll had begun to feu land adjoining the old village on which a good number of substantial houses could be built and that seven farmsteadings had been demolished to build park dykes, the farms themselves being let to one tenant – a reference to the creation of Dollar Bank farm.

The most important local happening of the time, however, passed unnoticed. In 1799 an elderly gentleman, probably staying with relatives at Solsgirth, called on the local schoolmaster, Mr McArbrea, at his school and house on the Burnside and talked with him about the provision of education in the village. During the talk the minister, the Rev. John Watson, was sent for and came to give his views. The occasion was so unremarkable that apparently neither could afterwards recall if the old gentleman even gave his name. In January 1802 John Watson received a letter from the Rev. Noah Hill, minister of the Gravel Lane Meeting House, Wapping, London, which read:

Rev. and Dear Sir,
With great astonishment will you read what I have the pleasure of enclosing, which is the last will and testament of Captain John

McNabb, late of Mile End, London. That he had thoughts of kindness to his Native Place, I had long known but had no idea of a Bequest comparable to what he has made. The Amount of the property of the Deceased cannot, at so short a period be ascertained, nor, indeed, can it soon be, as some part of it is afloat and there are long and intricate accounts to settle with Government, in which considerable property is concerned. Should these accompts be fairly adjusted and debts due to the Estate on personal security be paid – my opinion, and that of my brother Executor, is that the property of the Deceased cannot be less than Sixty Thousand pounds.

While you are struck with the magnitude of the trust, I shall join you and those in connection with you in fervent prayer that God who is not only "wonderful in working, but excellent in counsel" would so guide and direct you and your successors to the latest time, that this Great Charity may obtain its noblest end, the glory of God, the Redeemer's honour and the temporal and eternal good of all its objects. Mr John McNabb, who is one of the executors, is abroad with a ship of the Deceased in the Mediterranean. My friend, Mr Lepine, who is with me, joins me in every kind and pious wish. Believe me with due respect.
your sincere friend and Brother,
Noah Hill.

The letter also enclosed a copy of John McNabb's Will which, after leaving small bequests to his cousin, Marjory Edwards, late of Solsgirth, and to Hannah Jellard, his housekeeper, and his "lot, house and garden" to another cousin, John McNabb, on board "The Pitt," divided what was left equally between the said John McNabb and the parish of Dollar. The Dollar share was to be "laid in the public funds, or some such security, on purpose to bring one annualy income or interest, for the benefite of a Charity or school, for the poor of the parish of Dollar and shire of Clackmannan whier I was born, in North Britain or Scotland. That I give and bequeath to the Minister and Church of that said parish for ever,

Gravel Lane Meeting House - DM 1928

say to the Minister and Church Officers for the time being, and no other person shall have power to receive the annuity but the aforesaid officers for the time being, or their agent appointed for the time by them." His executors are named as Mr John Lapine of Hackney, the Rev. Noah Hill, and John McNabb, his cousin. The witnesses are John Gibson, Roger Hereford, and Thomas Higginson, and the will is signed John McNabb (L.S.) (Locum Sigillae = in place of a seal) and bears a thumbprint in the wafer provided for that purpose. It is dated the 8th of May 1800 and a codicil is added on the 12th of January 1802, the day of his death, signed with a mark and witnessed by Sarah and Elizabeth Dunscomb, leaving an extra fifty pounds per annum to Hannah Jellard.

Despite later comments that the phrasing of the will is amateurish it is a perfectly valid legal document and quite clear in what it intends. That the fund was to be used for educational purposes alone is made evident in that the smaller bequests are to return to the "Charity left to the parish of Dollar school".

Although Watson received the news of the legacy in January 1802 he made no mention of it apparently until March 1803 when John McArbrea, as Session Clerk, was instructed to copy the letter and will into the Kirk Session Minutes. The Session at this date consisted of the minister and five elders, James Gibson, James Christie, John Jack, Andrew Paton, and Robert Smith. They, in turn, seem to have made no mention of it to other parishioners. The lack of openness is puzzling. One obvious explanation is in the proving of the will – the cousin John McNabb contested the legality but the other executors forestalled him. The Session also contacted the Duke of Argyll's factor, John Ferrier, for help in the legal aspects of claiming the legacy, their principal worry being whether this would involve the outlay of money for, as they state, none were rich enough to afford this. Another reason may have been social for it was a time of famine and dearth and any announcement of a charitable bequest might have raised false hopes and claims.

The cousin, John McNabb, received his share of the legacy reasonably quickly and began to live in style, attempting to set himself up as a shipowner but he did not have his cousin's ability and, in fact, showed signs of insanity. He was eventually certified as insane after an Inquisition at Gray's Inn Coffee House in 1813 when Marjory Edwards was made Committer of his person. He died in an asylum at Hoxton on Christmas Eve 1817, his estate of £30,000 passing to Marjory Edwards, she leaving an estate valued at £200 to a "neice, Elizabeth Thiorais, spinster, lately residing in Russia, but now living with me" in 1824. Presumably most of the money had been passed over before.

The Court of Chancery with whom the Dollar money was lodged decided the principal was to remain in its care. It was to be invested in Government Stock, the interest being made available to the Kirk Session on condition they produced a plan for its use which would meet the conditions of the will. Mr Watson seems to have done his best to do this, making trips to London for consultation and to Edinburgh and Glasgow to look at charity schools such as Heriot's Hospital and Watson's Hospital. At one stage the

now elderly gentleman fell ill in Edinburgh and a locum had to be employed in Dollar. The Session also contacted the Argyll estate with the possibility of feuing ground to the south of the old church – that is the site of the present church, there being no road there till 1806. They also employed Robert Burn, one of the family of Edinburgh architects who later planned John Watson's (The Gallery of Modern Art) and Edinburgh Academy, to design a building to board forty poor boys and girls. It should be emphasised, and never seems to have been in the controversy surrounding the issue, that initially there was no money, the interest had to accrue and being placed in Consols would possibly only amount to £1500 per annum. Nevertheless the process of proving the Dollar right to the money seems to have been incredibly slow.

In 1808, the owner of Harviestoun and by this time Castle Campbell and the Argyll lands, Craufurd Tait, who, as an Edinburgh lawyer, must have known of the legacy and the Kirk Session's plan for it (which was essentially Mr Watson's), called a meeting of the local landowners – the heritors – and the parishioners to consider this plan. The heritors of the time were: Craufurd Tait, Colonel Campbell of

An Hospital for Dollar
Robert Burn ca. 1810 - DM 1935

Dollarbeg, John Duncanson of Sheardale, William Futt of Mains, William Haig of Dollarfield, Robert Marshall of Mains, Robert Pitcairn of Dollar, John Mathie of Mains, and John Moir of Hillfoot. They resolved that "the Erection of an Hospital for poor children would be a great misfortune, would discourage industry, and would tend to bring into the parish a number of poor people". They also resolved not to let their ground for the erection of such an hospital but approved of the provision of a Free School and declared their readiness, if necessary, to support the poor of their own parish in a decent and comfortable manner. They were, of course, frightened of ultimately having to foot the bill for a large influx of poor from outside. A great majority of the male inhabitants also signed a minute recording their disapproval of the Hospital, their ability and duty to look after the health and morals of their children without these being boarded, and their approval of the idea of a Free School for the parish.

Nothing came of it and in 1812 the somewhat patient parishioners convened another meeting, this time resolving to send a deputation consisting of John Burns, David Smieton, Henry Murray, William McLiesh, David McGregor, Andrew Paton, Robert Kirk, James Lawson, Andrew Sharp, Robert Malcolm, and Andrew Malloch, to see the Minister. In answer to their questions Mr Watson detailed the trouble he had been at for a number of years in the business, that the heritors in interfering had put a stop to it, that nothing had been done without legal advice and, the deputation expressing itself dissatisfied with the secret manner the Session followed as they had never once made it known to the parish in a public manner, he replied if they had done anything wrong it was unintentional. They met again the next day during which Mr Watson stated that:

> unless the parish seceded from Mr Tait's plan and agreed to his plan, which he said was agreeable to the will, we would never get it, and in order to prevent which he requested the Committee to call a meeting of the parish in order to adopt his plan, . . . Altho all the parish should leave me, and the Session should leave me, who have acted all along with me in the business – yet I stand alone for the poor of the parish.

Accordingly a meeting was called and another petition to both the Heritors and the Kirk Session was signed by the majority of the male inhabitants

stating that if they had been misled previously it was not their fault, and calling on the two bodies to unite so that they might be "the means in the hand of kind Providence, of bringing this great Blessing designed by the said donar into this parish for the purpose designed in his will".

It seems to have had little effect for a further year passed and then the Court of Chancery approved the Kirk Session plan for an Hospital and the legal issues appear to have been resolved. There remained the question of land and Mr Watson travelled to Edinburgh to "take counsel on the refusal of Mr Tait to implement the late Duke of Argyll's agreement respecting the ground intended for the Institution". Nothing came of this either for in December 1815 Mr Watson died, the appointment of the next minister falling to the owner of the Castle Campbell barony, Mr Craufurd Tait.

A few days after John Watson's death Tait received a petition from the inhabitants, conveyed by the merchant, John Gibson, requesting that Watson's assistant, Mr Brydie, be appointed. Mr Tait, however, had other plans:

> Dear Sir,
> I have just now received your letter dated the 18th, current, mentioning that Mr Moore of Lepcroft had assisted the parishioners of Dollar in drawing up a petition to me, for presenting to the church of Dollar Mr Peter Brydie, who has been for some short time past assisting Mr Watson, the late minister, and that you understand Mr Brydie would be acceptable to the parish. I have no doubt of Mr Brydie being a very good man, and it is a great mark of his ability having interested the parish so much in his favour upon so short an acquaintance. But there is a very excellent man, with whom I and my family have been most intimately acquainted now for more than these twelve years, and I have granted a presentation of the Church of Dollar in his favour. He is a religious and good man, of kind and obliging manners, and of great knowledge and learning; and I am sure I do not venture too far, when I pledge myself, that you and the other elders, and all the

parish, will, upon experience, find him to be a good minister and a kind friend. His name is Mr Andrew Mylne, and it is probable you and many people in the parish have seen him, as he has been frequently at different times living with me and my family at Harviestoun. Many patrons keep the parish vacant for six months; but I am sure that you and the elders will approve of my having granted the presentation without delay, since I know so thoroughly the worth and qualities of Mr. Mylne.

I am with great regard, dear sir, yours faithfully,

Craufurd Tait.

Thus there came upon the Dollar scene the Reverend and redoubtable Andrew Mylne. The excellent Mr Brydie, one is pleased to report, eventually became the minister in Fossoway.

Thus too the privileges of patronage in appointing over the congregation not only their spiritual adviser but also the principal trustee of the McNabb charity. Although presumably Tait and Mylne were in agreement over the general form the new school was to take, the internal academic structure would seem to have been wholly Mylne's, especially as by 1820 Tait was in serious financial difficulties and already considering the sale of Harviestoun. The Kirk Session now consisted of James Gibson, James Christie, and Robert Smith. None were a match for the forceful and dominant personality of Mylne although Robert Smith indicated his protests against some of Mylne's ideas by non-attendance. The parish also expressed its opposition in more vociferous form. Whether one approves of what Mylne did with the money from the bequest or not, he undoubtedly remains one of the greatest, and least acknowledged, of Scottish headmasters.

DR ANDREW MYLNE MA, DD, FRSA (1815 – 56)

Andrew Mylne was the son of Andrew M. Mylne, a fuller in Haddington, and his wife, Jean Harcus. Born in 1776 he was educated at the Grammar School there and by 1800 seems to have been running a school in his native parish. Around 1803 he was teaching in Edinburgh and had

contact with the lawyer Craufurd Tait, possibly as a tutor to his children. In 1807 at the age of 31 he entered Edinburgh University and graduated in

The Revd Andrew Mylne
Original Painting copied by Ian Campbell

1810 with an MA. Almost immediately he entered the ministry and in 1812 at the age of 36 received his licence as a probationer. From 1811 to 1815 he is listed as "Andrew Mylne, teacher, 2 Drummond Place (North Side). House: 3 Roxburgh Place." being known as a "teacher of high reputation in Edinburgh and the proprietor of a well-known English school in that city". He published a number of textbooks in Ancient History, Geography, English History, Astronomy, Spelling, and Grammar. He was also friendly with the Jedburgh born Sir David Brewster, Principal of the University and contributed several articles to that worthy's Edinburgh Encyclopaedia. It was Brewster, the inventor of the kaleidoscope, who joked that: "Dollar has acquired a threshing mill", Mylne being pronounced "Mill" at that date. An English school taught "English" as opposed to "Scots", a necessary acquisition for getting on in the world. From the dates it would seem as if Craufurd Tait was helping him to acquire the necessary qualifications to step into Mr Watson's pulpit and thereby become the Principal Trustee of the McNabb Bequest.

On being appointed minister in Dollar, Mylne immediately applied to Chancery to have the jurisdiction of the bequest, though not the money, transferred to the Kirk Session, and submitted a plea for the payment of expenses incurred by Mr Watson to be paid to Mrs Watson. These amounted to £614, a large sum for the time. This was agreed to and he convened his Kirk Session, now consisting of Robert Smith, James Gibson, and James Christie, as trustees, with Gibson's son, William, acting as Clerk. The bequest through inflation now amounted to £92,345 less legacy duty of some £9,000. £55,000 was declared to be principal to be invested by the Court of Chancery and some £37,000 to be interest, the latter to be put at the disposal of the new trustees for the setting up of the school. Only rough equations of money with present day values are possible but on the basis of wages and house prices a multiplier of two to three hundred would not be out of place giving a present day estimate of some six to nine million pounds for the interest alone. The use Mr Mylne and his Kirk Session put this to is described in the section on Dollar Academy.

Mylne continued on as minister and superintendent of the school for some eight years in an almost autocratic capacity arousing much resentment in the village. This came to a head when he issued an order that all tutors in attendance at private boarding houses were to take their charges to Sunday service at the parish church. Apparently two or three of the young men who acted in this capacity belonged to the Secession church and believed this would lead to their dismissal. A champion for their cause arose in the form of former Ensign Porteus of the 98th Regiment of Foot, now living at Mount Devon, who, on the 12th of August 1826, called upon Captain Pinkerton of the Royal Marines, now living at Devonside, who, with Mr Porteus, thereupon called upon Dr Elliot of the Royal Navy, now living at Belmont, after which all three called a meeting at Mr Henderson's inn to elect a deputation to call upon Dr Mylne and discuss with him an increase in the Kirk Session,

now apparently reduced to two elders with the local parish schoolmaster, Peter McLaren – Mr McArbrea having died in 1820 – acting as Clerk. Dr Mylne refused to see them as a body but offered to see them individually. Circulars were then circulated and meetings met. Dr Mylne announced that Peter McLaren would be appointed an elder. Another meeting was held and Robert Smyth, one of the elders, and 179 other inhabitants signed a protest against the appointment. On the day of the appointment Robert Smyth absented himself so no appointment could be made. Had it been, Mr Porteus had resolved to stage a protest against the completion of the proceedings in the church for "as soon as the precentor had finished singing the last line of the first psalm (which is always lined in Dollar church) I was immediately to commence giving out the line for the whole congregation joining in singing until dark, so as to defeat the election". "Lining" was where the precentor – there was no music allowed – sang each line for his audience to repeat. The other method was "run-on" where the next line was sung by the precentor while the audience was singing the last. The merits of the two systems were often the subject of heated debate. Even if hymn books had been available, one has to remember that many of the congregation would have been unable to read them.

Shortly after, Dr Mylne departed for London and Mr Porteus took it upon himself to write to the Lord Chancellor detailing the Doctor's crimes, to wit: collaring the Masters in presence of their classes, "a circumstance to be regretted as the masters are gentlemen (James Walker, English Teacher, and Peter Steven, Writing Master, excepted)"; throwing a child into the river, embezzling the Trust funds, overcharging fees, overpaying himself; and cornering the garden produce. Further, on Dr Mylne's return, he wrote him a letter as well pointing out that "your veracity is notorious for not being of the most exalted description" and that he, Mr Porteus, had "not converted Mount Devon into a brothel; nor is there any servant of mine so advanced in pregnancy, that she would be considered a disgrace to be seen in any family, and more especially in the house of one who ought to be the conservator of the morals of the parish". The last reference concerning the Institution gardener, one McNabb, brother to the Head Gardener of the Edinburgh Botanics, who was before the Kirk Session for having got with child a Sally Hunter, who, from this letter, seems to have been a servant in the manse. McNabb was dismissed but not before Porteus had claimed that he had been "convicted before the highest criminal court for an outrage unequalled in the annals of the law" without, unfortunately, specifying the crime.

A further public meeting was held in Henderson's Inn (The Castle Campbell Hotel) at which Mr Porteus advised petitioning Parliament. He took it upon himself to supervise the petition and one day proceeded to Edinburgh for this purpose. While he was in the cabin of the steamer a Mr Moodie entered and spoke to a Mr Marshall. Mr Porteus, recognising them, promptly lay down an a sofa and pretended to be asleep, whereupon he heard them discussing a special meeting of the Presbytery of Stirling at which Dr Mylne intended to ask assistance at Dollar to create a new batch of elders. When the meeting was held in the little Session House for this purpose, a large crowd outside gave vent to their emotions, while inside Robert Smyth objected to some of the names. On the Sunday following the new elders attended the Session House and, according to Porteus, were booed and hissed on their way in. The Elders, and Trustees of the Institution, were now the Rev Andrew Mylne, William Haig of Dollarfield, James Haig, Mr Erskine of Aberdona, Craufurd Tait of Harviestoun, John Tait his son, McArthur Moir of Hillfoot, Mr Clerk of Dollarbeg, Mr Duncanson of Sheardale, Robert Kirk, James Christie and the absentee Robert Smyth, who refused to attend. Indeed Dr Mylne seems to have worked a remarkable religious conversion among the local landowners in persuading them of the benefits of attending their local parish church.

Mr Porteus undaunted continued to plague the minister and after being, as he considered it, deliberately kicked on the shin in church by one Gilchrist, "a minion of the Doctor", threatened to throw the perpetrator over the balcony. A precognisance was taken on the subject and a warrant served on Mr Porteus then in Wales, from where he posted home in three days to be informed by his counsel, the great Henry Cockburn, that the Lord Advocate had deserted the indiction whereupon:

> As soon as it was known in Dollar, every demonstration of joy was exhibited by the inhabitants, who set to work in preparing a large bonfire with a flag, on which was inscribed "Victory over Conspiracy"; and paraded through the streets to the great trepidation of the Doctor and his supporters. In the evening the committee, along with my witnesses, spent a very happy evening in the head inn, congratulating me on my triumphant escape from Dr Mylne and his minions. While we were regaling ourselves within, the populace were enjoying themselves without in preparing an effigy of the Reverend Doctor, dressed in his canonicals, bedizened all over with labels containing all his crimes, and his £300 a year stolen from the poor, in conspicuous characters placed next his heart. After perambulating the village, they then carried the effigy to the manse, and in front of the windows it then underwent the last operation of Jack Ketch, who consigned it to the flames amidst the cheers of the crowd.

Mr Porteus now instituted a summons against Dr Mylne but desisted at the entreaties of his wife, promising her he would never again interfere with Dr Mylne and the affairs of the Trustees. The obsession was too strong and it was not to last. He later printed a pamphlet which he threatened to circulate and the long forbearing Mylne was forced to counter with his own which Porteus promptly used as a basis for another publication *The Annals of the Parish* containing some highly libellous statements.

Mr Porteus, having enlivened the monotony of Dollar existence for a considerable period, now disappears from view and it is not clear what happened. He seems to have been charged with libel and served six months in Saughton Prison in Edinburgh after which he may have died. *Gibson* remembered the family but not the father, and makes no mention of the feud. *Annals of the Parish* is well worth dipping into for the Ensign's gloriously inflated style if nothing else.

Despite his apparent unpopularity Dr Mylne nevertheless appears to have been able to fill his small church and in 1841 funds were subscribed for the building of a new church on the site of the old Kirkstyle cottages. The basic design was by William Tite, a London architect and member of the Board of the Globe Insurance Company, then in possession of the Harviestoun estate. Tite, the son of a Russian, was the designer of the Royal

Parish Church - DM 1906

Exchange; chairman of the Committee responsible for constructing the London Embankment (out of stone from Dumfriesshire!); first Chairman of the R.I.B.A.; and a major railway architect designing stations both in Britain and France, including the Caley in Edinburgh, and Carlisle.

No sooner had the new church been consecrated in 1842 than in 1843 came the Disruption, when at an Assembly at St Andrew's Kirk in Edinburgh in a protest over patronage – the appointment of ministers by local landowners – 193 ministers and elders withdrew from the Established Church and walking down to a hall at Canonmills constituted themselves into the Free

Church of Scotland, the number of ministers seceding eventually rising to 464. In doing so they gave up their churches, salaries, and manses in an incredibly brave defence of principle. Support for their action was vast and money was quickly raised to pay them and eventually to build new churches and new manses. In Dollar about one hundred members of the church seem to have become supporters of the new Free Church. The by now aged Dr Mylne played no part in the Disruption nor condemned those who did, but the minister of Muckhart, James Thomson, seceded and a little church was erected at Shelterhall to serve the two villages. Dr Mylne had married in 1844 and, from memoirs of the time, seems to have become much of an invalid towards the end of his life. He died in 1856, and though remembered as a somewhat terrifying figure in public life is also remembered as a much more benevolent person in private.

REV. WALTER IRVINE (1856 – 61)

Not much is known of Walter Irvine who only stayed a few years before removing to Kilconquhar in Fife.

REV. ANGUS GUNN M.A. (1861 – 1913)

Mr Gunn was a young and vigorous minister who had been assistant at Arbroath and he became much committed to village life. During his long ministry he became Chairman of the McNabb Trust and was much involved and very outspoken in negotiations with the Endowed School Commission over the provision of free education in the parish, when they refused to allow the Institution to continue providing it for those under ten years old. It was a decision that aroused much anger over unneeded interference with what had become a much loved and respected establishment. The younger Mr Mylne of the 1820s might have been wryly amused. Mr Gunn remained minister at Dollar for the rest of his career, serving for forty years.

SECESSION CHURCHES
THE ASSOCIATE SYNOD OF ORIGINAL SECEDERS

What is termed the First Secession took place in 1733 when Ebenezer Erskine of the North Church, Stirling, seceded with others over the patronage question and formed an Associate Presbytery. Later they split again in 1747 over the Burgess Oath, by which prospective burghers in the royal burghs swore to "maintain the true religion as presently professed in this realm", into the Burghers and the Anti-Burghers. Still later in 1799, presumably on the principle that nothing secedes like secession, the Burghers split into the New Light Burghers, who had adopted a testimony that viewed the Solemn League and Covenant in a "new light", and the Old Light Burghers. Whereupon the Anti-Burghers, in case they were found wanting in contumacity, did the same. In 1820 both sets of new Light Antis amalgamated, apart from a remnant which in 1827 joined the Old Light Antis to call themselves The Associate Synod of Original Seceders. All of which, believe it or not, is a simplified version of the secessions of the time. The Dollar adherents of this particular Synod worshipped in a grain store in the Old Town until they built a Chapel in Chapel Place in 1828. They made use of visiting preachers until the appointment of a Dr Wylie in 1831. He left in 1846, and again they had visiting preachers until in 1852 they united with the Free Church.

According to one account some of their congregation may have joined in a reaction against the Rev. Dr Mylne when, early in his ministry, he called a meeting to answer questions on the McNabb legacy. Finding his little church packed for the occasion, he subjected those attending to a long homily on duty, abruptly stopped, and then, announcing that as there had been no questions there was nothing to discuss, walked out. More in anger than sorrow some were said to have purchased a tent – probably a wooden pulpit – which they erected near Market Park and invited preachers from Edinburgh to hold services. Their congregation increasing they are said to have used the hayloft of the Castle Campbell Hotel.

The Old Secession or Auld Licht Chapel was apparently also used for the first Sunday School, attended by children from all the churches.

THE FREE CHURCH

The main secession over patronage, as described earlier, took place in 1843 after which a Free Church was erected halfway between Muckhart and Dollar at Shelterhall, the minister being the Rev. James Thomson. Free Kirkers from both villages and the area round about made their way there summer and winter. Lawson in his *Reminiscences of Dollar Academy, Church, and Sunday School* gives a full description of the services which from September to April started at 11 a.m. with a sermon followed by a lecture. From

Shelterhall Doorway - DAA

May to August the sermon started at 10.15 a.m. and the lecture was given after lunch, women and children in fair weather picnicking outside by the stream nearby while the men went to the "Sugar Inn" at Cowden or the cottage at Bell's Bridge for a dram. Resumption of services took place when the church officer, James "King" Somerville, held up the "ladle", a collection box at the end of a pole. Services in summer finished about 4.30 p.m. Lawson lists as members: Andrew Hood, farmer at Middleton, and his brother James of Lawhill, James Smith, Peter Cram, and Robert Kirk, the

Academy Trustee. The last, a local joiner and an imposing grey haired Kirk Elder, Lawson, as a boy, remembered seeing, a solitary figure in his apron, dancing furiously on the top of Gloom Hill to the strains of the Oakley band playing on top of the Castle Tower. In 1852 the Free Church congregation at Shelterhall united with the Original Seceders in Chapel Place. Many Free Church members now worshipped in Chapel Place and the congregation became so large that in 1858 they decided to erect a church of their own at the west end of Bridge Street. The Shelterhall church carried on until 1864 when it was razed to the ground and the stone used to extend the Dollar

West Church - DM 1905

church. The ornamental surround of the entrance doorway was built into the wall of the former East End Bowling Club in Lovers Loan. The Rev. Thomson, having married a young lady late in life, retired to Edinburgh where he died in 1874.

THE UNITED PRESBYTERIAN CHURCH

Another Protestant church in Dollar, the United Presbyterian, was started in a cottage above the Cross Keys junction in the Old Town by an Edinburgh china merchant, Mr Millar, who also built Sheardale House. Later the cottage was demolished and a meeting hall, Millar's Hall, built on the site. Around 1872 the congregation moved to a new church on the Burnside, the East Free Church, and the meeting house was used as a grainstore by the Gibson family. It has recently been converted from a garage into houses. On the merging of the free churches in 1910 their

minister, the Rev. W.B.R. Wilson, retired and the congregation merged with the West Church. After being under consideration as a Town Hall the Burnside church was bought by James Moir of Hillfoot and presented to the Parish Church as a church hall. For a period it was sold to the Academy for use as a dining hall but is now again in the possession of the Parish Church. As well as being a fine minister, the Rev. Wilson was also a fine scholar, acting as a sub-editor for that immense undertaking the *Oxford New English*

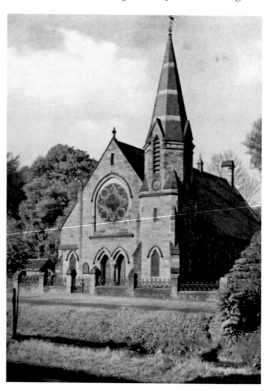

U.P. Church - DM 1909

Dictionary under that other Scot from Denholm, Sir James Murray. Mr Wilson edited the entries for T, C and W in particular and one room of his manse is remembered as being stuffed full of slips of paper. The U. P. Church was formed in 1847 by the United Associated Synod of the Secession Church (formed by merging the New Light Burghers and Anti-Burghers in 1820!) uniting with an earlier 1761 Secession, The Relief Church, which wanted relief from patronage.

THE SCOTTISH EPISCOPAL CHURCH

The Scottish Episcopal Church of St. James dates as a congregation from 1863 and owes its existence to the efforts of the Rev. A.W. Hallen of Alloa who established a mission in Dollar despite the opposition of the Bishop of St Andrews, within whose diocese it was. Internal politics were resolved when Dollar became an incumbency in 1877 with its own clergyman under the Bishop's jurisdiction. At first the minister and deacons of the Free Church allowed the congregation the use of their building and then later they used a prayer room rented from the estate of "the late Mr Stalker". The site for the present church was gifted by Sir James Orr of Harviestoun. After building commenced the gable end was blown down in the violent storm that wrecked the Tay Bridge and the builder went bankrupt. Building was, however, recommenced and completed in 1882, the architect being Thomas Frame of Alloa and the cost £2000. Although often referred to as the "English Church" it is, in fact, an original form of the Scottish Church which did not adopt Presbyterianism and retained its bishops and internal appointment system.

St James the Great - DM 1910

EDUCATION IN THE NINETEENTH CENTURY

THE PARISH SCHOOL

At the beginning of the century the parish school was still the main provider of education. This was not free. An Act of Parliament in 1803 prescribed a minimum salary of £22 Sterling per annum for a parish schoolmaster and the fees per quarter: 2/6d for English, 3/- for Writing, 4/- for Writing and Arithmetic, and 5/- for Latin. The *Account* of 1792 gives Mr McArbrea's salary as £100 Scots plus the interest on 500 marks donated by an Archibald Paterson, merchant in Edinburgh, in 1652, and 60 marks by "one, Kirk, in Dollar".

In 1819 the Trustees of the new Dollar Institution paid for an assistant to Mr McArbrea, his pupils now numbering around fifty. Many of these were possibly illegitimate, the Institution at first refusing to accept them but paying for their education at the parish school. As the ban against them lapsed so did the number attending the parish school but there always seem to have been a dozen or so attending, whether from dislike of the Institution or because they had not fulfilled the three-year residence provision laid down by the trustees for free education. The Institution continued to pay the schoolmaster an allowance for lack of custom. (Mr McArbrea died in 1820 at the age of 81 and is buried at Kilmaclock near Doune. The name is probably a variant of McCairbre, a small clan who were armourers to the Campbells and one quoted by Stewart of Garth as a clan which died out naturally rather than being exterminated. Nevertheless a descendant of Mr McArbrea from Australia visited the Academy in the 1970s.) Mr McArbrea was succeeded by Peter McLaren, whose spelling is celebrated by Peter Porteus as being deficient but who kept perfectly good Kirk Session minutes. In 1861 the master's salary was raised to £35 per annum. In 1855 the Commissioners to supply teachers to parish schools recommended that none be supplied in future to Dollar because of the existence of Dollar Institution and, in 1874, on the death of a John Clark the school was not resupplied. The arrangement was not to last long for in 1888, under the Endowed Schools Act, the Institution was forbidden to supply free education to those under ten years of age and accordingly handed over its Infant School on the Burnside, and provided room at the Cairnpark Gate for a new Board School. James Christie was transferred to become Head of the new school as were other teachers. After initial difficulties the schools existed happily side by side, although small fee-paying preparatory schools, notably those of the Misses Gellatly at Parkside at the top of McNabb Street and, later, Miss Bremner at Argyll House came into being. The Old Schoolhouse seems to have been used for different purposes, at one stage being the Working Men's Reading Room. It is now used for parish church functions. The Board School became the County Primary School with the doing away of School Boards in 1918 and in 1964 moved to new premises at Market Park under the name of "Strathdevon", while the old premises were taken over by the Academy as a Junior School.

Last School Board
Back Row: Messrs Cowan, Stenhouse, Haig and
Cram
Front Row: Revd WBR Wilson, McDiarmid (Ch),
Provost Mrs Malcolm, Mr Graham
DM 1919

DOLLAR ACADEMY

The story of Dollar Academy starts, as was related in the section on the churches, in 1799 when an elderly gentleman knocked at the door of the Old Schoolhouse, whether then one-storey or two is not clear, and asked to speak with Mr McArbrea. He wished some information on the provision of education in the parish and at some stage the Rev. John Watson was called in to give his opinion. The usual setting is given as the local tavern but Mr McArbrea in a later affidavit on McNabb's visit only mentioned his house. If

the elderly gentleman gave his name, neither Mr McArbrea nor Mr Watson seems to have remembered it. Two years later, in January 1802, Mr Watson received a letter from the Rev. Noah Hill of the Mile End Meeting House in London informing him that Captain John McNabb had left the interest on half his fortune to the parish of Dollar for a charity or school. As described in the section on the church, years of dissension between Mr Watson, the local landowners and the parishioners followed over the use of the bequest and it was not till Mr Watson died in 1815 and the Rev. Andrew Mylne was appointed in his place that Captain McNabb's "thought of kindness to his Native Place" bore fruit.

The Founder of the Academy, John McNabb, was christened in Dollar Parish Church on the 14th of May 1732. He was the son of Malcolm McNabb and Janet Cunningham who had been married in Dollar on the 26th June 1725 and who had two older children, Thomas, born in 1726, and Jean, born in 1728. Only in the case of Jean is a dwelling place given as being "in the broom", this being an area to the northeast of the Ramshorn still retained in the name "Broomcroft". Tradition has it that the birthplace was a house on a knoll in the second field on the right past Wellhall Farm. The Rev. Andrew Mylne gives the following account of McNabb's life in the *New Statistical Account* of 1841:

He attended occasionally the village school, and it is said he herded cattle, even after he became a grown lad, but being tired of this occupation, he set off one day to Kincardine, the nearest seaport, and engaged himself with a coasting trader. Afterwards he went to sea again and determined to try his fortunes on the deep. We are told upon very good authority that when he set out for Leith to board a ship there, he had not a farthing in his pocket, and that when he came to the Queensferry he was unable to pay his passage across, though the demand was only three halfpence. Out of this difficulty he was relieved by the kindness of a person who lived in Dollar and knew him. After crossing the ferry they both walked together to Edinburgh. They separated at Edinburgh, and at parting the kind acquaintance gave him sixpence to enable him to make his way to Leith, where he engaged himself to the master of a ship. While at sea he saved some money and afterwards became what is called a ship-husband. In this business he was very successful and amassed a considerable fortune. He came to London and settled in the neighbourhood. It was there that he added considerably to his former fortune by several fortunate speculations in buying stock. At his death it was found he had amassed a very considerable fortune, invested in ships and in the funds and other government securities.

Peter Steven, the first Writing Master, added to this in a letter to his daughter, Jane, using only commas!:

he was very economical, not using all his allowance of food and grog but selling them to his shipmates, whereby he had a few pounds saved, when he returned from his voyage that small sum he laid out on tobacco, soap etc., which he sold during his next voyage to his shipmates, his great sobriety, strict attention to duty etc., attracted the attention of his captain who promoted him, so that he had an opportunity of making money faster than before, in this way he went on until he had saved wherewith to buy a sloop of his own, and from one ship to another he went on till he had nine ships of his own which were chiefly employed in the transport service, at last he settled in London as an underwriter ...

A ship-husband was an agent appointed by the owners to attend to the business of a ship while she was in port. The accounts are not clear as to where he pursued this line of business and it is fair to assume that only later did he settle in London.

Lloyd's Lists give several J. McNabbs as captains of ships. He possibly captained "The Theodorick", sailing between London and Virginia, and another ship, called "The Randolph", trading again with Virginia and Maryland. A John McNabb is credited in the Owners' Lists as owner and part owner of eight known ships at different dates. These are "The Swift", "The Friendship", "The Nancy", "The Otter", "The Pitt", "The Rose", "The Maria", and "The Struggler". Four voyages in four of these ships between 1789 and 1791 were made by the notorious Triangular Passage and in each case the captains were changed in Jamaica, suggesting that the ships were being hired by slave traders, who, during these years, were renting every ship they could lay hands on as they believed a ban on slave trading to be imminent. The number of British ships so engaged jumped from 85 in 1789 to 144 in 1791. The elderly John McNabb was possibly hiring his ships out but was not, as rumour sometimes has it, a slave trader, being no doubt at this stage, his seafaring days over, safely home in London.

He died on the 12th of January 1802 at the age of 69, although his coffin plate records his age as 66. The funeral seems to have been a fairly substantial one for the time. In 1929, the Former Pupil and Dux, Andrew Drysdale, with the help of J.K. Husband, then Secretary of the London Club, was responsible for bringing the remains home to Dollar when his burial place, the Mission House at Wapping, was demolished.

The amount left by John McNabb in 1802 amounted to some £55,000 sterling. By 1816 when Andrew Mylne was appointed parish minister and, under the terms of the will, main trustee, it had grown to some £92,000. After legacy duty the amount of interest available for the charity to use was reckoned to be £37,325. Mylne at once questioned, through Sir Ilay Campbell, President of the Court of Session and, incidentally, father-in-law of Craufurd Tait, the right of the Court of Chancery to dictate the use of the money to Scottish trustees. The Court of Chancery then decided that while retaining the capital it had no right to dictate the use of the interest and it was made available to the trustees, the minister and Kirk Session of Dollar, for them to decide its use. Mylne could not have received the news of this before the 24th or 25th of June 1818. The first official meeting of the trustees of

Dollar Academy - DAA

Dollar Institution, as it was formally called, took place on the 26th.

The trustees consisted of the Rev Andrew Mylne, James Christie, James Gibson, and Robert Smith. Mr Mylne was appointed Agent and Cashier and Mr William Gibson, the father of the author of the *Reminiscences*, was appointed Clerk. Initially, Reading and English Grammar, Writing and Arithmetic, Latin and Greek were to be taught, and a Girls' School was to be set up. On the 2nd of July Mr Mylne reported he had engaged the services of an architect, Mr Playfair, then superintending the erection of the New College in Edinburgh, and a field on the south side of the public road west from the Kellyburn was chosen as a location. In August it was agreed that a Midwife and Surgeon be the first appointments for the parish and that the New Inn be rented so that classes might start. By the end of August it was agreed to accept the opinion of a Mr John Hay, planner in Edinburgh, that a better site would be Williamson's Park, and

arrangements were made to feu this from Mr Tait of Harviestoun; Mr Mylne was to insist on certain servitudes as to the building of houses and the preservation of trees to the West. A road was to be built from the Turnpike Road to the main gate (McNabb Street) and the houses there were to be neat and slated. While Mr Playfair preferred stone from the Cullaloe Hills in Fife, the Trustees insisted on the use of Sheardale stone to provide local employment and arrangements were made with Mr Tait to reopen the quarries. A Mr Martin accepted the post of Surgeon at £120 per annum and Mr James Walker was appointed to teach English. In November Mr Playfair reported on the tenders, the lowest, that of Beattie and Armstrong of Edinburgh at £9195, being accepted. Mrs Marshall was appointed midwife. In November Mr William Tennant of Lasswade was appointed to teach Latin and Greek, Mrs Brydie of Alloa was appointed schoolmistress, and Mr Hay was commissioned to draw up plans for the grounds.

In January 1819 accounts were paid for forms (benches), medicine and many pairs of shoes and the trustees declined to answer a letter requesting to know the amount of the legacy and the trustees' plans for it. They also paid a bill to the "Courant" for a paragraph contradicting statements made about the "Academy" in the public newspapers. In February it was reported that Mr Walker had commenced teaching at the New Inn (on the corner of Bridge Street and Devon Road) and that a charge of five shillings was to be made for those not entitled to free education. The Lord Advocate agreed that trustees could fill official positions but had, also, expressed the opinion that none was entitled to free education except those on the poor roll. The trustees, however, decided that as the numbers on the poor roll were very few, that they would include the greater number of the present population. Later in the month it was reported that Mr Tennant was now teaching Latin and a Mr Taylor temporarily teaching Writing and Accounts. In March tenders were accepted for a seven foot high wall round the grounds and a wooden arch (bridge) over the Dollar Burn on the old road from the Mains to the church. The park was to be ploughed and Mr Playfair was to obtain coins etc., to put into the foundations. In June a tender was accepted from Mr Beattie for the erection of eight houses to run from the principal building to the burn of Dollar (this was on part of the minister's glebe surrendered by Mr Mylne) at £525 per house. Mr de Joux from Geneva was appointed to the post of Modern Languages. In July the trustees paid the funeral expenses for a young apprentice, David Miller, killed by a fall of stone at the Academy. Arbitrers were appointed for salaries paid to trustees and it was agreed Mr Mylne was to act as Cashier and Agent but not be paid for the posts. Though the minutes do not record it, Mr Stevens of Edinburgh was appointed Writing and Accounts Master and a Mr Hogg also seems to have been killed during the erection of the building.

During 1820 instructions were issued for the commencement of the middle part of the building, the death of Mr McArbrea was reported, and the Sheriff-depute was contacted with regard to an advertisement fixed to the church door and resistance being offered by some of the parish to the teachers entering the building with their boarders. This is the only indication that the Cairnpark third of the building was in occupation and the teachers were taking in boarders. The walls between the teachers' houses were to be heightened (again the only indication some had been built) and a gate built in the north wall with a door on either side, one of which was to be blank. A statement was now issued with regard to boarders and feepaying pupils:

Boarders were to be allowed to attend, as they benefited the inhabitants by their expenditure on food and clothing and the children of the parish by their mixing with a superior rank which would improve their manners and affect a new stimulus to exertion in prosecuting their studies. All pupils had to reside within the parish and only those whom the trustees chose to include under the description of poor would receive education gratis, all others to pay 5 shillings to each teacher per quarter, Mr Tennant to be allowed to charge one guinea for Persic.

Academy Place - DAA

The old men of the parish were to be employed in cutting an aqueduct to bring water from the Slunk Well to the public building. Five stoves were ordered and it was agreed to make the ceiling of the Library panelled instead of plain.

During 1821 it was decided to complete the public building and make gravel walks, the wall of the sunk fence was to be heightened, a number of books were to be purchased as prizes, and Mr Bell of Perth was appointed Teacher of

Mathematics. In December as the work on the new building was finished it was decided that the clearing of the grounds and digging of drains could commence.

Thus the first two and a half years of the Academy, as it was commonly called, although

Old Library - DAA

Dollar Institution remained the official name for a hundred years. From the minutes we can gather that there was a certain amount of opposition in the village to Mr Mylne's plans for the school. It was to take several forms: a public meeting and petition, pamphleteering by Peter Porteus as described in the section on the church; protests at trustee meetings by two of the poorer trustees, Robert Smyth and Robert Kirk; and an advertisement in *The Scotsman*, by James Lawson, John Blackwood and others, accusing the Trustees of providing education for many at the expense of the poor and urging gentlemen not to send their children to the school. Despite the publication of a denial by the Trustees, this last action seems to have had considerable effect.

The opening of the school seems to have been quite informal, James Walker relating the story later of how after he had unlocked the door to the Cairnpark third a small boy dashed under his arm and was first into the school – thus, of course, illustrating that the school was for the pupils and not the teachers! The small boy was John Westwood, a poor but bright scholar, who took advantage of the horticultural training given and returned later as Head Gardener and Botany Teacher. Of the teachers mentioned James

Walker and Peter Steven remained for many years, Mr de Joux neglected his duties and under pressure resigned. Dr – as he now was – Mylne expressed a preference for native speakers of foreign languages (preferably Swiss as you could obtain three languages at least for the price of one) but found their temperament unsuited to his, as, in fact, was that of young Mr Bell, who was shortly after dismissed for allowing boys to play football in the grounds and not reading out the Principal's notes. Mr Bell went off to run a school of his own at Helen Place but, on retiring through ill-health, went to live at West Sheardale with his in-laws and there, as related, undertook the laborious task of working out the mathematical tables.

In 1826 under pressure Dr Mylne was forced to enlarge his Kirk Session to provide more trustees. Only one of the original three, Robert Smyth, remained and he refused to attend. The others were landowners apart from Robert Kirk, a local joiner. Mr Clark of Dollarbeg undertook the publication of *Statutes and Rules for Dollar Institution* which was published in 1828. The duties of the teachers were laid down as follows:

The English master was to teach English and English Grammar five hours per weekday and three on Saturday. He could employ one assistant. (Mr Walker's classes sometimes consisted of about 100 pupils and English meant English as opposed to Scots! He lived in what is now McNabb House in Academy Place. His tombstone is in the old churchyard and discloses an appalling list of his own children's deaths. Even so he has descendants in Canada.)

The Writing Master was to teach Copperplate Writing, Arithmetic and Book-keeping. He was to teach similar hours and also have an assistant. (Mr Steven was reckoned one of the best writers in Scotland. He also taught large classes and eventually built and lived in the house named Seberham).

The Latin Master was to teach Latin, Greek, Ancient History. and exercise his pupils in English Composition. He was also to teach Oriental Languages. (Mr Tennant was a cripple with a remarkable facility for languages – he supposedly taught himself Gaelic in three weeks. He eventually became Professor of Oriental Languages at St Andrews. He built Devongrove where he lived with his sister and is known as the author of a long poem "Anster Fair").

The Modern Language Master was to teach French, German, Italian, and Spanish for five hours on weekdays and two on Saturdays.

The Teacher of Mathematics and Natural Philosophy (Physics) was to teach Geometry, Land Surveying, Draughtmanship, Arithmetic, Algebra, Astronomy, Navigation, Ship Building, Gunnery, and Fortification – plus Mechanics and Natural Philosophy at an evening hour.

The Teacher of Drawing was to teach Landscape and Figures, Architectural plans and elevations, Machine drawing, drawing for Plasterwork, Cabinetwork and Weaving, Military Drawing and Fortifications, for four hours on weekdays. two on Saturdays, and one hour each evening.

The Teacher of Chemistry was to teach Chemistry as connected with the Arts, Natural History and Practical Mineralogy, Gardening and Husbandry.

There was also to be a School of Industry with a schoolmistress to teach sewing, plaiting, tambouring and lacework and a master to teach basketry, and the making of fences, seats, gates, doormats, brooms, beehives etc. (There is no indication that a master was ever appointed for the latter crafts.)

For these minor accomplishments the Head Academic Teachers were paid £140 Sterling plus

a house. They could take in boarders if they wished privately. Seven houses were eventually built in "Teachers' Row" (including one on the Burnside) for this purpose, wings having to be added at the back to the smaller ones which originally cost £525. Numbers 1 and 2 cost somewhat more.

The only children officially entitled to free education were those on the poor roll, but, as has been mentioned, since these numbers were very small, the Trustees agreed to admit the children of the poorer classes who had been resident in the parish for more than three years (this to stop an influx of poor from elsewhere). Industrious and well-behaved parishioners of the labouring class without the residential qualifications and richer parishioners paid fees under the following scale:

Annual Parental Income	Per class per quarter
Under £30	8d
£30 to £50	1s 6d
£50 to £75	2s 6d
£75 to £100	4s 0d
£100 +	5s 0d

The first comprehensive roll occurs in 1830. It shows:

	Boys	Girls	Total
Feepaying residenters	37	25	62
Boarders	19	1	20
Free scholars	78	48	126
	134	74	208

The only girl boarder at the time, Mary Turcan, resided with Mrs Brydie, the sewing teacher at her house in Institution Place (or Teachers' Raw as it was more vulgarly called).

The numbers taking different subjects were:

English	156	Writing	156	Drawing	41
Latin etc	42	Maths	7	Mod Lang	3
Geography	39	Sewing	39		

Geography was taught by the Librarian, Mr Martin, who built Springfield, History within the English and Latin classes.

The main instrument of punishment was the

tawse. Those (they tend to be referred to in the plural) owned by Mr Steven were "long and narrow, and when properly wielded were capable of twisting round the person in quite a serpentine manner". He was normally "an amiable and gentle man, but when put to it he delivered his attack with wonderful vehemence". His assistant, Mr Cameron, "smote hip and thigh", while Mr Walker "when about to administer justice to unfortunate delinquents frequently wound his left arm round that of his victim, at the same time firmly gripping his wrist with his hand, and at the rate of at least 180 strokes a minute ... the gyrations of master and pupil greatly resembled a couple waltzing". Dr Lindsay, later, punished with anything at hand but usually with his "large key of knowledge". The only one who seems to have been resented was a Mr Harrower in 1843 who threw his tawse, described as being of enormous length and breadth and with a numerous progeny of tails each armed with a veritable knot, at the offender, then pummelled

him, often compelling the victim to lay their hands flat upon the table. He was finally waylaid after school by one victim "a tall stout black fellow ... who sprang upon him with such force and fury as completely paralysed him. After pounding this cowardly braggart to his hearts content, he rejoined his comrades amidst triumphant shouting, and during the remainder of his school career was looked upon as a youthful village Hampden". Mr Harrower, who taught religious instruction, left shortly after.

In 1832 an Infant School was started in 6 Institution Place under a Thomas Russell and his wife, catering for those age 3 to 5. It stayed open till 6 p.m. in the summer although lessons ended at 5 p.m. Summer also saw picnics up Dollar Hill, no doubt rendered livelier by Mr Russell's bent for ventriloquism. Later a small building was erected near the Burnside to accommodate the numbers. Mr Russell eventually became an Inspector for the Poor in Clackmannanshire and a well-known Alloa auctioneer. Also in 1832 Mr

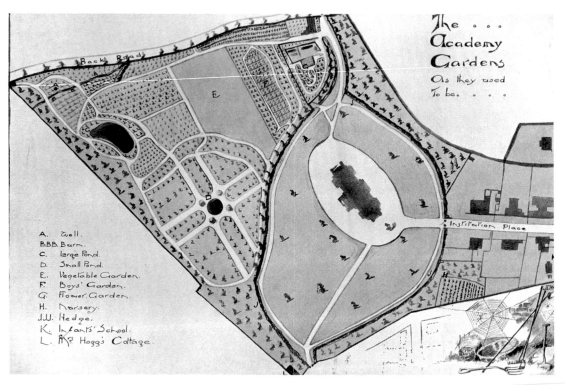

"Oeconomical and Botanical Gardens" ca. 1830
Plan by Jack Westwood - DM 1905

Gerlach, the successor to Dr de Joux, having had enough, found himself a job at Glasgow High and, according to the minutes:

> in the evening of last Communion Sabbath – on coming out of the Church behaved in the most disgraceful manner and to the great offence of the Congregation by insulting personally the Minister and by dancing down from the gate of the Churchyard to the bridge over Dollar Burn in the presence of the people retiring from Church.

He was duly replaced by a M. Duprez who promptly complained to the Trustees that "In the Academy of Dollar it will be allowed by anyone, acquainted with the same, that there is no discipline whatever – and for some time past smoking, fighting and swearing have prevailed within the precincts of the Academy ... the shameful conduct of five big boys being brought home lately in a cart tipsy at 11 o'clock at night has, unfortunately, not added to the reputation". In return the Principal complained bitterly of M. Duprez's habit of running down other masters in class and on his exhibiting tricks of legerdemain in Alloa, blazoning on bills his connection with the Academy. M. Duprez too departed after a quarrel with the Latin master, Mr Scott, over Joseph Bourne, a coloured boy, who boarded with Duprez. Mr Scott, having excluded Bourne from his classroom for bad conduct, was promptly besieged therein by both Duprez and Bourne and had, along with his class, to escape through a window, being further pursued and shouted at along Academy Place. In the investigation which followed Mr Scott was accused of calling Bourne a "smoke" which he strongly denied. *Stewart* says that Bourne, who had already been in trouble for drawing a knife on another boy, let fly a slate at Scott's head and was expelled. The records show both Duprez and Scott resigning, the latter as a form of protest against nothing being done about Bourne, only to find his resignation accepted. It did him no harm as he became Professor of Hebrew at Aberdeen. Racialism of any sort does not seem to have been tolerated, especially from members of staff. A later incident concerning remarks by a Dr Karlschmidt

about a half-caste boy, Daniel McIntyre, led to the teacher being dismissed. McIntyre went on to become a doctor and set up in practice in Doune. The earliest recorded pupil of mixed blood is Charles Heddle, son of an Orkney doctor and a Sierra Leone woman. He became a founder member of the Sierra Leone Council, advising the British Government on the Colony, made a fortune by being the first to process ground nut oil, and, later in life, married a French girl and retired to a chateau near Paris!

In 1838 the Trustees appointed a Botany Teacher in the shape of John Westwood, the small boy who had been first into the new school. The gardens of the Academy had been planned as "Oeconomical and Botanical Gardens" and Westwood set out to fulfil their title. A scheme for training a small number of suitable boys in gardening after they left school was to result in a number of excellent gardeners, an article in the 1906 *Dollar Magazine* listing:

> Mr McIvor, who had charge of the chinchona plantations in the Nilgiri Hills, India, where he introduced improved methods of culture and the barking of trees; Mr Ross, who had charge of the Government Gardens at Kew, from there went as head gardener to Constantinople, and afterward was engaged by Government to collect rare and valuable orchids from all the tropical regions of the world. After this he settled in New Zealand, where he has conducted a most successful and thriving "nursery" enterprise. Another, Mr Hogg, has been for many years keeper of the Great Park at Windsor. William Forrester, James Ferguson (Boxton), James Condie (Harrow), and James Clark, may also be mentioned as men from Dollar very well-known in the gardening world.

Recent years have also disclosed the career of James Sorley, a descendant of the weaver after whom Sorley's Brae is named, who became Head Gardener of Canada and laid out the grounds at Ottawa, as well as William McNabb, head of the Scottish Botanics. It is small wonder that we find among those attending Mr

John Westwood - DM 1905

Westwood's Botany Class the names of local landowners sitting with the children. They also occur in the Modern Language classes. Community schooling is nothing new.

In 1843, in his absence, Mr Haig complained of the Principal's ill-health and deafness and suggested he be retired on a salary of £50 but it was not seconded. Dr Mylne married late in life and his wife took devoted care of him in his old age. He seems to have become badly incapacitated and confined to a wheel chair.

In 1846 the Trustees decided to apply to Parliament to bring in an Act to increase the number of trustees and this was passed in 1847. The Trustees now consisted of: The Parish Minister, the Elders, the Lord Lieutenant and Vice Lieutenant of the County, the Convener of Clackmannan, the Sheriff of Clackmannan, the Patron of the Parish, 2 Representatives from Stirling Presbytery, the Principal of Edinburgh University, 2 Representatives of the Parliamentary Electors, and all the Heritors of the Parish. This last all-inclusive group unfortunately laid a governorship open to anyone able to purchase a small amount of property and seems to have been occasionally abused.

The new committee, as new committees will, attempted to sweep clean. Mrs Brydie was retired on £30 per annum, Mr Russell was dismissed for some unspecified reason and took up his new career as Inspector of the Poor, and an attempt was made to persuade Dr Mylne to retire on reduced salary. The Doctor may have been infirm but he was no fool and after pointing out he had been appointed for life was retired on full salary.

In July 1850 the Rev. Thomas Burbidge was appointed the new Principal of Dollar Institution, taking up duties in October. Born at Leicester in 1816, he was educated at Rugby, Repton, and Cambridge and was apparently at one time tutor to Dr Arnold's children. The circumstances of how he came to be appointed are not clear. He quickly established weekly meetings of the Masters and appointed ten monitors or prefects with powers to report indiscipline to him, suggested that the school be divided into a basic English school and a higher General school and recommended the charging of general fees instead of class fees to encourage a full day's attendance. He concludes his first report by recommending the Masters for their support and stating that he thought the school was in sound moral condition.

The amity was not to last. By February the Trustees were calling a special meeting to consider a petition from the inhabitants about letters sent by Mr Burbidge to a former pupil William Roberts which Roberts had forwarded to Mrs Martin, wife of the Geography teacher, with whom he had probably boarded. Unfortunately neither the letters – of which copies of three out of the four were circulated – nor the petition have survived, but the contents of the letters, which apparently made enquiries into the morals of the school, were considered sufficient to lead to a recommendation for Mr Burbidge's dismissal. The trustees split over the issue, the locals tending to be in favour of dismissal, while others such as Bruce of Kennet, Johnstone of Alva, Lord Abercrombie, and Sheriff Tait considered the condemnation unfair and refused to take part. Burbidge complained about the non-copying of the fourth letter which made the reason for his enquiry plain, the committee replying that "in regard to the prevalence of the vice to which the letters refer the objection was not that enquiries had been made but that they had been made in a manner which evinced a great deficiency both of sound judgement and delicate moral feeling" and that the fourth letter had been read to the committee. Dr Strachan, the local GP, probably summed up the real reasons for the criticisms when he stated to the committee that "he was not aware of any dissatisfaction among the parents until there were reports in the village of Mr Burbidge being a Roman Catholic priest", reports no doubt fuelled by his heinous habit of wearing his clerical gown in the street. The issue was resolved by Mr Burbidge tendering his resignation.

He became headmaster of Leamington College at Leamington Spa for seven years and vicar of Hexton, Hertfordshire for ten. From 1868 he was Chaplain at Malta and then Canon of Gibraltar, dying at the home of his wife near Pisa in 1892. He appears to have been a friend of Matthew Arnold and published a book of poems with Arthur Hugh Clough in 1849.

In his stead the Trustees appointed the Rev. John Milne, an Aberdonian, at the time Principal of Huddersfield College, and also apparently a clergyman in the Church of England. In his first report he suggested a curriculum similar to that proposed by Mr Burbidge. Under him the school settled down to seventeen years of solid achievement often referred to later as the "golden years". In 1854 a small primary school was established at the west end of the Sheardale cottages to save younger children crossing the Devon, the wooden bridges there often being destroyed. A Miss Snowdowne taught there for nearly the whole of its history, running night schools for adults as well. In 1863, with Milne's encouragement, Dr Lindsay, the teacher of Mathematics and Physics, Thomas Kirk, Classics (Hindustani) and John Brown, the Art Master, tutored four boys for the highly competitive Indian Civil Service examination. One hundred candidates competed for ten vacancies. The Dollar pupils came 3rd, 4th, 7th, and 8th. Such success had not been achieved before by a school and it caused a sensation far outwith Dollar so that the school became well known and a connection with India was established that was to last for the next hundred years. The Academy was later to become a recognised training college, the only one outwith London and Dublin, for Cooper's Hill, the Indian

Civil Service College founded in 1871 which in its fairly short existence took in 23 FPs, 7 gaining top diplomas. In 1865, it is pleasant to relate, the first four successful boys, A.N. Nimmo, A. Izatt, W.C. Rennie, and C. Black, sent money to the School Treasurer for a piece of silver to be presented to each of the masters who had tutored them. What happened to Nimmo and Black is not known but Rennie and Izatt were among the pioneers of the Indian Railway system.

In 1866 the West Approach was created forming a new main entrance to the school, the toll keeper at Devon Road complaining that carriages were whipping through the school grounds to avoid the tolls and Sir Andrew Orr of Harviestoun, on being graciously granted permission by the Trustees to make use of it, pointing out a little peevishly that he owned most of it. In the same year the first four Hong Kong Chinese boys known to be educated in Britain attended the Academy, along with four Parsee pupils as well. All wore their national costumes and one of the Chinese boys, when later a banker, presented the first cup to the school for competition.

Dollar Rules 1852 - DAA

Sir James Dewar - DM 1902

Dr Milne was apparently an immaculate but rather portly gentleman; known as "Porky", not only for his portliness, but on account of on his one day taking a French class instructing a pupil on how to pronounce "pourquoi". A highly efficient headmaster, he frowned on "penny dreadfuls" – trashy magazines usually of a "Western" nature, smoking and the use of firearms – the latter apparently easily available locally at 7s 6d a time. Masters of his time included Dr Lindsay, described variously as having a grim sense of humour in that he punished with anything that came to hand but particularly with his large "key of knowledge" and as "a giant physically and intellectually". He kept a large number of boarders at Brooklyn and all pupils vouch for him as a magnificent teacher. David Gill, the noted astronomer, confessed during a year with Lindsay he never opened his textbook on Euclid but that when he did he knew Euclid off by heart. He gives pupils of the time as the Swettenham brothers, Governors of the West Indies and Malaya; Dewar, the physicist who first froze air, invented the vacuum flask and, with Abel, invented cordite; Mair, an eminent mathematician; Briggs Constable a well-known politician; Cranston, Provost of Edinburgh; Smith, the ironmaster at Stirling; and Izat of the Indian Railways. Dewar stated that Lindsay first stirred his interest in physics. Lindsay apparently

was in line for a professorship but some objection came from the Dollar area. He seems to have had a drink problem and J.A.W. Dollar remembered him later, after he left the Academy, as a great black figure on the Back Road muttering to himself and concluded that "much learning had made him mad". Elected to the Governing Body as a representative of the Parliamentary Electors he resigned as a teacher when the other governors passed a motion to exclude employees from acting as governors. Kirk who could teach Latin, Greek, Persian, Urdu, and Hebrew is described as strict and eccentric. He too resigned in some quarrel with the governors and went to Canada although his family remained in Dollar. "Cocky" Brown, diminutive and natty in his artistic corduroy jacket and intellectual dark spats, was a great friend of Dr Lindsay. He laid much emphasis on the bringing of bread for rubbing out, most of which got eaten, and punished by belabouring pupils with his port crayon or pencil case. The writing master then and for long after, was "Black Jack" Douglas, so called because of his skin colour. A masterly penman – his daughter was to win a premier prize in the art – he was remembered for his decorative white shirts and his habit of teaching clutching a bunch of spare pens which would be plunged into the what he termed "the beefs" of any male caught leaning out of his seat. Billy "Schlaps" Watson, another much regarded master, apparently was landed with his nickname after an early threat of punishment. It is extraordinary how much the various methods of corporal punishment tend to be remembered, usually without rancour unless they were delivered unjustly. Lines are often more resented – Dr Milne had a set of these published on posters and seems to have been the first to prescribe their writing out as a punishment – while sarcasm is never forgiven. Dr Milne retired in 1868 having had Parkfield (Heyworth) built as a boarding house for boys. Such was the excellence (and cheapness) of a good Dollar education that many large families came to settle in the town, among them Milne's Aberdeen relatives. Two, Alice and James Cadenhead, were sent down as parlour boarders to their uncle. Although it only lasted two years young Alice had a great time, being treated with the utmost decorum by the boys, her letters home being recently privately published by a descendant. James went on to be a noted Scottish painter. Regrettably both Dr Milne and his wife died in 1871 and are buried in Dollar Kirkyard beside a stepdaughter. They were held in high regard and in 1872 Former Pupils instituted the Dux Medals in memory of their headmaster. Frank Swettenham, later Governor of Malaya – and, presumably, the "Swetman" who gave Alice a birl on the ice at the skating pond – on his visits to Dollar always visited their grave.

The Rev. William Barrack, also from Aberdeen, succeeded Dr Milne as headmaster. Again an efficient principal, memoirs tend to say little personal about him. In 1869 a hall, designed by the notable architect, John Burnet, was added to the rear of the Playfair Block. Although attracting some criticism it now seems preferable to an alternative plan to build another storey on top! Dr Barrack resigned in 1878, probably over the reinstatement by the Governors of some pupils he had expelled, to become the first headmaster of Kelvinside Academy and he was replaced by Dr George Thom, the first non-clerical Principal and apparently the first to be referred to as "Rector". The advent of easy communication by the new railway and the intro-

duction of compulsory primary education in 1872 seems to have gradually led to a vast increase in numbers, 1014 being recorded in 1876/77, comparable to the present roll in 1998. Heaven knows where they put them all, the only buildings being the main Playfair Block and Hall, the Infant School, and Sheardale School. The numbers broke down into:

Infant School	224
Sheardale	44
Evening Classes	40
Lower School	279
Upper School	427

While the new state primary schools were building after the 1872 Act the place of charity schools in the scheme of things was being debated, it finally being decided that it was the Government's duty to provide free education for those of compulsory school age and that charity schools would cease to provide it. It was a decision that was to lead to many of them, particularly the large city schools such as Heriot's and the Merchant Company group – Watson's Girls and Boys, Stewart's, and Gillespie's – eventually becoming private. In Dollar's case it applied to those under ten years of age and the school handed over its Infant Building and ground at the Cairnpark Gate for the erection of a new Board School. The trustees argued against the change strongly but were overruled and when under the Endowed School Act they were asked by the Scotch Education Department to draw up a new governing body they declined to make recommendations. The Education Department thereupon drew it up for them.

The Governing Body was now to consist of the following trustees: 1 from Kirk Session, 2 from Clackmannan County, 1 from Kinross, 3 from Dollar School Board, 1 from Edinburgh University, 1 from St Andrews University, 1 alternately from the School Boards of Alloa and Tillicoultry, 1 alternately from the School Boards of Clackmannan and Alva. The funds were also limited very strictly to scholastic purposes.

The new board met on the 1st August 1887 and proceeded to sweep very clean. The Infant School was handed over to the newly elected

Dr Thom and Staff
Messrs Campbell, Smith, Masterton, Cooke, Oswald,
Spence, Douglas, Christie, Malcolm, Cownie,
Lauder,
Dron, Snowdowne, Thom, Geyer, Brown and
Cruickshank
DAA

Parish School Board and the primary teachers dismissed – although presumably re-employed by the new School Board, James Christie becoming head of the Board School. The Sheardale school was closed and the teacher, Miss Snowdowne, dismissed. The janitor was moved out of his flat in the Academy and into 6 Institution Place. The Gardens were reduced in scope and only the Head Gardener, Mr Blackwood, and an old assistant, Mr Hynd, were left. The boxwood hedges were grubbed out, the ground was levelled and grassed, the large pond – on the site of the Boys' Pavilion – was filled in and a displenishing sale of equipment and plants took place. Only the walled garden and Ladies' Pond were retained. Mr Westwood had, thankfully, died in 1875. The Governors tried to continue to pay retirement allowances to Mr Douglas, Miss Snowdowne, and to make one to Miss Crombie, but, being debarred from doing so by the Education Department, were blamed for their meanness. The allowances seem, however, to have eventually been paid. In 1890 they applied for a coat-of-arms but, as it was to cost £50, designed their own to include a ship (for John McNabb), the lion rampant, and the torch of learning. A selection of mottoes was submitted

"Anybody else for tennis?" 1892 - DAA

and "Juventutis veho fortunas" (I carry the fortunes of youth) selected. An inscription was also carved on the pediment of the building to John McNabb (using the spelling Macnabb). A road was made from Cairnpark to the school and a small gate erected and the greenhouses were demolished, the materials being used to help

Academy Gardens
Dr Mylne's Sundial 1829 - DM 1913

build a new workshop. Finally they managed to have the £55,000 principal of the McNabb legacy transferred from the jurisdiction of the Court of Chancery to their own.

Astley Piggot remembered from this period teachers known as "Bottle Brush" Montgomery, "Warrior" Leitch, "Daddy" Hand, and "Froggy" Bonne, who may have been the French teacher whose wife, a large German lady, kept discipline for him. Janitor Campbell ran drill classes every morning from 7 to 8 a.m. using the Volunteers' muskets which, as a treat on the last drill of the season, were primed with powder and banged off. Marbles tended to be illegally introduced and in one well-remembered incident one D'Auvergne Findlay's tamping-rod winged its way in the direction of Parkfield Boarding House. It was also the Janitor's task to round up "kippers" (truants) and one of the beech trees in the Back Road was known as the "Kipper Tree" as its higher branches provided excellent comfort and concealment, Astley Piggot also remembered Chinese pupils with penny farthing bicycles running challenge races to the bottom of the brae to Tillicoultry and

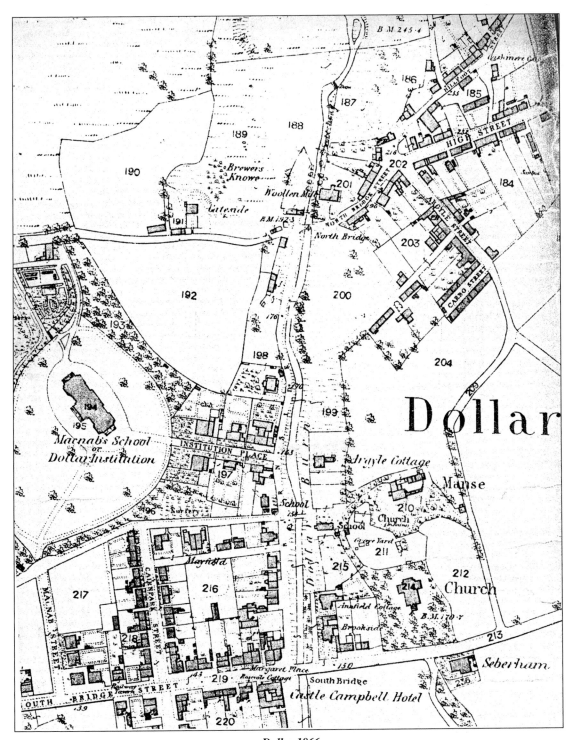

Dollar 1866
The first Ordnance Survey Map - DAA

presenting the winners with diamond shaped medals, some two by three inches, made of silver. Visits came from circuses; an illusionist presenting "Pepper's Ghost" – the projection of a figure under the stage onto the stage by the use of mirrors; the Diorama of Canada, in one of whose scenes the tail of a donkey actually moved!; and Forrest Knowles, an itinerant actor and reciter. Pigott also recollected an FP's gift, the "Library Lioness", a stuffed animal with a detachable tail which invariably found its way to the wrong end, and which was later consigned as a whole to the school furnace by an exasperated headmaster. Lectures and visits to historic sites were provided by joining the Dollar Association.

THE GLEN AND MILL GREEN

THE MILL GREEN

The Meal Mill in Mill Green was presumably that of the Barony of Campbell to which all tenants would be thirled – made to take their grain for grinding. The miller would take a portion of the hard-earned grain for himself as a charge and, consequently, millers were habitually

Mill Green and the Castle - DMus

disliked and regarded as dishonest. As an extra chore the tenants were also liable to keep the mill and its stones in good repair.

The overgrown foundations of the mill lie in the centre of the green over to the east slope near the steps. Excavations by the Academy in 1979 produced remains going back to medieval times. The mill wheel seems to have been powered by water brought from a dam below the present

waterworks weir and conveyed in a wooden trough or "trows" above ground to the mill. The last known miller was a William McLiesh early in the 19th century after which the buildings deteriorated into a slum, at one time inhabited by a Meg Monteath and Jean Grewin, and two lame young men, Jamie Skip and John Greig.

Gibson relates the story of how William McLiesh carried a petition from the townsfolk to the Duke of Argyll asking him to grant the use of the green for bleaching purposes to the village, the request being granted. By the middle of the 19th century, however, the green appears to have been used for grazing, complaints being raised about damage to fencing done by visitors to the Glen. Early in the 19th century Tait of Harviestoun, to test the power, erected on the stream from the Bog Well a large waterwheel some thirty feet high, which had been used to pump out the mines on the Kelly Burn. It was broken up in 1836. Formerly under the care of the Town Council the Mill Green is now looked after by Clackmannanshire Council. Silver birches were planted along the bluebell path at the time of the Silver Jubilee and a plaque on a stone commemorates a visit by Princess Anne in 1979.

DOLLAR GLEN

The idea of constructing a path up Dollar Glen seems to have occurred to several people around 1860. Up till then the shortest way to the castle had been made by a narrow path, now nearly overgrown, leading from the present quarry carpark entrance to the top of Hempy's Falls and then up the slope by zigzag steps worn in the turf to the Castle garden. More doughty spirits could descend to wade the bed of the Sorrow and climb by Kemp's Score as was done by Sir Walter Scott and the Blairadam Club on their first visit in 1818. They revisited by the easier route in 1828. Dr Andrew Mylne descended the Score more rapidly than he intended but being, in his younger days, adamantine proof, recovered after a few days in bed. There are supposedly steps under the mud and debris that clog the cleft.

The proposal to open up the Glen was taken on the 9th August 1864 by a Committee consisting of Dr Strachan Senior, a local doctor; Mr Stalker, builder; Mr Brown, Academy Art master; Dr Lindsay, Academy Science master; Mr Cousin, shopowner; and Mr Bradshaw, the bookshop proprietor and a relative of the publisher of the famous Railway Guide. A public meeting was held in the Parish Schoolhouse and the above committee was appointed plus Mr Westwood, the Academy Botany teacher and Gardener; Mr Horn, a Devon Railway engineer; the prominent townspeople Mr Wardlaw, Mr Cadogan of Belmont and Freshfield, and Mr Davies. Later John Strachan Jnr, Mr T.S. Bradshaw and Mr James Christie, Academy teacher and poet, were invited to join them. Sir Andrew Orr, the owner of Harviestoun and the Glen, gave approval, as did Mr Cairns, the tenant of Dollarbank, and Mr George, tenant of Gateside. Peter Stalker and David Horn surveyed the footpath, at no small danger to themselves, and Mr Westwood acted as Arbitrer. Money was collected round the doors. Mr Macfarlane in Dunfermline, who seems to have been the owner of Gateside, was contacted regarding possible entrance by the cottages where the present golf clubhouse stands. The work was to be completed by the 1st March 1865.

Apparently Mr Macfarlane did not give access for the footpath first commenced at a little quarry at the south end of the entrance to the Glen and extended to the bridge at the junction of the burns, access being gained by going down the present path from the waterworks on Castle Road to where the small overgrown quarry can be discovered on the right. The offer of James MacCallum, quarrymaster at Tillicoultry, to contract for the work at 9/2d per chain to the first bridge and the rock between the two bridges at 1/6d per yard was accepted.

By the 1st January 1865 £67 5 4d had been collected and £42 2 6d expended. MacCallum further contracted for "the footpath on west side for first chain 1/6d per yard, then up to where the bridge crosses 1/2d per chain, and for the one that goes up the Glen past Castle Campbell towards Sochie Falls 6/- per chain". Two wicket gates on the quarry road and two stiles over the fences between the washing green and quarry were built while a complaint was made to the Rector, Dr Milne, on the destruction of ferns at Kemp's Score.

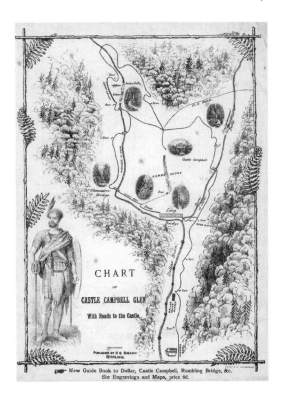

Early Plan of Dollar Glen - DMus

The first phase of the work was completed and it was decided to hold an official opening on Friday, 26th May 1865, the entire length of the footpath to Sochie Falls then being 3254 yards with bridge lengths of 165 feet.

Despite some rain nearly a thousand people collected near the entrance at the little quarry at 7 p.m. on the 26th. The Dollar Flute Band headed the procession and afterwards marched through the town. After several speeches the whole gathering proceeded up the path to its utmost limits expressing joy and delight at the ever-changing scenes. Thereafter some eighty of the company gathered at the Castle Campbell Hotel at 8.30 p.m. and, having paid their one shilling and sixpences, proceeded to partake of supper, Dr Strachan acting as Chairman and Mr Brown and Mr Westwood as croupiers, all enjoying themselves greatly. Among the speeches was one by Mr Christie on the ancient fortalice of Castle Campbell. Mr Christie also composed a song on the Glen which was sung by Mr Deany.

No doubt heartened by this support for their endeavours, at an inspection of the path on the 20th of June the Committee determined to cross the burn by a bridge to gain "access to an eminence on the west side where a delightful panoramic scene is to be witnessed and on which it has been suggested 'The Old Old Story Seat' be placed". This is a reference to a fundraising talk,"The Old Old Story", given by the humorous lecturer, Mr George Roy, the previous April. The extension was completed by July and on the 29th a general picnic was held at the termination of the path, Messrs Ewing and Lamb attending with their pipes. The path was now complete but there remained two main problems, better access and upkeep. Better access was eventually provided in 1867 when Sir Andrew Orr bought the Old Woollen Mill and offered entrance there, a bridge providing access to the west bank at the corner of the bleaching green and another further up across to the original start of the path, much as the bridges do at present. This was washed out in the flood of 1877 when a witness saw the bridges heading rapidly downstream. Thereafter the path seems to have followed its present course through the Mill Green.

Money for the upkeep of the path was raised by means of a series of Lectures and Concerts extending over several winters. Among those giving talks were Mr Roy again, Dr Strachan, Dr Hunter, Sheriff Tait, Andrew Wilson and a Mr Ballantyne. For Mr Roy's second lecture, which commenced the series, policemen were engaged, members distributed themselves to maintain order, and nails were inserted in the window frames. It seems the youth of the town were no better behaved then than now. Sheriff Tait's lecture, which was delivered in the Mission Hall in the Old Town and concluded the 1867 season, was on the subject of "Dollar, Past and Present" and drew a large audience. Sir Andrew Orr presided and the listeners included all the local bigwigs – James Orr, Dr Milne, James Tait, James Leishman, John McArthur Moir, James Blair, W.J. Haig, and John Bald Harvey of Glendevon. The original of the lecture was found some thirty years later and enthusiastically published in 1894. In 1870 Mr Ballantyne was invited back – three guineas to be offered – to lecture about New Year

time: "it being suggested that if Mr Ballantyne can make the lecture somewhat more sensational than the last, it may be, on the whole, quite as satisfactory to the young folk"!

"Mr Ballantyne" would seem to have been R.M. Ballantyne, the author of *Coral Island*, *Armpit: the Young Viking*, and other Victorian moral tales. This was presumably the occasion when someone remembered him practising his muscular Christianity at the Skating Pond in a series of dashing manoeuvres culminating in a jump across the banking which separated it from the curling rink.

Many of the place names were bestowed by the Committee. Entering the Glen the path ascends to a small promontory which had a seat placed upon it to give views up and down the Glen. Climbing further on the right is the site, cut out of solid rock, of yet another seat, named as "Rest and Be Thankful". At the junction of the burns, the Burn of Care to the right flows over Hempy's Fall (an original placename which is either named after the hedge-sparrow or a

Upper Sochie Falls - DMus

relative of Tam Baird) and the path ascends through a small glen to a flight of steps leading to the Castle. A detour to the right, now overgrown, led to a view of the long fall now known as Craiginnan Falls (alternative names suggested being Turnpike Fall or Argyll Cascade). The other path from the junction led over the Long Bridge, past the original Kemp's Score or Cutt, up Windy Edge (where a large boulder fell and jammed in 1962), across the Glencairn Bridge to view the Glencairn Falls (the name taken from the old name for the Glen of Sorrow) to the Lower Sochie Falls where there was another seat. The lower path then leads up the Burn of Sorrow to cross by a bridge to the Upper Sochie Falls, much reduced in height by a fall of rock in the 1950s. (Sochie – place of the willows – seems to be an old name for this area.) Another seat was placed here. The path then ascends Jacob's Ladder to where a modern seat replaces "The Old Old Story Seat". The path continues to where the highest bridge crosses a narrow defile at Nelly's Dell, a spot much admired by Dr Strachan's daughter, later Mrs Hinton Stewart, and chivalrously named in her honour by the Committee. The path then returns to the castle high above the chasm which leads to Sochie Falls.

In 1866 Dr Henderson of Muckhart offered a camera of some sort, probably obscura, to the Committee but the offer had to be declined owing to the difficulty of siting and superintendence, and in 1867 Sir Andrew Orr agreed to the opening up of some parts of Castle Campbell ruins "with the view to making interesting discoveries. All openings to be built up again." A year later this was taken further, the Committee agreeing to Sir Andrew's suggestion that they might look after the Castle. Fundraising concerts and lectures continued. Some complaints were made by Mr George and notices were erected at the entrance: "No Dogs Allowed" and "Visitors Leaving Footpath are Liable to Prosecution".

After this there seems to have been some dissension. No meetings are recorded for the latter half of 1871 and none at all for 1872, the next meeting being on the 8th of January 1873 when Dr Strachan for some reason gave an account of his connection with the laying of kerbstones on the principal street of the town and

a Mr Gibson was to be contacted on the exclusion of the public from the ground in front of the Castle near Kemp's Score.

In March Mr Gibson and Mr Ferguson stated the present arrangements, whatever they were, could not be interfered with at present. There the first Book of Minutes ends.

What happened after this is even less clear. A Minute exists for the 19th February 1874 from which it appears that interviews had taken place between the Chairman, Secretary, and Sir Andrew Orr and that Sir Andrew had suggested making a charge of admission for the footpath. The Committee expressed their view on this as follows:

In accepting office the Committee confidently hoped to be the means of providing a source of permanent enjoyment for the people of Dollar, access to which would be free from pecuniary restrictions. From the date of their appointment the committee have zealously endeavoured to secure the object originally aimed at: and in furtherance of that object have raised and expended a sum amounting to fully three hundred pounds. The committee do not feel inclined to express an opinion as to the propriety or probable results of taxing strangers on visiting the Glen and Castle Campbell, but they would earnestly recommend that the inhabitants of Dollar, who resort to the footpath with a view to pleasant relaxation in seasons of leisure, and who have done so much to provide this enjoyment, should be exempt from any such tax. The committee will be happy to see any measure adopted which may tend to increase the amenities of the Glen and the fine old ruin with which it is connected; and they hope to hear that, whatever arrangements are made, Sir Andrew Orr will kindly comply with the wishes of the committee as now expressed.

A reply was, however, received from Sir Andrew's factor that:

Sir Andrew was quite of the opinion that

Long Bridge - DMus

Glencairn Bridge - DM 1925

the best way of raising funds to keep the walk and the Castle in proper repair was by levying a small tax at the foot of the wood to admit to the Glen and Castle, and that his intention was to keep the whole in proper repair, and if funds admitted, to still further improve the walk and the Glen, as well as keeping up the old building of the Castle. He will therefore relieve the committee and take the management in his own hands by his factor, which he hopes will suit the purposes of all parties much better.

The committee further protested against the possible charge to Dollar inhabitants but Sir Andrew again replied through his factor:

he was sorry that the committee should view with such apprehension the very small charge it is intended to make for the Glen and Castle with the object of putting and keeping these in somewhat better order than they are at present ... he hoped that on reconsideration the committee would see it in that light, and go hand in hand with Sir Andrew in the change about to be made.

To this the committee seem to have made no response and their work was terminated. How the new system worked and for how long charges continued to be made is not recorded. Sir Andrew or his successor, his brother James, certainly had extensive repairs carried out to the Castle in 1874. But Margaret Donaldson remembered from her childhood in the early 1900s notices warning of danger and that the bridges had badly deteriorated. It seems that they were later repaired but fell again into disrepair during the Second World War.

The Glen and the Castle were handed over to the National Trust by a later member of the family, J. Ernest Kerr, in 1950, the town, under the leadership of Provost Cowan, having raised £1,100 in response for a plea for £500 to repair the bridges and footpath. The committee in charge consisted of Provost Cowan, H. Bell, P. Mitchell, N.A. Pett, J.A. Lambert, A.R. Pyott, G. Blair, R.K. Holmes, J.S. Brydie, and J.A. Miller.

Since then the Glen has been looked after by the Trust with the help very often of Service Units in the repair of bridges. Recent years have seen the proliferation of wooden catwalks to replace sections where the path has eroded, a flight of steps from the new quarry carpark, a particularly ugly massive wall around the little promontory, and a somewhat enthusiastic planting of trees below the top of Castle Road and the Castle car park, an area till now deliberately kept clear to allow unimpeded views of the castle. In a short time, unless action is taken, this "classic view" of the Castle which appears on postcards and guides will be much obscured. In 1998 the Long Bridge and the Glencairn Bridge which gave access to the Windy Edge Gorge were removed when the Trust, after a fall of rock took place, became anxious about being sued. Viewpoints are promised but will only make a small substitute for the thrill of plunging into the awful declivity with its possible dangers. In fact no accidents have been recorded in that particular area although they have taken place elsewhere. One suspects that the originators of the Glen Walk would shake their heads over our contemporary fears.

Windy Edge - DM 1925

THE DEVON VALLEY RAILWAY

Before the advent of the railway, travel from Dollar was tedious and difficult. Early in the nineteenth century *Gibson* could remember walking to Alloa and then taking the five hour Earl of Mar coach to Glasgow where it drew up at Mein's Hotel in the Trongate, owned by the brother of Mrs Tod of Argyll Street. Travel to Edinburgh was usually made by boat from Alloa

Opening of Dollar Section
Devon Valley Railway, 1st May, 1869 - DM 1929

to Granton, the first regular steamer on the Forth being the "Stirling" in 1813, followed by the "Morning Star" and "The Lady of the Lake", built at Kincardine. Two rival companies merged to form The Stirling, Alloa, and Kincardine Steamboat Company. By 1841 the railway had reached Lancaster and, via stage coach from Edinburgh, it still took two days and two nights to reach London. Eventually the railway reached Falkirk, a coach running from Tillicoultry to that town, and then it was extended to Alloa by 1850. In 1851 a branch line extended to Tillicoultry at Glenfoot and shortly after into Tillicoultry itself. It was to be another eighteen years, however, before Dollar was connected. A separate branch line to Alva opened on the 3rd of June 1863. Fortunately the great gangs of uncontrollable navvies that had been a law unto themselves were a thing of the past and had evolved into more law abiding working parties so that the valley was spared the worst excesses of the railway mania years.

The Devon Valley Railway was built in two

sections by two railway companies. The first section from Alloa to Tillicoultry was built by the Stirling and Dunfermline Railway Company who owned the Alloa – Dunfermline line. The portion from Alloa to a temporary station at Glenfoot about half-a-mile from Tillicoultry was opened in June 1851 and continued on to Tillicoultry the same year. (An intermediate station was opened between Sauchie and Fishcross in October 1873, closing in September 1930.) This railway company was taken over by the Glasgow Railway Company in June 1858 and this in turn was later taken over by the North British Railway Company in August 1865.

In 1858 a new company named the Devon Valley Railway Company was incorporated by an Act of Parliament on the 23rd July 1858 with power to extend the railway from Tillicoultry to Kinross to join the main line at a station called Hopefield. The first sod was cut near Rumbling Bridge by Mrs Adam of Blairadam on the 4th of August 1860 in front of some 1400 spectators.

The first section of the railway opened was the $6^1/2$ miles from Hopefield (Kinross) to Rumbling Bridge, the opening being done by W.P. Adam, M.P. of Blairadam.

Financial difficulties led to delay and construction at the other end of the line started in August 1867 on the $2^1/2$ miles between Tillicoultry and Dollar. Originally several bridges over the Devon had been planned for this section but eventually costs were reduced by the simple expedient of building embankments and changing the course of the river, most notably at Taits' Tomb where the riverside family cemetery was left stranded in the middle of a marshy field. The Tillicoultry – Dollar section opened on the 1st of May 1869, the 11.15 a.m. train from Alloa, complete with directors and officials of the North British Railway, simply continuing on to Dollar. The official party carried on by coach to Rumbling Bridge, returning in time to connect with the 4 p.m. Alloa to Stirling. On arrival and departure the party were photographed by Mr

Dollar Station with Porter, Peter Dudgeon - DM 1904

Bradshaw of Dollar. The public service commenced on the 3rd of May. The first stationmaster was a Mr McNess and one of the early employees was Peter Dudgeon, who became a popular local character and whose cry of "Do – lar!" was said to be heard from the top of Dollar Hill. Local views of the opening were ecstatic:

> One may expect that the gay, and withal aristocratic village, will be flooded, during the summer months, with visitors, that Castle Campbell will not remain a thing looming in the obscurity of guide books, but become a realised fact to hundreds and that the picturesque Rumbling Bridge, with its attendant, the superb hotel, will come in for an increased share of patronage. Much discussion has taken place as to the future of that tried friend the Dollar Coach, now placed in the background, many seeming to think its occupation may be gone. Even if that is so, the spirited proprietress of the "Castle Campbell" should place the old favourite between Dollar and Rumbling Bridge, and thus still keep up her connection and popularity with the travelling public.

The "old favourite" which ran between Tillicoultry and Dollar (not to Rumbling Bridge), was a two-horse bus, the best known driver being a John Reedy, credited with the shout, "The machine's broken down! You will all have to come out!" in moments of desperation. Alas it did not long survive the opening of the final stretch of line. This final section of 4¹/₂ miles from Dollar to Rumbling Bridge was the most difficult but most imposing of all. From Dollar the line curved to the south over a nine hundred yards long embankment, containing 110,000 cubic yards of sand and stone, before it crossed the Devon by a six span viaduct, the track being carried on malleable iron lattice beams with iron handrails. It then climbed the hill to a summit of 350 feet on a gradient of 1 in 70, before entering a seven hundred yards long cutting, eighty feet deep, which involved the removal of 130,000 cubic yards of rock and soil. After this it crossed the Gairney Burn, 110 feet above the river by a magnificent viaduct

The Last Train 1964 - DMus

consisting of six arches of forty five feet span each, constructed with stone from Devonshaw Quarry. The full line from Alloa to Kinross, measuring thirteen and a half miles, was opened with celebrations on Saturday April 15th 1871 when an excursion train, consisting of two saloon carriages, six first-class carriages, and one third-class for the local hoi-polloi, travelled the entire route. Thereafter some five to six trains were run in either direction daily, apart that is from Sunday, for in the early days such a frivolity as train travel on the Sabbath was banned apart from the curious exception of a train commencing its journey from England on the Saturday being allowed to complete its journey and uplift passengers. Glasgow and Edinburgh could now be reached, via Alloa, in around two hours from Dollar. The stations on the Devon Valley Line were Alloa, Sauchie, Tillicoultry, Dollar, Rumbling Bridge, Crook of Devon, Cleish Road (later named Balado in June 1878), and Hopefield Station in Kinross which was renamed Kinross Junction in October 1871. Hopefield was sited on the junction of the branch line with the main line but was repositioned 200 yards further north in 1890 when the main line was doubled on the opening of the Forth Bridge.

The forecast of an influx of visitors was fulfilled and visits to Rumbling Bridge, Castle Campbell, and the Academy Botanical Gardens became common. An unforeseen consequence as far as the Academy was concerned was, for a short period, a massive increase in the number of pupils attending.

The Devon Valley Railway Company was

amalgamated with the North British on the 1st January 1875 and the North British Railway Company became part of the London and North Eastern Railway Company on the 1st January 1923 under the Grouping arrangements introduced by the Railway Act of 1921. On the 1st January 1948 under the Nationalisation arrangements of the Transport Act of 1947 it became part of British Railways.

The line closed as a railway for passenger traffic in 1964 but continued to carry coal from the Dollar Mine till its closure in 1973. Proposals to run it as a private railway with a terminus at the mine – the station by this time having been demolished and housing built in the station yard – met with local opposition and British Rail removed the track.

During the 1950s a magnificent photographic record of the Devon Valley Railway – probably one of the most complete of any former railway line – was made by the late Peter Wilson of Heathcote, Dollar, who died in 1992. The photographs are now stored in the Dollar Museum.

Two comic incidents are supposedly connected with the railway. One was that of a small terrified child on his first trip who wanted to know why, "The hooses are a' runnin' awa'", and the other of a train drivers' strike when the train was being operated by an amateur who had difficulty stopping at the platform much to the exasperation of the stationmaster, who, after much shunting back and forward, finally shouted: "Bide where you are, Jock! We'll shift the station!".

THE DEVON VALLEY FLOOD OF 1877

Although the flood of 1877 had spectacular effects in Dollar, its main brunt was felt in Tillicoultry, an eyewitness description of it coming from W.C. Benet, a native of Tillicoultry and a former teacher at Dollar Academy, then home on holiday with his young bride from North Carolina where he eventually became a judge.

The flood occurred on the 28th of August after a few days of only slight showers. In the early morning there was only drizzling rain although it was extraordinarily dark and gloomy with clouds of a pea-soup colour. About 8.30 a.m. Benet heard a woman screaming in the streets: "The Dam-head's burst!" and found the street in commotion. In the High Street a torrent from one to four feet deep was flowing eastward and the millworkers going home for breakfast could hardly cross. Most seemed to think it was caused by destruction of the dam but Benet found on looking up at the hills that the "front of Tillicoultry Hill looked like a waterfall so gigantic as to dwarf Niagara ten times multiplied. The water was coming from the very top, the skyline of the hill. This phenomenon could not be accounted for by the bursting of a dam, a thousand feet below. Nor could that have anything to do with what was seen on Ellieston Hill to the east of Tillicoultry Hill a great cataract raging down its face in a straight line from the hilltop to the valley, a resistless torrent whose water had never run before digging its own channel in its course".

The roadways on either side of the Tillicoultry Burn from the Heid o Toun Brig to the Middle o Toun Brig were washed away and the channel of the burn piled high with boulders, some of them tons in weight. One house had its gable end washed away; another was flooded. Two people were killed. A Mr Hutcheson, a mill owner whose works lay on either side of the burn above the Heid Brig was standing on the small bridge within the works talking to William Stillie, a dyer, when a young woman, Isabella Miller, passed them. They heard a roar, looked up, and found a ten foot wall of water upon them. Stillie was swept a hundred yards downstream to where the flood was pouring over the Heid Brig. He managed to gap the stanchion of a window and held on until he was rescued. Hutcheson's body was found the next day half-a-mile down the burn buried in gravel, the girl's two days later, well down the Devon, her white arm outstretched from the sand in which she was buried. Hutcheson's works were wrecked. The weaving shed with its heavy machinery had totally disappeared while the Heid o Toun Brig was in ruins. The whole valley of the Devon seemed transformed into a lake.

Next day Benet went exploring up Tillicoultry Glen to find the cause of the flood. The Damhead had not burst but was filled to the brim and for a hundred yards back with sand and gravel. On going up the Daiglen Burn he found large holes on either side, some twenty feet across and as deep into the side of the hill, scooped clean out, from the lips of which broad beaten tracks of flattened grass led down to the burn. He then climbed further into the hills as far as Maddy Moss but found nothing untoward up there. On returning over Helen's Muir, however, to the top of Ellieston Hill, he found another great hole, this time on flat land, which was filled with water, while the scar in front of the hill was in places fifteen to twenty feet deep, the fields at the foot a scene of desolation. After this long tour young Benet got home at twilight.

The flood at Dollar was also described in detail by an unnamed eyewitness who had intended to go fishing. After 7.30 a.m. it suddenly became very dark and torrential rain fell for about an hour. When he went out he found the burn like a river and a low rumbling sound in the distance. On the Bleaching Green, the Glen bridges and trees were hurling past and boulders were being tossed around like toys. On the Burnside the flood was tearing away the banking

Houses after the Flood 1877 - DM 1950

at the bottom of Sorley's Brae though the rain had much abated. Remembering a previous flood in the 1850s which had done the same and that the houses there had been built on top of the coup which had eventually filled the hole he and Peter Snowdowne, the joiner, went to warn the inhabitants of the danger but they paid little attention. Shortly after, the railings and garden wall fell and the inmates took fright and fled. A few minutes later the top section of the front of the first villa fell outward across the raging flood

to be followed by the second, third, and fourth divisions. Although all the stone bridges were in danger they stood up well but the railway bridge was completely wrecked and choked with trees and boulders, a considerable part of the flood being diverted along the railway westward and flowing into the "Dead Waters".

The younger Dr John Strachan, although not a direct witness, recalled that having spent the night at Solsgirth he was driven home about eight or nine in the morning and found the Muir Mill Burn in flood and even the little burn at Ramshorn overflowing. Torrents of water were rushing down the fields at Dollarbeg. At the Rackmill the Devon was, however, only moderately in spate. On the Burnside two houses had their fronts swept away. The adjoining houses of Oakbank and Argyle Cottage were intact but the road was gone up to the garden walls. In the ruined houses the tables laid for breakfast could be seen but much furniture – tables, chairs, and sofas – had been swept downstream, some wit insisting that a piano, sweeping along was heard to play the then well-known tune "Doon the Burn, Davie lad." The bridge at the railway was completely blocked for a week under four or five feet of debris. Dr Strachan found evidence of the flood as far east as Baldie's Burn and westward as far as Alva, reckoning it must have covered some eight miles east to west and five miles north to south. He too could recollect a similar flood in the 1850s before there were buildings on the East Burnside when a great hole was torn out of the banking, a hole later used as a free coup for many years. He remembered his father's house – Rose Cottage in Academy Street – being flooded to such an extent he could sail about on a old door in the kitchen. He also recollected a tremendous hailstorm later on the 2nd of July 1897 and which too was selective in its damage. At Newrawhead inhabitants were wheeling hailstones out of their gardens by the barrowful and burns were filled to the brim with them. Plants at Broomrigg remained completely untouched while those at Belmont were completely destroyed.

Gibson commented that a similar flood with water foaming over the hills occurred on the 2nd of August 1883 with this time its fury concentrated on Tillicoultry and Alva. J.A.W. Dollar recollected D'Auvergne Findlay snatching a young child out of the way of the 1877 flood at Dollar. The wall opposite the road from the West Lodge to Harviestoun collapsed under the pressure of water and its replacement still has holes at the bottom to let water through should another flood occur.

DOLLAR TOWN COUNCIL

Towards the end of the century it seemed to some in the village that Dollar, in common with many other towns of its size, should form itself into a Burgh. An attempt to do so in 1887 was defeated by lack of support, many fearing it would prove too expensive. Three years later another attempt was successful and the Sheriff declared Dollar a Burgh. The first council meeting took place in the St James Hall or The Athenaeum, now part of the Strathallan Hotel, on the 16th of March 1891, and the local chemist, James B. Henderson, was elected Chief Magistrate. Two years later a change of law allowed him to adopt the ancient title of Provost.

An immense task faced the new Town Council in the provision of lighting, roads, water, a sewage system, and rubbish collection. Some public gas and oil lamps existed but were extinguished at 11 p.m.; there was virtually no maintenance of roads; a Water Association existed but only supplied part of the New Town, the Old Town and other parts of the New depending on wells; the sewage system and rubbish collection systems were primitive. With very limited resources the only public servants affordable were a part-time Town Clerk in the lawyer J.S. Henderson, a part-time Chamberlain, and one labourer. Nevertheless in the pride of being an independent burgh it created itself a seal in 1893 incorporating Castle Campbell and the motto "The Pleasant Seat of Learning." By 1896 it was able to afford three labourers and appointed a Burgh Overseer. The coming century would strain its often meagre reserves and, inevitably, make its members the target for both praise and blame.

James B. Henderson
First Provost of Dollar 1891-93 - DMus

Edmiston M.M. Breingan
Last Provost of Dollar 1971-75 - DMus

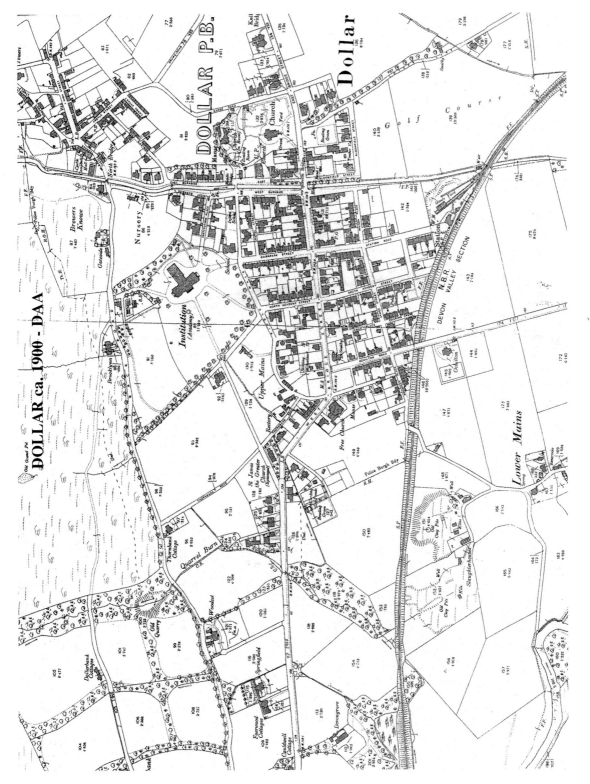

DOLLAR ca. 1900 - DAA

THE TWENTIETH CENTURY

DOLLAR PARISH

The beginning of a new century appeared to augur little change in parish life. Parish economy was still very much dependent on agriculture and changes here during the first half of the century were steady and slow. Looking back the most obvious difference was the increasing dependence on the internal combustion engine. Hundreds of thousands of horses were shipped to the Continent during the First World War and only a favoured few ever returned. The tractor began to fill the gap. In the 1920s it appeared on the more forward-looking farms and the tractor pulley gradually replaced the engine shed. Elevator lifters for potatoes were also introduced in the 1920s and the mechanical planter in the 1930s. The first continuous sucking milking machine was invented as far back as 1891 with the pulsator following a few years later, while the first combine harvester was that introduced in 1932 by Lord Balfour at Whittingham in Lothian. Nevertheless on most farms in mid-century manual labour was still required for such tasks as singling and weeding crops, cattle rearing, and milking, with large amounts of occasional labour being periodically required for other tasks such as harvesting grain crops and "howking tatties". The success or failure of the harvest due to weather was still a matter of major concern and often an item of front page news. As the century progressed the pattern of estates began to alter. In the 1920s the Moirs left Hillfoot and the Dobies left Dollarbeg. The bleachworks at Dollarfield ceased in the 1930s and the old house burned down during the war. While both the Harviestoun and Cowden estates increased their holdings their central dwellings moved to Aberdona House and Arndean and the respective "Castles" were demolished.

With the subsequent green revolution in the development of new varieties, fertilisers, crop sprays, and farm machinery, the labour element in farming was reduced to a minimum, often being contracted out, while over-production has led to the absurdity of grants for leaving land uncultivated and unused and for the planting of hill areas with often unnecessary blanket forestry. Connections between the town and neighbouring farms have consequently been lessened and, with the rise of the motor car, Dollar town has become increasingly a form of dormitory suburb.

DOLLAR TOWN

The publication of *The Dollar Magazine* quarterly from 1902 onwards with its policy of combining both Academy and Town events helps to give us a commentary on local happenings.

Haymaking at Glendevon - DM 1944

Unfortunately, however, while its early numbers contain reminiscences of the 19th century, the enthusiasm for writing such did not continue, nor has this century produced a Gibson, Stewart, or Lawson to provide a badly needed personal recollection of times past.

At the turn of the century much concern was expressed about the cost of gas lighting and in 1901 the Town Council entered into an agree-

Coronation as well as inaugurating a presentation to Peter Dudgeon, porter at the station since its opening thirty-three years before. (Both his sons did well in life and showed their appreciation to the Academy for their education there with gifts over the years including, as well as money, an organ, the first cine-camera and projector, and the first radio.) Water was piped into parts of the old town in 1904.

Boer War Celebrations ca. 1900 - DMus

ment with Crompton and Co., to establish an electric generating station in Dollar. By 1904 some all-night electric lamps were lighting the streets along with the gas lamps, leading to complaints about the proliferation of poles carrying electric cables. Worse was to follow when a year later telephone poles were being erected as well and a suggestion was made that those in the main streets be disguised by planting trees near them. (The gas lighting was much improved in 1908 with the provision of in-candescent mantles.) In 1902 the council were also engaged in arranging festivities for the

In 1907 a change of law allowed the election of woman councillors and Lavinia Malcolm, wife of the English master at the Academy, was elected to be the first woman councillor in Scotland. To mark the occasion a massive landslide took place on the front of Dollar Hill. A year later the son of a farmer at Brewlands, Alexander Stewart, now a farmer himself at Tenterfield in Australia, made his first annual Christmas gift of £20 for the poor of Dollar.

1910 saw the raising of money for a memorial to a favourite doctor, Dr Spence, who had been involved in an early motor accident and

Lavinia Malcolm
First Scottish Woman Town Councillor and Provost

subsequently died. It was to take the form of the Town Clock at the bridge. His daughter, Effie, remained in contact with the Academy until the late 1980s. The other doctor in town, Dr Strachan, was joined in his practice by a Dr Cameron and his own son-in-law, Dr Beveridge. A year later the town was again involved in Coronation celebrations for George V. Arrangements were made for a march from the Academy to the Church with the planting of an oak tree outside the latter, a Fancy Dress Cycle Parade, an Old Folks' Dinner in the Drill Hall, a Children's Tea at the Institution with the presentation of Coronation medals, and finally a Cake and Wine Banquet in the Masonic Hall. In 1911 A.M.J. Graham took over the duties of Town Clerk on the death of Mr J.S. Henderson, his uncle.

Proclamation of Accession of King George V
by Provost Green 1910 - DM 1910

In 1913 Mrs Malcolm presented a Provost's Gold Chain to the Burgh, the incumbent at the time being Provost Green. Shortly after, however, Provost Green and Bailies Anderson and Waddell resigned in protest over remarks made in a poll concerning the possible purchase of the U.P. Church on the Burnside, which had become vacant, for use as a Town Hall. Mrs Malcolm somewhat reluctantly accepted the Provostship after efforts to make Mr Green change his mind had failed and, thus, in doing so became the first woman ever to be elected Provost in Scotland. The U.P. Church was subsequently bought by J.M. Moir of Hillfoot and presented to the Parish Church as a Church Hall.

The First War naturally saw the town buckling down to all sorts of war work from forming a Local Recruiting Committee, a Red Cross Working Party, a Dollar Temporary Convalescent Home Committee, to a Committee for Growing Vegetables for the Royal Navy. The Academy Endowment funds were placed in War Bonds, 600 Black Watch were given temporary accommodation on their march from Glen Farg, the Scotchie and Ladies plantations were cut, and the parish minister, the Reverend Armstrong went off to be a padre. Life was not all hard work. Musical entertainments were put on including an operetta; Dollar Association lectures continued; and the Castle Campbell Hall was "transformed" by the lessee, Miss Armitage. War Weapons Week in 1918 raised £13,751. On peace being declared a Service of Thanksgiving was held in the church. No town war memorial was erected as most of the parish dead had been pupils of the Academy, the names of those who were not being added to the Academy memorial as well.

After the war Mrs Malcolm was re-elected Provost. In 1919, however, with Mrs Malcolm ill Provost Green again took over the provostship, Mrs Malcolm dying the following year. School Boards were abolished and the County took over the administration of not only the Primary School but also the Academy. Council Housing began and in 1921 during a coal shortage Kerr of Harviestoun gifted the parish the plantations on Sheardale for fuel. Stewart of Tenterfield died in

*Unveiling of the Academy War Memorial -
DM 1921*

Australia in 1923 leaving six daughters and a £1000 gift to Dollar, the interest to be used for the poor at Christmas. Born in the shepherd's cottage at Brewlands he had gone to Australia aged 22. In 1925 a water supply was made available to all parts of the town. The Parish Church was rededicated in 1926 after enlargement and redecoration and Mr Guild of Glenquey was reported dead, his family having farmed there for a hundred years. In 1923 the school had attempted a performance of *The Mikado* with a cast of teachers and pupils in place of the annual Boys' Concert and this, along with play readings and one-act performances by the Dollar Association may possibly have sparked off a series of Gilbert and Sullivan productions starting with *Iolanthe* in

Dr John Strachan Jnr, GP - DM 1927

1927. 1928 saw a telephone exchange installed, a talk by Miss Christie on the new medium of radio, a steam railway car, the formation of a Drama Club, a performance of *The Gondoliers*, and the felling of the two large trees on the Burnside near the foot of Sorley's Brae. It also saw the death of Dr John Strachan Jnr at Netherby, age 88. He left two sons, George and Arthur, the latter running a boarding house at Brookside after retiring from India and writing a series of books about shooting tigers, the final one being entitled *Mauled by a Tiger*. He was also a painter of miniatures and an editor of *The Dollar Magazine*. Dr John's daughters were Mrs Beveridge, Mrs Maughan, and Miss Strachan. In 1929 came the provision of a new stone bridge at

"HMS Pinafore" - DM 1929

the Rackmill, and a performance of *HMS Pinafore* to be followed in 1930 by *The Mikado*.

The 1930s saw further operettas, *The Yeomen of the Guard* 1931, *Patience* 1932, *The Pirates of Penzance* 1934, and, finally, *The Sorcerer* in 1935. Whether they then ran out of actors or out of Gilbert and Sullivan is not clear. The Drama Club meanwhile are recorded as performing *The Admirable Crichton* in 1933, *Quality Street* 1934, *Arms and the Man* 1937, and *The Farmer's Wife* 1939. The first "Kirking of the Council" took place in 1931, an event possibly occasioned by the presentation of ermine robes for the Provost by Mrs Butchart. Meanwhile the Council were busy with slum clearance, "Carbo", the row of miners' cottages running down from Argyll Street, being demolished in 1935 to be replaced with Council housing. They ran into opposition, however, in 1938 when they proposed the feuing of Mill Green as a park, a poll showing 69 for and 172 against, people complaining about the cost to the rates and the attraction of the "wrong type of people" – whoever they were. An underlying reason among many would appear to have been fears that the area would be "civilised" with the grass cut and such facilities as picnic tables and swings provided! Festivities relieving the grim period of the Depression included the Silver Jubilee of 1935 with a Church Parade of the Town Council and Town organisations along with football matches – Shopkeepers v. Old Crocks! – in the morning, a Fancy Dress parade led by Sauchie Town Band and sports for the children in the afternoon, shop window displays, more sports in the evening, Bridge Street illuminated with Japanese lanterns and fairy lights, and the Castle and Academy floodlit, the day being commemorated with the planting of three hawthorn trees, gifted by the Girl Guides, on the Burnside. Such a day had to be repeated in 1937 to mark the Coronation, this time with medals and mugs for the children. As the grimmer prospect of war loomed an Auxiliary Fire Service was formed in 1939.

The war years saw the blackout, rationing, and formation of a local Home Guard; Dollarbeg was taken over by an Anti-Aircraft Battery; Polish soldiers camped in Market Park; the hills were used for training secret agents; an American Liberator crashed on Whitewisp and three Spitfires crashed into the side of Dollar Hill. A Town Broadcast took place in February 1942. Again committees and organisations to help with the War Effort were formed and, in common with the rest of the country, the town lost its railings in a scrap drive. The Academy saw a large increase in children, some presumably sent to Dollar for safety. After the war in commemoration of those who had lost their lives the Memorial Gardens at the corner of Devon Road and Bridge Street were created in 1947 and a memorial stone, designed by G.H. Paulin, FP, the sculptor of the school memorial some thirty years before, was erected. A Committee, under Provost Cowan, was also formed to raise money to reinstate the bridges and paths in the Glen which, along with the Castle, was gifted by J.E. Kerr to the National Trust in 1950.

The 1950s saw the beginning of the housing boom. In 1952 a fifth of the houses in town were Council Houses and in that year building started at Craiginnan. Private houses were also being built at various sites; the Back Road, the Burnside, the Tillicoultry and Muckhart Roads, and Waddell's Field (Bogton Park). The Market Park was purchased by the Council and the Mill Green was still in use by courtesy of Mr Cullens of Dollarbank. The 1953 Coronation celebrations included a Fancy Dress Parade with the inevitable bicycles, TV for the Old Folks, Open Air Dancing on the Burnside, the planting of a tree at the Memorial Gardens and the cherry trees up the Burnside. In 1954 the Academy purchased the British Legion Hall, the Queen's Wood was planted, and building was commencing at Tod's Field (Kellyburn Park), with 30 Weir houses also being erected at Craiginnan. In 1956 communion flagons were stolen from the parish church, and the old inn at the Ramshorn was demolished. The following year the Academy was floodlit for the Mylne Centennial, and Strachan Crescent commenced building.

In 1960 J.E. Kerr of Harviestoun died at the age of 82, his daughter, Mrs Grant, succeeding to the estate; new houses were being built on Castle Road; and the Academy Rector, Harry Bell, was dismissed. In 1961 the main Academy building went on fire and classroom accommodation had to be found for pupils in various halls in the town while it was rebuilt. The Bell enquiry found his dismissal "justifiable". Private housing continued building on the Glebe and at the top of Hillfoot Road in 1962 while in 1963 came the visit to the town of the Queen and the Duke of Edinburgh. The Railway closed to passenger

Coronation Night on the Burnside - DM 1953

The Ramshorn Inn at the A977 junction - DM 1913

traffic in 1964 and the new County primary school, Strathdevon, opened at Market Park. 1966 saw the demolition of the old Manor House at Upper Mains and of the old Vicar's Bridge over the Devon when its parapet collapsed. In 1967 the Drama Club was re-formed with a performance of *On Monday Next* and has continued to thrive ever since.

With the restructuring of Local Government the Town Council was abolished in 1975, democracy apparently being served by the election of one representative to the Clackmannan District Council and one to the Regional Council. In an attempt to maintain some form of local identity a Community Association was created which in its short life started the Town Gala and laid the groundwork for the creation of an elected Community Council in the hope, often proved somewhat vain, of being able to influence local government. Another focus for town aspirations was the Civic Trust which was largely responsible for much of the town being declared a conservation area. The most damaging result of the reorganisation as far as the town was concerned has been the inability to run its own affairs and the political shortsightedness of the Region in abolishing the 1932 arrangement with the Academy over subsidising fees for the parish parents, leading to an increasing number finding themselves unable to send their children to the Academy founded for their benefit.

The 1970s saw the creation of large private housing schemes to the northwest of the town at Moir's Well, the floodlighting of the castle for the Castle Gathering entertainment in 1972, the sad loss of two Academy FP army officers, Stewart

Gardiner and Bill Watson, in Northern Ireland, the Silver Jubilee celebrations of 1977, and the visit of Princess Anne in 1979. With the closure of the Dollar Mine in 1973 came also the final closure of the railway with the consequent demolition of the buildings and the uprooting of the rails, the former railway line being turned into a walkway. In the 1980s another housing scheme commenced at the Ness near Kirkstyle, and the town was provided with a new and somewhat flavoursome sewage system (shortly to have the flavour removed) while nearly all traces of the coalmine at Westerton miraculously vanished. The River Devon for a brief period became worth fishing before succumbing to more pollution. Dollar Museum was founded with the help of the Church in the Old School House before moving

The Queen and Provost James M. Miller 1963 - DMus

to the old Brunt Mill, now the Castle Campbell Hall (at the top of East Burnside by the entrance to the Mill Green). In the early 1990s yet another housing scheme was built near Devongrove. Despite promises made on the closure of the railway, bus transport continued to be reduced making life difficult for the young, the old and the disabled. In the 1990s Mitchell Court was erected on the old Gasworks site and more shops

Princess Anne - DAA

vanished. Clackmannanshire again became a separate region or county, a new, somewhat inconvenient, Community Centre was erected at Market Park, and promises to provide additional recreational space for both the living and the dead have yet to be fulfilled.

PROVOSTS OF THE BURGH
OF DOLLAR

James B Henderson	1891-1893
David Westwood	1893-1896
Richard Malcolm	1896-1899
John Drysdale	1899-1902
Morten Fischer	1902-1908
James B Green	1908-1913
Lavinia Malcolm	1913-1919
James B Green	1919-1925
Stewart F Butchart	1925-1931
Christopher E Allsop	1931-1937
Robert Waddell	1937-1939
John Scott	1939-1943
Percy Walton	1943-1946
Alexander M Cowan	1946-1950
John C Shaw	1950-1953
John Hewitt	1953-1956
John Muckersie	1956-1962
James M Miller	1962-1965
Harold Moss	1965-1968
William Y Galloway	1968-1971
Edmiston M M Breingan	1971-1975

TOWN CLERKS

John S Henderson	1890-1911
Antony M J Graham	1911-1953
David Graham	1953-1975

The Last Town Council 1975
Back Row: Philip Coutts, David Graham, William Henderson, William Kavanagh, David Beveridge,
Peter McGrouther and Alexander McIver
Front Row: Harold Moss, David Tait, Edmiston Breingan, Alexander Harrison and Gavin Macdonald

THE CHURCHES IN THE 20th CENTURY

MINISTERS AND PRIESTS 1790 - 1998

Church of Scotland	Secession Churches			St James' Episcopal
	Original Seceders	**Free Church**	**U P Church**	
John Watson 1790-1815			Founded by John Millar of Sheardale 1849	
Andrew Mylne 1815-56	J A Wylie 1831-46	Jas Thomson 1843-64		
Walter Irvine 1856-61	**Union Synods and Dollar 1852**			*Priests and Rectors*
Angus Gunn 1861-1913	Daniel Wilson Probationer 1852-54	Mr Rattray assistant 1861-64	John Campbell (missionary)	A W Halley 1863-1867
	E Brown Hill 1856-63			N Lawrence 1867-1873
	West Free Church 1859			Alex. Troup 1873-1878
	Geo. H Knight 1863-78		**Burnside Church 1872**	Henry Maskew 1878-1906
	Robert Paul 1878-1910		Wm B R Wilson 1872-1910	Wm Gwyther 1906-1912
	Union Free Churches 1910			Wm C Louis 1912-1921
	A Easton Spence 1910-1919			J Wood-Smith 1921-1932
Robert Armstrong 1913-1920				H Sutcliffe Hay 1932-1939
Robert McLelland 1920-1929	Peter D Gray 1919-1936			John L Stretch 1939-1950
Union of Church of Scotland and Free Church 1929				Pat. D Broun 1950-1953
Parish Church		**West Church**		
J Stobo Glen 1929-1948		George R Logan 1937-1942		John L Stretch 1953-1970
Andrew Hughes 1948-1975		Joseph Lynn 1942-1952		M Paternoster 1971-1975
		John M McKinnon 1952-1975		Wm Glazebrook 1975-1982
Union of Parish and West Churches 1975				Hugo D Petzsch 1983-1986
Arthur R C Gaston 1975-1989				G Macgregor 1987-1991
				C Sherlock 1991-1998
John P S Purves 1990-				G Grunewald 1998-

THE PARISH CHURCH

The Minister of the Parish Church at the turn of the century was the Rev. Angus Gunn. A native of Aberdeen he had been appointed from Arbroath by the then patron of the parish, Sir Andrew Orr, in 1861. Among his other duties he was Chairman of the Board of Governors of the Academy for over forty years and served on the School Board for the Primary School. *The Dollar Magazine* of 1910 gives a full account of the ceremony and praises sung at his Jubilee in 1910. He died in 1913. *Stewart* says of him "in his younger day he was smart, goodlooking, highly educated, apt to teach, full of enthusiasm, the enemy of every oppressor, and the willing champion of all who were oppressed ... the young minister of Dollar was a very Savonarola, who could make the guilty tremble in the midst of their iniquities, and the unclean quake in the midst of their sensual festivities." J.A.W. Dollar is slightly more acerbic: "Gunn was the great theological artillerist of those days, and his sermons volleyed and thundered. He married a Mrs Boothby, whose youthful son had a thin time; so had I, and mutual misfortune made us close friends". (Dollar for a time was in a boarding house!) He was presumably the minister Margaret Donaldson (Peggy Wright) described as "very stout and wore an ostentatious gold-watch chain across his waistcoat. Though a notable trumpet in the face of the Lord, his eating habits left much to be desired; his front was liberally spotted with the remains of previous meals and soups. He, poor creature, was known (without animosity) in the village as 'Chains & Slavery'." Which makes one wonder what it nicknamed one "with animosity". He was followed by Robert Armstrong who went almost immediately into service as an army padre for World War I. He moved to Kilconquhar in 1920 and was replaced by another padre, Robert McLelland. During his term of office he started what *The Magazine* calls – a "Boy Scout Battalion", and a Literary Society. He was also involved in the setting up of an organ fund, and must have played a large part in the extension and refurbishment of the parish church in 1926. He moved to Rutherglen in 1928 and died in 1929 at the early age of 39. He was followed by the Edinburgh-born J Stobo Glen, who served from 1928 to 1948 before moving to Kildonan. His replacement was another Edinburgh man, Andrew Hughes, who had served in the Orkneys and Jedburgh, before service in India and Ceylon during World War II. He was responsible for the founding of the Boys' Brigade in 1957, the Girls' Brigade (formerly Guildry) in 1959, and for the installation of the perpetual lantern, designed by Ian Campbell, to mark the Mylne Centenary in 1956. He resigned earlier than need be to allow for the union of the two Church of Scotland congregations on the 21st of January 1975 under Arthur R.C. Gaston, born in Warwickshire and educated in Bute. With the union the West Church was sold and the Parish Church used its prerogative to repurchase the old U.P. Church from the Academy to serve as a Church Hall. The old Manse was also sold and the minister's residence moved to the other side of Manse Road. These changes along with the refurbishment of the Old School House have given the church a complex of buildings and enabled it to extend its activities. Mr Gaston answered a call to Geneva in 1989 and was replaced by the present incumbent, the Rev. John P.S. Purves, in 1990.

The Parish Church, opened for worship in 1842, had a rear gallery added in 1862 and two side galleries added in 1875, the latter two a gift from James Orr of Harviestoun. The Chancel to the rear was added in 1926, and the refurbishment included new pews, an organ gifted by Robert Stenhouse, a pulpit gifted by the Academy pupils, a font from the Sunday school, and an Eagle Lectern from the Academy governors, this last being stolen in 1981 but recovered by the police. The Reredos was a gift from J. Calvert Wilson, an Academy teacher, and the Tapestry, designed by Adam Robson and executed by Miss J. Dunn, was gifted by Miss J. Wright of Woodcot. The Porch, one of two proposed, was added in 1966. The Session rooms to the rear of the church were renovated to mark the 150th Anniversary in 1992.

The large chancel window was gifted by the congregation to commemorate the fifty years service of the Rev Angus Gunn. Two small colourful windows here, designed by Adam Robson and Jennifer Campbell, were the gift of the Macnamara family. The window, representing

St Columba, in the nave was gifted in memory of Alexander Wardlaw. The other large window commemorating the Union of the West and Parish churches was again designed by Jennifer Campbell and Adam Robson, being the gift of Jane McLeod, the widow of the Rev. H. McLennan. Regrettably the maker not only varied the design but made the colours too dark.

THE SECESSION CHURCHES

The United Presbyterian Church on the Burnside only seems to have had one minister, William B.R. Wilson, from 1872 to its amalgamation with the other Free Church congregation at the West Church in 1910 when he retired. His alter-ego, as mentioned previously, was as a sub-editor in the production of the *Oxford New English Dictionary*. His manse was at Springfield.

The incumbent of the Free or West Church at the beginning of the century was the Rev. Robert Paul who had come from Coldstream in 1878. The early issues of the *Magazine* contain excellently researched articles by him on local history, notably those on Castle Campbell and the Witches of Glendevon. He died in 1910 and the union of the Free Churches took place under A. Easton Spence, an Aberdonian. Like his counterpart at St. Columba's he volunteered for war service and died at Cologne in 1919. He was replaced by the Stirling-born Peter D. Gray, who had ministered in Edinburgh and Musselburgh. He was minister in 1929 when the larger part of the Free Church in Scotland re-united with the Church of Scotland so that, in effect, from then on there were two C. of S. congregations in Dollar. He remained until 1936 when George R. Logan took over from 1937 to 1942 before going to Dumfries. He was replaced, in turn, by the Rev. Dr Joseph Lynn who had been an Army Chaplain for thirty years and gained the C.B.E. for his services. He served from 1942 to 1952 when his place was taken by John M. McKinnon with the unusual background of being not only an industrial chemist but also having served with bombers in the Royal Flying Corps of World War I. He had also been a missionary in South America before serving twelve years in Glasgow. On his retiral in 1975 the congregation voted to merge with that of St. Columba's. Rev. John McKinnon celebrated his 100th birthday in 1998.

The West Church built in 1858 had its original simple plan added to with two wings in 1864. It was sold for conversion to houses on the amalgamation of its congregation with that of the parish church. Its brass War Memorial plaque and Cradle Rolls were installed in the parish church but regrettably a plaque in memory of the Rev. Robert Paul, designed by the noted architect, Sir Robert Lorimer, seems to have perished in the change.

ST JAMES THE GREAT

Little information has survived on many of the vicars of the Scottish Episcopal Church, probably because few tend to stay long in such a small charge. Nevertheless, possibly because of its smallness, there is a close family feeling about its congregation. The exception in length of service was the much-loved Canon Stretch who felt impelled to return after the tragic accidental death of his replacement Patrick Broun in 1953.

The church was completed in 1882. Windows within commemorate Sir William Raeburn, the Glasgow ship owner, and his wife; Julia Armitage; Philip Findlay; and Canon Stretch. The font is a memorial to Archbishop Archibald Tait of Canterbury, youngest son of Craufurd Tait of Harviestoun.

PLACES AND PEOPLE

The main reminiscences of life in Dollar in the 19th century were written by William Gibson, George Lawson, and John Stewart. Their own family histories demonstrate something of the advantages of the provision of education by the Academy, at least as far as the male members are concerned. For the girls the situation is less clear as their futures in such a male-orientated working society lay mostly in marriage and the no less important influences an educated background would have on their families.

William Gibson's grandfather, James Gibson, came to Dollar from Blackford at the end of the 18th century and set up in business starting a general store in two cottages above the Cross Keys junction on the site of a hall now converted to housing. Later, having prospered, he built a house and shop further down the brae – recently also converted to housing – bearing the date 1806 where he ran what his son described as "an emporium for almost everything". He died in 1819 and his son, William, carried on the business becoming around that date the first Clerk to the Trustees of the new Academy. William and his wife had twelve of a family, five dying in infancy. Of the five girls, three married, and of the two boys James married into the mill-owning Archibald family of Tillicoultry, and William married a Jessie Prentice of Stirling. William apprenticed himself as a draper in Dunfermline and Glasgow and when his father built a shop at the corner of the Burnside and Bridge Street in 1829 the sons took it over as the drapers: J. & W. Gibson. James continued in the business becoming an agent for the Edinburgh and Leith Bank (later the Edinburgh and Glasgow), and factor for the Harviestoun estate. His son, John, succeeded him as factor and banker in 1846 and was bank agent when it became the Clydesdale Bank in 1868, being eventually succeeded by his son. William left in 1843 to set up in business for himself in Milnathort, four years later moved to Tillicoultry to learn mill management, and a year later set up with his brother-in-law the firm of William Gibson and Co., owning the Craigfoot and Dawson Mills. His son eventually took over the business and William retired to write his memoirs.

George Lawson was a relative of the Gibsons.

His great-grandfather also came from Blackford and set up as a brewer in Glendevon. He died shortly after, leaving a widow and a large family, his widow being Emily, sister of James Gibson, who brought her to a house in Dollar nearly opposite the Gibson shop. One of the sons, James, appears to have become a flesher on the Cross Keys junction and another of the family, Charles, became a draper in Bridge Street. The George Lawson of the memoirs is a son of the latter who set up as a draper in Alloa on his own account running a business there for forty years, during which time he was closely connected with the Chalmers Church Sunday School. He retired, firstly to Dollar serving as a Commissioner and then Councillor on the first Town Council, before finally ending at Selkirk where his daughter taught mathematics.

John Stewart's father was a farmer at Monzie in Perth. On returning home by the Castle and Glenquey one day he noticed a large building being constructed in Dollar and enquired of Andrew Sharp, the smith, what it was. From him he learned of the new Academy and on returning to his wife and young child, he talked with her about it and they changed their intention of renting a farm at Foulford and rented one in Dollar instead. There they had another twelve children, ten of the thirteen reaching maturity. Of the five girls one died young, one remained single and the other three married. Of the five boys the eldest, Peter, took a university degree at St Andrews, taught at Carnock, and then became minister of Gilmerton in Edinburgh from 1862 to an early death in 1873. John followed the same profession and became minister of St Bernard's in Glasgow for many years. He died in 1895 aged 65, his wife dying at the age of 39 as did three children, the eldest being 8. A brother, Alexander, went to Australia and founded a large farm at Tenterfield in NSW. Later in life he sent money home every Christmas for the poor of Dollar. Robert became a doctor and also went to Australia, settling in Ballarat. Charles seems to be the farmer mentioned by Gibson at Pitgober and Donald became a grocer in Cadogan St, Glasgow and served on the City Council. Not a bad record of accomplishment for a hill farmer's family crowded into their small cottage at

Brewlands on the brow of the hill above the Castle.

Of these *Gibson* takes us back to the beginning of the 19th Century, *Stewart* and *Lawson* to the middle and later. Other contributors to this section, which includes the early years of the twentieth century, are Charles Muil, Margaret Donaldson, J.L. Findlay, Astley Piggott, and J.A.W. Dollar, all of whom contributed letters and articles over the years to *The Dollar Magazine*.

*Gibson s*tates that in the early years of the 19th century there were few houses, apart from the Mains farmtouns, west of the Old Town. The elderly lady quoted in *The Dollar Magazine* as remembering the copper miners also recollected at that time five rich braw lairds who subscribed to a weekly paper passing it round among themselves, one of them with silver buckles on his shoes and at his knees and a cane with a green tassel. She also remembered an upper class of tradesmen with among them: a Provost, a Bailie, a Knight, and (somewhat obscurely) a Bonaparte.

A later inhabitant of the Lower Mains was the remarkable scholar Andrew Clark born in 1856, son of a farm labourer, who lived there with his grandfather, John Bowie, and went on to win numerous prizes at Oxford. After a short academic career at Oxford he left in 1894 as his wife disliked university life and became vicar of the village of Great Leighs in Essex, mastering, in addition to Greek and Latin, French, German, Italian, and Spanish. During the First World War he undertook the keeping of a detailed diary of life in the village which he deposited in the Bodleian Library volume by volume. When discovered by Dr James Munson in the 1980s it consisted of 92 volumes containing over three million words. Dr Munson published a necessarily very much abbreviated version under the title: *Echoes of the Great War* in the 1980s.

In the Upper Mains the Williamsons of the Manor House have already been noted. Later

The Old Town - DM 1939

occupants of the house included an eccentric relative of Dr Walker, the surgeon for the poor appointed by the Academy, and John Breingan, son of Duncan Breingan, who lived at Sheardale and who had been one of those who walked daily down to school at the Academy before the Sheardale school was founded. The others noted as later inhabitants of the Upper Mains were a David Kier, a David Lambert, the Allan family, who built a house there after leaving Dollarbank and who later farmed Glendevon Castle, and Laird Izat, whose family, like many others, took full advantage of the educational opportunities provided by the new academy. One son became an accountant in Glasgow, another ran a chain of grocers' shops there, a further son ran an English agency (whatever that was) which seemed to give him a life of leisure, while Alexander was one of those who succeeded in the Indian Civil Service exam and went on to earn the title "Honourable", eventually purchasing Ballilisk at Muckhart for his retirement. Members of his family also followed their careers in India, notably his son, Rennie, who gained a knighthood for his services. The house at Thornbank was at one time occupied by Daniel Macbeth after whom the nearby wood was named.

The Back Road remained the main road till 1806 and, apart from the Gateside Inn tenanted by the Wright family, one of whose sons, John, became minister of the Free Church in Kinross, one or two small cottages appear to have bordered it. One cottage at the Low Burn, according to *Gibson*, was inhabited by a well-known character "Muckle Jean" Christie, who ran a Dame's School and whose method of teaching reading when a pupil met a difficult word was to advise her to "Hip (skip) it, daughtie". The terrace of four houses with iron balconies, known as "Brooklyn", which replaced it was built by the noted Academy teacher Dr Lindsay. Another cottage along here seems to have been inhabited by a member of the Blackwood family as one of the tenants of the Banks until the amalgamation of the small farms in 1801. On the site of the present Golf Club House, built by another Academy teacher, William "Tasker" Masterton, as a private boarding house, a cottage – seen in an early photograph – was occupied by two Sinclair

sisters, while another built into the side of the Knowe was the residence of an old woman, Christie Mitchell, who sold toffee or gundie to the schoolchildren and was known as the "woman wantin the nose". Opposite, where the bungalows now stand, on the East Burnside was a larger house, later known as "Greenfields" from the owner of a market garden that was there, but reputed to be the property of the baron bailies of old. Udney's plan of 1793, however, marks no house on the site but shows the land as belonging to Dr Burns of Gateside.

Across the burn on the left, the building, which is now divided into Dollar Museum and flats, was originally the "Brunt" or "oo" Mill, Dollar's second woollen mill. The first mill, built about 1800 by James Gibson, Robert Pitcairn, and John Burns, lay on the same site but parallel to the burn. It was demolished in 1820 to make way for the new mill erected by William "Brunt" Drysdale of Alva and run by his son Robert. It

The Top of the Burnside (undated) - DM 1902

was later bought by Peter Stalker and at some time managed by a Willie Walker or Wilson and later by a Mitchell. Although possibly originally waulk mills for fulling or beating the cloth of local weavers *Gibson* states that both these were chiefly carding and spinning mills, some of the fleeces being pony-trekked from Blackford, the finished yarn being made into cloth for local use by weavers throughout the village or sent to Alva for manufacture. Some was sold at market at Monzie and later Perth. The lade for these mills lay roughly along the route of the present path, a dam lying across the first bend of the burn in Mill Green and the water being conveyed to the mill wheel above ground in a wooden trough known as "The Trows", a source of fascination and danger to the village children. Dr. Mylne protested at the letting of the effluent into the burn during the day and a large pond was constructed behind the mill to hold it until nightfall. Later, after it was purchased by Sir Andrew Orr around 1865, the second floor was removed and the building was converted into a hall for meetings, the small windows being joined to form long vertical ones. It seems to have served various purposes around the end of the nineteenth century, later being known as the Volunteer Hall, used on Sundays by a Mrs Bell (Sir Andrew's sister) for Salvation Army meetings and possibly by a Miss Bell for those of the Plymouth Brethren. It seems to have been used by the Volunteers as a drill hall and also at one time been named "The Bijou", the bioscope for early film shows, members of the audience being provided with fans to flutter as an antidote to the flickering films. Later, after the First War, it became the headquarters of the British Legion being known as The Legion or Castle Campbell Hall. It was later bought by the Academy for use as classrooms and then sold to be converted to flats and Dollar Museum in 1991. The wool industry never developed in Dollar the way it did in Tillicoultry and Alva, possibly because at the end of the 18th century there was no local laird to push industrial development, apart from Haig at the Bleachfield, and because in a sense the Academy took over as the industry of the village. A scheme in 1836, presumably prepared by the Globe Insurance Co. which owned Harviestoun at the time, for damming the Burn of Sorrow above the castle and erecting thirteen mills on the present golf course came to nothing. Possibly it was only a demonstration of the potentiality of the estate for selling purposes.

Opposite the hall lay a two-storeyed house occupied, according to *Gibson*, by Mrs Burns, from which a row of cottages stretched some way down the East Burnside, tenants of which included a Mrs McNaughton, shoemaker; Alexander Wardlaw, a mason; John Christie, the beadle, remembered for placing the "spokes" to

carry a coffin outside the door of the deceased and ringing the "deid bell" in front of the funeral procession; and Robert Forrester, the unofficial postman and precentor at the parish church, whose sons all became schoolmasters.

At the top of the brae the Gibson house and shop was sold to the first William's assistant, Alexander Wardlaw, and later to a John Hunter. It continued as a business down to recent years as a grocer's shop before being converted into housing. Alexander Wardlaw, mason, and his brother, John, an ironmonger in the small shop at Chapel Place on the Burnside, both related to the Wardlaws of Pitreavie, lived in the house opposite the Gibsons. Above this was one owned by John Blackwood, a weaver, which had a "loom shop of considerable size". The Blackwoods – John, James known as "King", Robert, and Tom – also formed a renowned fiddle band. One of John's sons, Robert, emigrated to Canada, became a teacher there, and frequently wrote home to local papers under his school nickname of "Ebony".

A local inn, The Cross Keys, stood on the south-west corner with Argyle Street but was demolished in 1936. The present Lorne Tavern, named after the heir to the Duke of Argyll, was a bakehouse owned by David Tod – the Tods also owned or rented Tod's Field, now gentrified into Kellyburn Park. Mrs Tod seems to have been the energetic partner, running an extensive bakery delivery business with carts throughout the county. She was a sister of the owner of Mein's Hotel, once the most well-known in Glasgow. The Tods' barn also known as "Dickie's Barn"

Dollar Fair - DM 1906

was the main venue for dances, especially during the annual Dollar Fair. The legal entitlement of fairs was actually four but only the Autumn and, particularly later, only the Spring fairs were eventually of any importance. For these, the great events of the year, stalls were set up in the High Street by local traders and incomers. The cattle were originally on display in the field now occupied by the Academy Preparatory School but were later transferred to a field east of Argyle Street. Horses were on display at the Upper Bridge. The day usually ended with brawling between the Tillicoultry and Dollar youth. In the twentieth century stalls and roundabouts later moved down to Bridge Street and the Market Park. The Fair, much reduced, finally ended its days at the Lower Mains. *Lawson* gives a good description of it in his time with the stands around the "Cross"; the Academy pupils pouring up at 4 p.m.; the "Dollar Derby" up the High Street between two cripples, Jock Greig and Cripple Skipp; and the colourful selling tactics of Salmond, a well-known Kirkcaldy confectioner. Other travelling excitements to pay visits at the turn of the century were Bostock and Wombell's Menagerie (the sons were at the Academy), Pinders' Circus, Mander's Waxworks, and Biddulph's Ghost Illusion.

Around the square of the "Cross Keys" – a cottage linking the Gibson's shop and the attractive crow-stepped house, at present occupied by Willy Crawford, has been demolished – lived "Deacon" William Gibson and John Drysdale, a proprietor of Hillfoot, the entrance to Mill Green here being known as "Hillie's Close". Going up the Hillfoot Road the present shop at the junction was run by a James Lawson, while the converted hall was the original U. P. Church, known as Millar's Hall, used as a grainstore after the church moved to the Burnside about 1870. The section of road at the foot of the brae was known as "Craigie's Brae", the house which once lay at the foot being owned by a Mr Guild, the last tenant of Craiginnan Hill Farm. The large house at the top "The Towers" was built by Peter Sinclair, an Edinburgh builder, in 1866. The house, variously known as "Viewbank", "Sandbank", or "The Croft", which crowns the hill known as the Broomie Knowe, was at one time lived in by John

McIver, a cattle dealer and father of the farmer at Lawhill, remembered as preferring to go barefoot on occasion as he had done on his cattle driving.

Up Castle Road at Blinkbonny lived young "Cork" Sharp, the smith, while his father, Andrew, "Old Cork", lived above the forge at the house below the present waterworks. The site of the waterworks itself was once a row of small cottages.

Coming down the High Street, which has mostly been rebuilt in recent years, a house at the top on the left was the home of William Rutherford who married a Jenny Mathie, Jenny

The Broomieknowe - DM 1922

confessing it "cam on me a' o a dint!" after a courtship of thirty years. Her father "Provost" Mathie – the Mathies claimed to have been Provosts for 300 years – lived close by here, being, along with the Baron Bailies – John Marshall, James Sharp, and John Drysdale – the last ghosts of the Barony of Campbell. A Joseph Marshall lived in a house on top of a byre in which lived a Peggy McDovan, and which is still called "The Luggie" – a word meaning a small cottage. Where the rather gracefully assembled group of slant-roofed modern council houses stand was a dwelling known as "The Royal Circus" which seems to have been a house of ill-repute. The owner of Hillfoot, John Moir, having lectured one of its inhabitants, Belle McCrabbie, on her loose life and drinking habits, was promptly chased down the street with a broom for his trouble. In revenge he bought the property and had it demolished. Tradesmen in the area in the middle of the 19th century are given as David Halley the cooper; Peter Cram the grocer; Mrs Oliphant the baker; Peter Wilson another baker, famous for his pies, fifteen of which were scoffed one after another by a Blairingone worthy at a Dollar Fair; Py Bell the china merchant; Robert Kirk the joiner – he was an Academy Trustee who stood up for the poor – while his wife Peg ran a grocer's shop both here and later in the New Town; Peter Lawson the butcher; Andrew Stenhouse the tailor – both he and Peter Cram married daughters of a "Laird" Jack of Lower Mains; a Mr Beveridge and a Mr Hunter both saddlers; and a Mr Russel another grocer. In one of the closes lived Robert Lyon, the Alloa and Dollar carter. Opposite the Lorne Tavern dwelt Alexander Stalker and his son, Peter, cabinet makers. Peter won an enormous order for the refurbishment of Cortachy Castle near Kirriemuir for the Earl of Airlie and for a while the town was apparently full of joiners and cabinet makers until a great caravan set out one day for the north. He also made a cricket bat to the description of young Richard Bell who wanted to start playing cricket at the Academy. Neither had any idea of the wood required so it was made of walnut because it would "look nice"! Most of the south side of the High Street was demolished – not without argument – as unsafe in the 1960s.

Argyle Street seems to have been originally known as the Drum Road and one or two original cottages remain. Leading down to the Burnside is Sorley's Brae, named after a weaver who built a number of cottages there. A descendant or relation, James Sorley, became Head Gardener of Canada. Further along, on the same side, was a street named "Carbo" (coal) with a row of cottages for miners, presumably originally working "The Stair Pit" over by the present Ness.

Argyll Street - DM 1913

Carbo Street - DMus

Carbo deteriorated into a slum and was demolished in 1935 to make way for council housing. On the opposite side of Argyle Street the cul-de-sac of Cowan Terrace was built on Fiddlefield, a field said to have been bought by a local fiddler, Johnny Cook, with the prize money he won at a fiddling competition at Argyll House in Edinburgh.

THE NEW TOWN

With the completion of the new road which was to become known as Bridge Street in 1806 and the siting of the Academy to the west of the Dollar Burn in 1818, the shopping and business centre of the town began gradually to shift to this area, one of the first buildings to be erected to take advantage of the increase in traffic being Henderson's Inn, later called Robertson's Inn from a son-in-law, and still later The Castle Campbell Hotel. It rapidly became the centre for meetings and ran the local coach services for many years. One of the Robertsons seems also to have started the "Oak Inn" on the Muckhart side of the Kelly Burn. *Gibson* states that in the early days the only grocers in the New Town were a John Swan and Hugh Munro, the latter also known as a watchmaker, while the only draper was Charles Lawson.

Cairnpark Street was known locally as "Puddledubs" because of its usual condition. It presumably owes its name to a large cairn said to have been demolished to provide stones for bottoming the new highway, the field also being known as Hutton's Park. To the north of this lay Williamson's Park which became the grounds of the Academy. In the 1841 census it seems that all the houses in this area, wherever they lay, were lumped together under "Cairnpark Street". The cottage that lay where the Academy Janitor's house is sited was a pub during the building of the Academy and a skew-putt from its roof ends bearing a toddy ladle has been preserved in the wall of the present building. The pub quickly became a sweety shop with a change of clientele and was run by three sisters, Mary, Beany, and Jeannie Christie, aunts of the teacher and poet, James Christie. J.A.W. Dollar said of the family:

How they all lived I have never been able to understand. But live they did on the exiguous profits of their tiny trade, loving and maintaining one another: always cheerful, and radiating abroad their kindly spirit like a bright light in a naughty world. Of all the Scottish characters it has been my privilege to meet in seventy-eight years of earthly pilgrimage, their's was perhaps the finest – without physical beauty (two were badly disfigured by smallpox), without

charm of voice or intellect or education, without even the attraction of youth and abounding vitality, they conquered the respect and attachment of all ... Dear old James Christie was their male counterpart. For him the kindliness of heart was often masked by an abrupt and combative manner. I saw the other side in after years: his industry, perseverance, and endurance, the courage with which he faced the world on a totally inadequate salary and the disappointment of a son who failed to realise his father's ardent ambition.

A warm tribute from a former President of the British Veterinary Society, whose London practice had held five successive warrants to the royal family. James Christie's eldest son was Robin, but how he disappointed his father is not known. A younger son, John, was Goods Manager for the L.N.E.R. in Glasgow and gained the O.B.E. for his charitable interests.

The New Town from the Church Tower ca. 1870 - DM 1929

111

Bridge Street ca. 1900 - DAA

A cul-de-sac, Chapel Place, off Cairnpark led to the Auld Secession Church, now transformed into two villas named Mayfield. The one-storeyed cottage was built by a Mrs Maclean and Park House was occupied by Mr Kirk, the Classics master at the Academy, Although a brilliant linguist, after some quarrel with the Academy governors, he went to Canada but Mrs Kirk (a Gibson sister) apparently stayed on. A Dr Arnot built a house to the east and opened up the road to the Burnside. The main buildings on the other side of this street are The Strathallan Hotel, formerly The Four Seasons, part of it being before that the St James's Hall or The Athenaeum, a centre for many lectures and entertainments as well as the first venue for the Town Council meetings. Charles Muil remembered the duo of Bobby Anthony and Daisy Robertson performing there. Bobby later transposed himself to "Mark" and became a writer of popular songs in London and a friend of Noel Coward. Along with W.K. Holmes he composed the Academy school song. Several brothers were at school – Armenians from Penang in Malaya their original name was Anthonian. Alongside the hotel for many years

there was a log hut used this century for various town activities. Behind the hotel lies the former Masonic Lodge, now the Scout headquarters.

Bridge Street obviously contains a variety of houses and shops built at different periods. Leading down from the bridge, however, if one discards infilling of gaps, removal of gardens and added shop-fronts, there are a number of similar buildings, presumably erected by some entrepreneur of the time, with a central doorway, two windows on either side and three above, all similar to the The Railway Tavern, named as such on the 1866 O.S. Map in anticipation of the completion of the line in 1869. This map also shows Station Road as a cul-de-sac with the Post Office marked in its present position.

Charles Muil listed the shops he could remember as being in these two streets in the early 1900s. Station Road contained: Green's, hairdressers; Beattie, fishmonger; Cousins', butcher; Mrs Edmonds', sweets; Brand's, grocer; Glass, baker; McFarlane, greengrocer; Miss Rutherford, Post Office; and Brown, draper. Bridge Street he remembers having: Waddell, butcher; Morrison, shoe shop; Hall, draper;

Henderson, chemist; Minnie Saunders, tuckshop; Howden, plumber; Rettie's, baker; Young, grocer; Morrow, grocer; Miller, stationer; Young, draper; Muckersie, stationer; Roxburgh, plumber; Fraser, jeweller; Gibb, draper; Drysdale, jeweller; Beresford, hardware and fishing tackle; C & J Robertson, ironmongers and wood merchants, beyond the bank; Snowdowne and McAlpine, joiners. Margaret Donaldson, an artist, recalling early childhood memories from about the same time remembered in Bridge Street from the east: the Old Toll House; a Miss Armstrong "formerly on the stage" in the next house; the "Gentlemen's Club"; Miss Roy's sweetshop; Minnie Saunders' tuckshop; a billiard saloon; a public house; a cycle repair shop; Miller's, newsagents; Town Council Offices; Muckersie's; Robertson's hardware shop with its bridge; a painter Donaldson with a brother who was a competent artist; Bennet a baker; and Nancy Brown's dress shop with its rocking horse in the window at Christmas. Academy (McNabb) Street, she thought, contained Howden's the plumber and a bakehouse while Station Road had the Misses Glass, bakers; McConchie's, saddlers; the Post Office; and Green's the hairdressers. The Burnside had Gibbs', draper; Cowan's the grocers; a small ironmongers, and "two ladies at the top who lived in a lovely cottage and sold flowers." Many of these businesses remained with the original families until recent years. Of the ones mentioned Green's were probably the successors to a Bruce Hay, a barber of the earlier days noted for his personality and jokes. Green's, though their Dollar shop has been let in recent years, expanded to Stirling, Dunfermline, Falkirk and Edinburgh. Miss Rutherford, an Academy teacher, helped her brother out in the Post Office which he ran for a long time. Gibb's was the successor to Gibson's at the corner of the Burnside and was taken over as McConchie's new hardware store after a fire destroyed their shop in Station Road. A son of Beresford emigrated to Canada and became a surveyor and a member of the Winnipeg State Legislature. Muckersie's (now Barnett's) were the successors to Thomas Bradshaw, a relative of the Bradshaw of the Railway Timetables so often consulted by Sherlock Holmes, and himself a publisher of

Dollar Guides and prints. The Muckersies continued the printing tradition. Minnie Saunders was famous as a retreat for Academy pupils, especially boys. A poem is dedicated to her in *The Dollar Magazine* No.2 in 1902. She retired to Blairgowrie in 1925. Of these shopowners the Greens, the Cowans, and the Muckersies supplied Provosts to the Burgh. David Graham, whose detailed recollections (now in Dollar Museum) deserve to be published on their own, remembers the fire in Station Road in August 1935 which started in Giannandreas' café and destroyed adjoining shops as well.

Colonel J.L. Findlay listed the inhabitants of the East Burnside around 1870, commencing from the old woollen mill, as follows: the Volunteer Hall; the Norfors; the Lockharts; Mrs Hutton; the Maclennans and the Lows (later MacHardies) in the houses damaged in the flood; the three Misses Gellatly (later replaced by the Drysdales); Mrs Young; the Findlays themselves in Argyle Cottage; Mr Bisset; the Workmen's Club (the Old Schoolhouse) with the Blair Family at the back; the U.P. Church; Mr Levack who lived previously in Jersey House; Mrs Dunlop; Mr Walls, secretary to the Scottish Episcopal Church, (later a Mr Clubbie). Round the corner in Bridge Street a bungalow occupied by the Mackays and across the road Mr Gibson at the Bank. A Mr Turcan, who left a great deal of money, lived in the last house east of the burn. Besides the many family children he lists thirteen boarders living with them on that side of the burn.

On the West Burnside a Mr Wilkie then occupied the Hotel, and the Gibbs the corner shop. Snowdowne the joiner had the yard there, now David Tait's, which was the scene of an exciting fire put out with much help, Findlay's father organising the schoolchildren with buckets. Next day they were all told to report to the bank for their rewards, those passing up full buckets from the burn receiving 2/- and those passing down empties 1/-. J.L. Findlay received a shilling with which he bought of all things a photograph of the Academy schoolteachers! After Snowdowne's were Drysdale's grocery; a family, Fells, who went to Australia; Wardlaw's the ironmonger and fishing tackle shop; the Storrars (previously the Rev.

Troup of St James's); on the corners of Academy Place, Mr Douglas in number 6 and, opposite, Mr Spence; then Mr Malcolm who took over from Mr Macdonald in the boarding house facing the Burnside; and, finally, Greenfields plant nursery. Of the Findlay family J.L. was an army padre for

DOLLAR INSTITUTION AND TEACHERS.

T. A. WATSON. J. G. BONNE. A. D. SPENCE. J. DOUGLAS.

S. COOKE. J. CHRISTIE.

J. L. MACDONALD. J. SYMMERS. DR. BARRACK. J. BROWN.

D. E. MONTGOMERY. R. MALCOLM.

DOLLAR, FROM THE SOUTH BRIDGE.

W. G. CRUICKSHANK. P. SNOWDOWNE. D. G. KINMOND. D. P. OSWALD.

Dr Barrack and Staff
as purchased by Master Findlay - DAA

many years publishing his memoirs as *The Fighting Padre*. He presented a stained glass window to St James's in memory of his brother, Philip. Another brother D'Auvergne, remembered for firing off his ramrod on Janitor's parade and rescuing a child during the flood, became an architect in Canada. He, too, became a Colonel with the Canadian forces in World War I. Both brothers won the D.S.O.

McNabb Street was built as the way to the first and main entrance of the Academy, the houses accordingly to be "neat and slated!" Alas,

the ground opposite the gate to the east had been speculatively bought by the builder to the Academy and he shortly after went bankrupt. Ownership of the ground was doubtful and it remained for many years a local coup and an eyesore. Number 9 was built in 1860 by a James Baillie, a local joiner, with a lane leading to the workshops at the rear now used by the Academy. Either he (or a son) was a skilled musician and church organist whose choral concerts were marked features of the year. The house was bought in 1954 by W. Kersley Holmes and his sister, Olive. The Holmes family had lived at 21 Station Road with a room kept darkened for pet owls. One of the houses near the Academy was the home of a Mr Vaughan who had apparently settled there after coming home from Australia. Another of those with a large family who had "discovered" Dollar as a provider of good education at a reasonable rate he advised his sister, a Mrs Tattersall, to come to Dollar as well and both families were well known in the district. It was to Vaughan's that a casualty was taken after a tremendous snowball fight lasting hours between the Academy pupils from Dollar and Tillicoultry, and *Lawson* remembered as an apprentice serving Mrs and a Miss Vaughan in Gibson's shop on Bridge Street when an ox burst into the shop and created chaos. He also mentions the tragic death of Mr Vaughan who, on feeling unwell in the middle of the night, went down to take some tonic but, mistakenly took some monkshood instead. A son, Henry Vaughan, became an architect and along with his cousin, Henry Tattersall, and some young London friends tried to form a London FP Club but the scheme fell through as most of them found their jobs were taking them away. Henry Vaughan went on to practise architecture in America and is, in fact, one of the three main architects connected with the recently completed Washington Cathedral within which he is buried.

The boarding house, Heyworth, formerly Parkfield, was built as such in 1868 by John Milne, the third principal of the Academy. After his death in 1871 it was taken over by the Gellatly sisters as a private preparatory school, then as a boarding house by Mrs Heyworth until 1925. Mrs Heyworth, as a widow, had come from Yorkshire to have her family educated at the Academy, running a boarding house at Holmlea and then Southville before buying Parkfield. Her son, Geoffrey, was to make his mark as an allrounder and 1912 is often referred to as Heyworth's year. He was wounded in the First War and eventually, in later years, became badly crippled. A story goes that his mother was determined to get her sons into the firm now known as Unilever and went down to Lever House to request an interview with Lord Leverhulme himself. She was told that this was impossible as he was busy but undaunted she seated herself in the hallway, much to the annoyance of the staff, until his Lordship passed through on his way out whereupon she accosted him. Her sons Lawrence, Geoffrey, and Roger all became directors of Unilever, Geoffrey becoming Chairman in 1941 after commencing in 1912 as a clerk in the accounts department at 12/- per week. He was ennobled for his work on many Government Committees and Commissions. An older brother, Frank, not an FP, was a lawyer and a sister became headmistress of Tiverton Girls' School. Lord Heyworth left a substantial legacy to the school in his will. Parkfield was later purchased by Miss Mathie and Miss Armitage. Miss Mathie died in 1931 and Miss Armitage carried on until 1946 when it was bought by the Academy Boarding Houses Association. The gate at McNabb Street, as stated, was the original entrance to the Academy. To its west side was a gatekeeper's cottage, long lived in by a Mrs Hogg, the widow of a workman killed during the erection of the school. She, too, was a seller of gundy – toffee which was pulled until it attained a required consistency. The cottage was demolished when the road junction was altered.

Further west along Bridge Street the handsome building (80) was built as the strictly teetotal Gentlemen's Club with a large billiard hall on the top floor. Later it did duty as a surgery for the Doctors Galloway. An old photograph shows a sign outside advertising "Refreshments, Cyclists". Mitchell Court (1997) has replaced the Dollar Garage which lay above it as well as the remains of the old Gas Works behind. Why the double-villa across the road, lately Dewar Boarding House, originally known as Aberdona,

took the name of the house at Sheardale is not known. It was run as private boarding houses by Mr Alsopp and Mrs Strachan before being taken over by the school. Its twin, at the corner of Devon Road, which is known as Freshfields, possibly after a director of the Globe Insurance Company which owned Harviestoun, occupies the site of The New Inn or Big Toll House, a business venture of Tait of Harviestoun, which did not succeed. Dollar Academy started here when Andrew Mylne rented it in 1818 to start classes while the school was being built. After this it was taken over by a shoemaker, James Miller, who employed around twenty men.

The Toll House proper was a small white cottage which stood opposite the Devon Road (88/90) until it was demolished in 1933 and replaced by the villas. The toll keeper complained about the coaches evading duty by whipping round by the Academy grounds after the West Approach was completed in 1865. The house up from this (86) was the first Post Office,

Bridge Street, Gentlemen's Club on left
DMus

run by a Miss Philp, who also dispensed drinks. The Memorial Gardens were created after World War II and seem at an earlier date to have been laid out as a putting green. Jersey House, down Henderson Place, was for many years the Town Council offices and local library. It was originally built by an owner of a brickworks as a demonstration of his wares. Close by, last century someone was allowed to build a tiny house across the end of the road here creating a cul-de-sac out of what was originally part of

Manor House Road or the Middle Walk leading down to Lower Mains.

Devon Road was not the original approach to the town from the south. After crossing the ford at the Rackmill the road led up to the present branch to Lower Mains where another branch turned east to the foot of Lovers Loan, this leading into the Old Town by the old Kirkstyle on the site of the parish church. The Devon Road seems to have been extended north to Bridge

The Old Toll House, Bridge Street - DM 1913

Street at the building of the 1806 turnpike. Ochilton House was built by Haig of Dollarfield in 1820 and the road for years was known as Ochilton Road.

It is not clear when Dewar Street was named after the inventor of the vacuum flask. In 1900 the eastern section was named Wilson Place, the centre section James Street, and the western section with its little row of brick workers' houses Prospect Place. The present Campbell Street was James Place and its continuation to the south was, curiously, Charing Cross. The present number 25 Dewar Street was once the local police station. Traces of old place names are evident on buildings in other parts of the town.

Proceeding further down Bridge Street and Harviestoun Road the row of houses on the right is Charlotte Place named after one of the daughters of Leishman of Broomrigg who must have put money into their building. The cottage at the west end was built by a Mr Malloch, manager of the Bleach Works and a cottage that lay at the east end belonged to a William McLiesh, the former and last miller of Mill Green. Another Leishman daughter is com-

memorated in Helen Place, the group of three houses on the right just before the Quarrel Burn bridge. It was at one time a brewery and also a school, Broomfield, run by the first mathematics teacher at the Academy, Andrew Bell, after his dismissal by Dr Mylne.

A series of large houses built in the early 1800s lies along the road to Tillicoultry. Woodcot, in whose driveways Strachan Crescent was built in the 1930s, was built by Dr Walker, the second surgeon for the poor appointed by the Academy. He was succeeded by his nephew. Springfield was built by Thomas Martin, the first Librarian and Geography teacher. These would be for taking in boarders. Devonside was built by a Captain Pinkerton. It was later lived in by the McCall family; the second Rector of the Academy, Thomas Burbidge; and the U.P. minister and sub-editor of the Oxford Dictionary, W.R.B. Wilson. Mount Devon was the home of Ensign Porteus, the bane of Dr Mylne. Belmont for long belonged to the Elliot family. Broomrigg was at one time occupied by a Mrs Young and then by the Rt. Hon. David Erskine, a relation of the Earls of Mar and Kellie before being taken over by Major General Leishman, who added the two wings and, presumably, the white facade. Three of the Leishmans went to Australia and founded the small settlement of Dollar there. Across the road, Devongrove was built by the crippled Professor William Tennant of Anstruther when he was the first Classics master at the Academy. He became Professor of Oriental Languages at St Andrews but occupied it, with his sister, until he died. Later it was occupied by the Ewings. Further out on the way to Tillicoultry, past Belmont, the two-storeyed cottage still called The Horse Shoe was a smiddy with a horse-shoe doorway. The smith was a James Drysdale who also had a smiddy at the old Kirk Style.

LEISURE PURSUITS

The nineteenth century was to see a great increase in organised leisure pursuits. Apart from the inevitable hunting, shooting and fishing among the gentry, there is no early evidence for organised games in Dollar. A form of scratch football was played among boys – Dr Mylne complaining in the 1820s of fences being broken by practitioners. One curious custom, prevalent in Scotland, may have taken place annually in the schoolhouse when pupils brought along cockerels and the classroom was turned into a cockpit. Defeated cockerels were stoned to death and became the property of the schoolmaster. What he did with them all heaven knows. Some form of "games" may also have taken place in the summer. Those at Alva appear to go far back. Bell recollected that around 1850 he saw a large number of men, women, and children from Tillicoultry swarming along the road to Dollar, the men trundling a large cannon ball in a form of game which might have had local connections.

The earliest recorded game is that of curling, the Dollar Curling Club being instituted in 1828 and becoming a member of the Royal Caledonian Club in 1844. It appears to have commenced play on the large pool on the site of the present pavilion in the school grounds, reminiscences recalling that some of the early masters were fervent "roarers", even calling for candles to complete their games. A second club, the Devonvale, was founded in 1845 and admitted to the Royal Caledonian the following year. The clubs merged under the name of The Dollar & Devonvale Curling Club in 1847 with a dinner at Henderson's Inn, their headquarters being the Devonvale's Curling Stone House at the east end of Williamson's Haugh, the "Dead Waters" Skating Pond.

This skating pond was created around that time by voluntary subscription – even school boarders were "volunteered" – and a field was obtained for use from the Globe Insurance Company which then owned Harviestoun. The field was banked round and annually flooded and did service for a hundred years after. Annual subscriptions were paid and tickets issued for which one could, according to reminiscences, enjoy evenings of skating with bonfires and Chinese lanterns, munching hot pies and buns supplied by a local baker's van. One pupil remembered, as mentioned elsewhere, the author, R.M. Ballantyne, showing off his muscular Christianity by leaping the bank between the skating and curling ponds. Old maps show a number of curling ponds in the district,

notably that at Hillfoot House now overgrown but known to children as the Paradise Pool, indicating the annual probability of several weeks of hard frost. The Skating Pond was last flooded at the request of the Academy Rector in the 1970s. Since then, with the change in weather patterns, it has hardly been worth flooding even if the location of the sewage works in one corner still renders it practical. The field tends to flood in heavy rain and a pool which often forms there indicates an old bed of the Devon.

In 1856 the Curling Club built themselves a new pond and Stone House to the west of the haugh – its outline still visible – and in 1868 it built a four-rink pond on ground obtained from Sir Andrew Orr of Harviestoun on the north-east side of the railway embankment, presumably that

The Dead Waters Skating Pond - DM 1929

pool lying low down by Devongrove and known for many years as "Ewings' Pond". When Sir Andrew died in 1874, his successor, his brother James, refused to allow more than a year's tenure and the club asked Haig of Dollarfield for space at the Lower Mains, Mr Orr agreeing to take over the Club House and erect another one at the Mains for £24 10s. The new pond was to the east of the brickworks. It was not a successful site being liable to overflooding and on Mr Septimus Leishman of Broomrig offering £100 and Mr Haig granting a site near Marischal Villa a new pond was built there in 1885. The Committee was also offered a rent of £4 per annum for its use in the summer for Lawn Tennis by Mr J.A. Gibson, and a proposal was made to build a joint clubhouse but this proposal was declined when Mr Leishman again supplied the needed funds. Electric lighting was installed in 1908. Rendered useless by weather the Curling Pond was replaced in recent years by the Curlers' Court residential housing scheme, the Curling Club playing its matches elsewhere on indoor rinks.

The Lawn Tennis Club has, however, survived in much the same area. The game was introduced as a novelty to fill in the intervals at the All-England Croquet Club Championships at a place called Wimbledon in 1877.

Despite the first recorded Scottish game of cricket taking place at Schaw Park, Sauchie, in 1785, adult cricket in Dollar is not recorded until July 1866 when a match was reported between Kinross and Dollar, Dollar winning by an innings and 31 runs. A Club is not recorded, however, till June 1903 when it was formed with R.B. Main of Broomrigg as President and A. Muckersie as Secretary. The School Governors offered the use of the school pitch for July and August. In December 1903 the Club obtained from the ever-generous Haig of Dollarfield a

The Curling Pond c. 1898 - DMus
Left to Right: I Gibson, R Clark, J Henderson, J Wyles, R Cownie, G Thom, J Taylor, F Hall, W Henderson,
J Hunter, R Malcolm, C Kinloch, R Paul, J McGeachan, W Spence, W Smith, W Cruickshank, J Cairns,
M Jack, A Henderson, G McLeod, A Morrison

The West Tennis Club - DM 1922

pitch at Craiginnan Park and the first full season of 15 games was played. The fortunes of the Club thereafter varied according to the players available. From 1906 to 1912 it was in abeyance, had a short revival and then lapsed due to the First War. Revived in 1920 it functioned spasmodically before another full revival took place in 1932, players being mentioned then including Percy Walton, the Hewitts, Davidsons, Lyons, Fletchers, Sutcliffe Hay, John Muckersie, and John Munro. After the Second War the club again faded, playing only a game or two a year, until at the suggestion of Harry Bell the Academy Rector, it was thoroughly revived with John Muckersie as Captain and has remained active ever since sharing the use of Bowfold Park with the school.

Fishing curiously appears to have become an organised sport in order to protect the fish. We find the Rev. Watson lamenting in *The Account* of 1792 that the salmon were decreasing by the

Dollar Cricket Club - DM 1937

improper use of spears. By 1900 the poachers had turned their attention to trout with the use of nets and dynamite. Accordingly to try and save the fish it was decided to form a Devon Fishing Association with an annual subscription of 2/6d. The first President was Mr R. Archibald of Beechwood, Tillicoultry, and the Secretary was Mr James Wilson of Sunnyside, Alloa. With the decrease of pollution salmon have again of recent years been making their way up the Devon although there has been a general falling off of their numbers throughout Scotland in the last year or two.

The first Golf Course in Dollar was in fields down by the Kelly Burn, the nine holes running from the Market Park – the site of Strathdevon School – over the woods and the banking to Tod's Field, the present Kellyburn Park. The Course started in 1886 and was later demoted to being the Ladies' Course after a second course was formed at Gloomhill on the site of the housing schemes at Moir's Well. The grass on both was kept short by sheep and cattle and both courses had to be abandoned when the farmers required the land for cropping. After a lapse a committee was formed with Provost Fischer, Colonel Haig of Dollarfield, Mr Kerr of Harviestoun, Dr Spence, ex-Provost Westwood and Messrs Dougall, Green, Macbeth, and Stanhouse, to form a course on the Banks of Dollar. Mr J.S. Henderson agreed to act as Secretary and a nineteen years' lease of part of the Banks and Gateside was taken and Brewlands House – the former boarding house run by Mr Masterton – was rented as a club house. £600 was raised by the people of Dollar and Mr Kerr gave £400. The entire length of the course, designed and supervised by Ben Sayers, was three miles, a direct track being cleared for a width of seventy yards, whins being uprooted, marshes drained, and rocks blasted, the fragments of these being turfed over in small knowes. The annual subscription was to be one guinea for gentlemen and 10s 6d for Ladies and Green Members, that is those under eighteen, artisans and shop assistants – such members being restricted, of course, from the Club House and competitions. A scarlet blazer was de rigueur for gentlemen.

Bowling commenced around 1870 when John Robertson built a green to the east of his premises down Lovers Loan, complete with Bowls House and fountain (still there). It was entered by the old doorway to the Free Church at Shelterhall which he had purchased and preserved. The Castle Campbell Bowling Club flourished there until 1893 when a dispute arose over the lease and the Club leased land from Mr Haig of Dollarfield adjoining the Curling Club, the required money raised by selling shares and running a bazaar. The total original cost was £339 1s 9d. (What the 1s 9d bought is not detailed.) The formal opening took place on the 31st May 1894, Mrs Dobie throwing the first jack. A Ladies' Room and kitchen were added in 1952. The Club continues to flourish not only for bowls but as a social centre.

Opening of Dollar Golf Course 1906
by the Countess of Mar and Kellie - DMus

The Bowling Club - DM 1914

DOLLAR ACADEMY IN THE 20TH CENTURY

The provision of education in the parish at the beginning of the century was in the main supplied by the Board School, with its new building at the top of Cairnpark Street as well as the old Institution Infant School, which took children to the age of ten, and the Institution itself, still known locally as the "Academy", which took them from that age on. First impressions of school often remain the strongest and the names of the Infant Mistress, Miss Scott, outside whose house at the west end of Chapel Place every morning a contingent of little girls dutifully waited to accompany her to school in complete silence, Miss Lyon, and Miss Rutherford, who also helped her brother out in the Post Office, are remembered along with that of the Board School headmaster of the time, Mr Begg, who even merited a rhyme, no doubt a traditional one adapted and carefully chanted at a distance:

Bairdie Begg's a holy man

He gaes tae Kirk on Sunday.
Prays the Lord tae gie him strength
Tae wallop the kids on Monday.

Besides these, for the more refined types, a number of small private preparatory schools existed. The most well known of these was that run by the Gellatly sisters, first at Oakbank on the Burnside, and then at Parkfield (now Heyworth) at the top of McNabb or Academy Street. The diminutive Jemima was the driving force and not averse to using the tawse on unruly boys but not, happily or otherwise, to great effect. Their school ceased in 1906. Another school was run by Mrs Maughan, a daughter of Dr Strachan, at West View (next to the West Church) and, later at somewhere named Eslington. It does not, however, seem to have lasted long. Yet another school opened in 1911 run by a Miss Norris, while Miss Murray and Miss Lindsay ran a seminary to which a Mrs Kennedy and daughters came to run dancing classes every Spring. A Captain Rolland came to

Panto Group, possibly the Board School - DAA

teach fencing and gymnastics to the boys of the Academy, although the latter subject tended to be taught by his son on account of the Captain's rotundity. Margaret Donaldson also remembered around this period another dancing teacher called Mr Hunter who played the fiddle and demonstrated the steps; "one flourish of his bow and the admonition 'tae dae it nate' and we were off. God help the simpleton who did it 'wrang'. One skelp on the knuckles with the fiddle bow made sure you'd never make another mistake". A pamphlet exists in Dollar Museum advertising another school run by the Rev. Levack at Devon Lodge on the Muckhart Road but how long this functioned is not known. Later Miss Bremner was to run another successful school at Taprobane (Argyll House) which was eventually taken over by the Academy in 1932 and formed the basis of a new Academy fee-paying Preparatory School.

The Rector, possibly the first to be so-termed, of the Academy at the turn of the century, Dr Thom, known variously as "Tim" or "Caractacus" retired in 1902, perhaps on account of his wife's health for she died a year later. A popular lady, she was known as "Wahoo". On retiral Dr Thom ran Brookside as a boarding house. In his place Charles Dougall was appointed Rector. A native of Kippen and a brilliant mathematician he was an authority on Burns and published both a biography and an edition of Burns' poems. From the evidence of his own poems in *The Dollar Magazine* he was also an accomplished versifier. He proved an excellent headmaster instituting minuted staff meetings and a pupils' committee, and allowing in his first year a determined group of young ladies to talk him into starting a Hockey Club, tutored by the gym master Sergeant McGeachan. "Geach" appears to have been the second gym instructor appointed, the first being a Crimean War veteran with a bayonet scar on his nose known as "Daddy" Hand. McGeachan, as a member of the Volunteers (later the 7th Argylls), went off to the Boer War – Charles Muil remembered going down to the station bearing Chinese lanterns to welcome them home and also later to wave to the popular hero general, Lord Roberts ("Bobs") of Kandahar, as his train passed through. He recalled as well his mother's face,

one of her sons already killed, as he went off on a train to the First World War. "Geach" too went off to that War but was invalided home and died shortly after. His last words are recorded as being: "The British Army".

After years of "Janitor's Drill" a corps (also connected to the 7th Argylls) was formed in 1903, to be officially inaugurated at a full dress inspection by Lt.Gen. Sir A. Hunter on the 24th June 1904. It consisted of 3 Officers and 86 Cadets, the C.O. being the Head of Art, Captain P.D. Lauder. In a democratic vote they had decided on a kilted uniform, with Glengarries bearing a version of the school badge. The enthusiasm was such that three years later they set out to build a shooting range at Lawhill, the concrete target bunkers of which are still to be found. The sound of shots combined with his initials seem to have led to their C.O. being nicknamed "Ping Ding". Few must have expected their mock battles in the so-called "Cuddy Corps" to turn to reality within a few years.

The start of Dougall's term of office also saw the successful launching of a combined Town and Gown Magazine, *The Dollar Magazine*, in 1902, after several earlier attempts. The first Editor was, almost inevitably, Dr John Strachan Jnr, member of the Glen Committee, founder of the Dollar Club, the Dollar Academy Club (in 1870),

School Uniform, Senior Girls 1902 - DAA

the Scientific Association, the Naturalists' Field Club and general pater familias of the town.

To add to the list of nicknames, teachers of the

period were "Tasky" Masterton, "Jeems" Taylor, "Billy Goat" Annand, "Great" Scott, "Dicky" Malcolm, "Ping Ding" Lauder, "Crookie" Cruickshank, "Jock" McGrouther, and "Sammy" Wyles. "Jock", strangely enough, had been appointed singing master and then had taken charge of the workshops. He organised the annual "Boys' Concert", which took the form of a Minstrel show, to raise funds for the Sports, in the days when even coming second in an event earned an inscribed medal. The Sports, purely for Boys, were arranged by the FPs at the end of April.

The Headmaster's Class of boys (University entrants) for 1905/06 is often quoted as being a remarkable but also ill-fated group, most of them dying young. It contained Hector Hetherington, later Principal of Glasgow University, and William Robieson, later Editor of the Glasgow

Corps returning from Camp
SF Butchart and J McGeachan - DM 1909

Herald. The girls also accomplished a remarkable feat a year later in the British Empire Writing Competition of 1906. "Sammy" Wyles

CS Dougall and Staff ca. 1905
Back Row: ?, J McGeachan, A England
Second Row: J McGrouther, A Collyer, W Annand, J Taylor, J Scott, D Low, J Henderson, PD Lauder, T Young
Front Roiw: S Butchart, R Malcolm, Miss Runciman, "Granny" Watt, CS Dougall, J Johnstone, ?,
W Cruickshank, W Masterton - DAA

was the Writing Master, good writing still being a highly prized accomplishment not yet superseded by the new typing machines – "typewriters" being the male clerks who worked them. Under his tuition Winifred Greenhalgh and Jessie Walker came first and second in the Junior Class; Mary Greenhalgh and Muriel Miller first and third in the Senior Class; and Grace Livingstone and Jessie Page first and second in the Advanced Class, Grace out of 7,000 entrants winning the prize for the best handwriter in the Empire. Exhibition Day continued, as it had done since the founding of the school, but now with a programme of speeches, short plays, a staged Boys' Debate (written by the English master and committed to memory!), prize giving, and an exhibition of boys' gymnastics over the "horse" known as the "Senior and Junior Cuddy". "Uniform" for the younger boys was a Norfolk jacket, breeches with long stockings, and boots – generally waterproofed with lard. Shoes and Eton collars were for Sunday. Girls' costumes were less regimented and Exhibition Day fashion was a topic long before the day. Although there were no school captains the Rugby and Cricket captains did duty as such.

In 1907 the governors decided to lower the seven-foot-high south wall of the Academy, to top the reduced wall with railings and at the same time to erect a stone and iron carriage gate at the top of Cairnpark Street, similar to the original at McNabb Street. The gate at Academy Place was also possibly erected at this date. The boys acquired a luxurious new pavilion in 1908 to replace the old cottage which they had previously

The New Sports Pavilion - DM 1908

The Old Sports Pavilion - DM 1908

used, and a new Science and Domestic Block designed by the firm of Sir Rowan Anderson was built in 1910.

In 1914 there came the Great War with some 800 FPs serving in the forces, of whom at least 166 are known to have been killed and some 60 Military Crosses or their equivalent gained. The photographs of the dead were long displayed under the balcony in the old hall.

The Pipe Band was started in 1913 and one of its early members was Lim Kar Taik from Burma who won the Gold Medal for piping. In Rangoon he was known as Scotty Chin Tsong. Apparently he died in the Hukwang Valley during the retreat from Burma after the Japanese invaded during the Second World War.

The centenary of the founding of the school was marked in 1918 by an official change of name from Institution to Academy and the buying by FPs and parents, completed in 1920, of the Bowfold or Bowshot Park which had previously been rented as a sports field. Possibly as a result of the increasing independence of women in the War, the first Girls' Sports were held in 1918. In 1921, a War Memorial, a bronze entitled "Youth" mounted on Woodburn stone, designed by the FP sculptor, George Paulin, son of the minister at Muckhart, was unveiled. It bears the name of his brother. Among other memorials, such as those at Muckhart and Milngavie, he also designed the Argyll Memorial and the 51st Division Memorial at Beaumont Hamel.

In 1922 the school became insolvent. During the previous one hundred years little thought

Science and Domestic Building - DM 1910

seems to have been given to the long-term future of the school, the interest from the McNabb legacy being spent yearly. In 1881, for example, the income was £4,724 comprising £2,235 from the McNabb endowment, £1,750 from fees, and £739 from other sources. Expenditure was £4,605, £3,705 of which was for salaries. In 1887 when the Governors achieved control of the principal of £55,000 it seems to have been poorly invested. Fees too seem to have been kept at a minimum without thought of building up an emergency fund. With war-time inflation the once apparently munificent salaries of the Dollar staff had sunk well below the level of even the state school salaries. In 1918 an Act abolished School Boards and brought local education (e.g. the Board School) under the administration of the County Councils and, in 1919, a National Minimum pay scale was introduced which would have cost the Academy an extra £3,600 per annum. Under an Act of 1908 Counties were empowered to take over any such schools in difficulty and the Governors applied for this to be done. Accordingly in 1922, but backdated to the 1st of January 1921, the school was taken over by Clackmannan County Education Committee which left the Governing Body in position but replaced the now defunct local board members with ones from the Authority and added a parental representative.

Charles Dougall retired in 1923. His son, Charles, an FP, was badly injured and became a prisoner of war, after having the dubious distinction of being shot down by one of

Richthofen's circus! His daughter, Betty, married John Hogben, FP, who ran the Moray Press. Dougall was succeeded by Hugh Martin, a native of Peebles, educated in Edinburgh and Glasgow and a Snell Scholar of Oxford, who was then serving as Headmaster of Madras College at St Andrews.

To all intents and purposes, as far as pupils went, little would essentially have changed. Indeed what might be taken as the marks of an independent school – Head Boys and Girls, school uniform, and even the school song – composed by Mark (Bob) Anthony and W.K. Holmes in 1926 – were introduced during the twenties. To some of the Former Pupils, however, things appeared differently, and in a letter to *The Dollar Magazine* in 1924, Di Wardlaw, the wife of another FP, "Mick" Mitchell, (both had been in India), voiced her complaint that the former pupils had never been consulted or approached and thus commenced a campaign to bring the school back under independent governorship.

In 1927 a Boarding House Association was formed to bring the Houses under the direct control of the Academy, a process which started with the buildings owned by the Governors and was gradually extended to the purchase of the larger private Boarding Houses. It was not completed till after the mid-century. In 1925, the redoubtable Mrs Heyworth had retired and Parkfield was taken over by Miss Mathie and Miss Armitage.

In 1929, on one of his annual 1,000 mile round Britain bicycle pilgrimages, Andrew Drysdale visited his sister, Mrs Paull, in London and took to searching for John McNabb's burial place. He found it in the original Mission Hall at Wapping then about to be demolished, the coffins in the vaults being sealed in with concrete. He promptly roped in Kevin Husband, Secretary of the London Club, and Husband set in motion a claim to McNabb's remains. Eventually after much bureaucratic entangle-ment the FPs were allowed their claim and after an appeal for funds the bones in the disinterred coffin were cremated and the ashes placed in a casket made from the lead in which the coffin had been covered. Attempts at arranging transport and a ceremonial home-

The Academy Coat of Arms 1918
with original bookmark and the arms designed in 1888 - DM 1926

coming falling through, Kevin Husband eventually drove the casket north in the back of his car. On arrival he presented it to a somewhat astounded headmaster who did not know what to do with it. After some discussion Mr Jack was prevailed upon to wheel the casket down to the bank in a barrow for safekeeping while the governors made up their minds. Eventually it was decided to inter the casket above the door of the school and at the same time replace the rather nondescript entrance doors with bronze ones bearing an inscription also composed by Mr Husband. A ceremony in keeping with the occasion took place in 1931. Kevin Husband later went to Australia where he married a direct descendant of Peter McLaren, the Dollar parish schoolmaster in the 1820s. The small replicas of the Edina cup were a bequest of the Husbands.

Meanwhile Di Wardlaw's initiative had spurred former pupils into action and an approach was made to Clackmannan County Council, which was not averse to the idea of handing the school back but sensibly stipulated, as a safeguard, that a fund be established sufficient to ensure the school's survival. £22,000 was raised by the early 1930s – an incidental bonus being a large block of shares uncounted in 1922 – and the school was officially transferred back to the new Governors of the Trust (J.E. Kerr of Harviestoun being Chairman) at a ceremony in 1934. The County also entered into a Scheme by which they paid half of the fees of pupils in the Parish; the other half of the fees for those unable to afford them was paid by the school under a Foundation

Grant, much aided by a legacy of £16,000 from an FP who had spent his early life in South Africa and Australia, J. S. Drysdale. In 1932 Miss Bremner's Prep School at Argyll House came on the market and this was purchased to establish a new fee-paying prep school for the Academy, the first headmistress being a Miss Falconer.

Hugh Martin resigned in 1936 to become Headmaster of Daniel Stewart's and was replaced by Harry Bell. Born in Aberdeen, he held degrees from there and Cambridge and at the time of his appointment was the headmaster of Elgin Academy. In his initial year the first shooting team was sent to Bisley, the first swimming gala took place at Alloa, Prep School sports were introduced, a new procedure was laid down for morning prayers, and the pitches at Thornbank were rented. In 1937 a Preparatory School building was officially opened. In 1938 refugees from the Sudetenland were in residence at Dollarbeg en route to Canada and the Academy undertook their tuition in English. The McNabb quint was dropped the same year, five boys houses being considered an awkward number for competitions. In 1939 Aberdona Villa was purchased and renamed Dewar.

At the beginning of World War II in 1939 the school roll was 448 with 39 prep pupils. By 1944, with parents seeking a safe haven for their children, it numbered between 660 and 690. Harvest Camps, Berry Picking, Tattie Howking, Make Do and Mend, Wings for Victory, Fire Watching, and the Blackout became the order of things. Peter Wilson recollected the entertainments

The Prep School. William Kerr 1936 - DAA

of the time "Cosmopolitan Pie" and "The Vital Spark" as well as the booing of the Marseillaise when France surrendered and the refusal of the pupils at prayers to sing the hymn "Praise the Lord, ye Heavens adore him" because the tune was that of the German national anthem, although others of the time have no such recollection. The school also provided much of the material for the Town Broadcast in 1942. From 1945 to 1947 a son and grandson of the Ethiopian Emperor Haile Selassie attended the school. The son, Sahle, died in 1962 after serving as a diplomat and the grandson, Desta, was killed in the Ethiopian coup. During the war the school, with the rest of the town, lost its railings in what proved to be an unnecessary drive for scrap metal. Seventy Former Pupils are known to have been killed in the war, their names being added to the War Memorial.

With peace came a period of expansion, with perhaps a somewhat over-ambitious plan being drawn up for future building. Parkfield Boarding House was acquired and two "temporary" classrooms – intended to form the basis of a new dining hall – were built to the rear of the school. The girls were finally gifted a pavilion in 1953 to replace the "Hen Coop" which transmigrated to Newfield where it met a vandalised fiery end. Additions were made to the Science block in 1953 and again in 1957. The County renewed its commitment to paying parish fees in 1958 and Kinross also found it economic to pay the fees of nearby senior secondary pupils to the Academy. Under Harry Bell the reputation of the school stood very high. It was added to through the

Transfer of School from County to Governors - DM 1934

Harry Bell and Staff 1948
Back Row: Mr Strachan, Miss Blair, Miss Thomson, Mrs Gregg, Miss McPhee, Miss Davidson, Miss Forrester,
Mr G Smith, Mr McGregor
Third Row: Mr Todd, Mr Philip, Mr Hogg, Mr Munro, Mr Foggie, Mr Waters, Mr Gidney, Mr Walker,
Mr Jardine, Mr Mitchell
Second Row: Miss McKendrick, Mr Dishington, Miss Ritchie, Mr J Smith, Mr Cordiner, Mr Milne, Mr Taylor,
Mr I Campbell, Miss Peat, Mr D Campbell, Miss Duthie
Front Row: Mr Anderson, Mr Donald, Miss Skinner, Mr Calvert-Wilson, Mr Bell, Miss Williamson, Mr Walton,
Miss Scott, Mr Junks
Seated on ground: Miss Watson, Miss Craig - DAA

popularity of broadcasting, as a school team had become the first Scottish school to win the Radio "Top of the Form" competition, a highly prestigious achievement in those days. It should be added that it was also the first Scottish school to be invited to take part in the T.V. version in 1952 but was knocked out in the first round by an all-girl team! In 1954 Mrs Strachan gave up boarding at Brookside, the Academy Association boarding houses at that time being McNabb, Mylne, Tait, Argyll, Parkfield (Heyworth) and Dewar – all boys, Playfair for girls, and, privately, Mrs Tennant's Rathmore for boys and Mrs Montgomery's Rosemount for girls. The British

Legion Hall was purchased the same year for more temporary classrooms. The school appeared to be in a flourishing condition and it was, therefore, something of a shock when the Governing Body dismissed Mr Bell in 1960. Both the dismissal and the subsequent enquiry made headline news in the Scottish daily papers and aroused heated emotions in the teaching profession generally and in the village.

The reason for the dismissal of Harry Bell was, ostensibly, his appointment of a Head of Department without having the appointment approved by the Board of Governors as was laid down in the regulations governing the school.

Mr Bell's counsel insisted, however, that it stemmed from a personal vendetta directed by certain governors against Mr Bell because of his expulsion of some boys for drunken behaviour after a party. The pros and cons of the argument were thrashed out in the enquiry and in public – the minutes of one of the Governors' Meetings going mysteriously missing during the proceedings. Finally the Scottish Secretary announced that the enquiry had found that the dismissal was "reasonably justified". On looking back it seems somewhat incredible that, as Mr Bell was due for retirement in six months, some agreement could not have been reached and saved the Academy the resulting adverse publicity.

As if the Bell case had not been enough, at a quarter-to-eight on the morning of the 24th of February, 1961, the main school building, the Playfair Block, caught fire and within a few hours, despite the efforts of the Fire Brigade (and the senior pupils who had to dam the Dollar Burn to provide them with water) the interior was gutted, the greatest loss being the Library with its

books, among them a valuable collection of rare Scottish volumes. It says much for the school, under the Assistant Rector James Miller, and the village (but no doubt to the disappointment of some pupils) that hardly a day of teaching time was lost, a variety of premises from the school squash courts to local halls being pressed into service. The Prep. School was taken over by the senior school and its teachers and pupils were bussed daily to what the pupils, at least, remember as a few glorious years at the then empty Harviestoun Castle. As if to add insult to injury, shortly after in January 1963, the Prep. School went on fire as well, but only one end was damaged. While insurance covered the reconstruction of the school, the Governors decided to appeal for funds to add further facilities, mainly in the reconstruction and enlargement of the comparatively untouched Hall.

The question of the next headmaster now arose, an appointment made difficult by the fact that the teachers' organisations including those of the headmasters had interdicted the post when

Dollar Academy Fire, 24th February 1961, 7.55 a.m. Photo by I. Smith - DM 1961

Interior of Library after the Fire - DM 1961

it was advertised after Harry Bell had been dismissed. There were several applications nevertheless, among them, eventually, one submitted from an unexpected quarter: the Headmaster of Melville College, Graeme Richardson, an Oxford graduate and former housemaster at Fettes, realising that Harry Bell could never be reinstated and that Dollar Academy desperately needed fresh leadership, saw it as an educational challenge to try and heal the scars. Before he applied, however, he sounded out professional opinions and, on being assured that if he took the job, the embargo would not continue, accepted the post when it was offered. Needless to say, those who gave assurances found they could not hold to them, and among many his motives seem to have been completely misunderstood. As he was already the headmaster of a highly successful Edinburgh school he could hardly have been accused of furthering his career in taking up the now dubious rectorship of Dollar, yet this is what happened. He faced a daunting task, finding opposition both within the school and in the village. (Indeed, he used to relate the story that when it was announced that he was leaving Melville he was visited by a deputation from his Junior School bearing the proceeds of a collection to augment his salary and persuade him to stay, but that on his first avuncular visit to the Dollar Infant class, as he was departing, one small boy, prompted by some irresistible impulse, took a flying kick at his posterior!) Nevertheless, over the years the wounds caused by Harry Bell's dismissal healed and he left a healthy and progressive school for his successor to inherit.

During his headmastership there came the visit of the Queen and the Duke of Edinburgh to the town and school in 1963, and, in 1965 he had the satisfaction of presiding over the opening of the reconstructed Playfair Block and new Hall by Geoffrey Heyworth, now Lord Heyworth of Oxton.

The new building was a modern steel and concrete structure of three floors instead of two, standing within the cladding of the old. The reconstruction was not a complete success, the Library retaining the inconvenience of the old one without the compensation of its beauty, while the acoustics in the Hall have caused many a professional singer to blench. The stage too was completely enclosed with a door in the back wall and no stage lighting, the architect apparently believing it was only to be used for morning assembly and examinations, and some hasty and unsatisfactory emendations had to be made. The story also goes that the plaque commemorating the Royal visit had to be hastily recast as the architect's name was in larger letters than that of the Queen.

Along with the non-segregation in classes of boys and girls came the first mixed Sports in 1965. In the following session the first play was performed in the new hall, to be followed over the years by many others, including musicals after 1980. In 1969 a group of senior pupils organised the school's first charity walk in aid of the new Shelter Charity for the homeless. It raised £2,400 – a magnificent sum at the time – and began a reputation for raising money for charitable purposes which few schools can equal. A Games Hall was opened in 1970 and plans made for a new swimming pool on the site of the old Manor House, partly financed from the bequest of Miss Alice Gibson, the direct descendant of William Gibson the first Clerk to the Academy Trustees. A Girls' Section of the Corps commenced in 1973.

During the sixties a number of other well-known FPs died, among them: the sculptor G.H. Paulin, whose later works included busts of the Queen and the Duke of Edinburgh; Sir Rennie Izat who had followed his father in a successful career with the Indian Railways; W.K. Holmes who had contributed so much to the *Magazine*;

Barry K. Barnes, who along with James Hayter ("Mr Pickwick") contributed to stage and screen; Sir Hector Hetherington, former Principal of Essex and Glasgow Universities; and Di Wardlaw whose letter had led to the reestablishment of the Academy Trust.

Graeme Richardson was succeeded in 1975 by Ian Hendry, a native of Forres, then Headmaster of Dunoon Academy. The school at the time faced an uncertain situation in that the new Region intended to renounce the Trust Scheme of 1958 by refusing to pay half the fees of the pupils of the parish. The Governors were then faced with handing the school over to the new Regional Authority, much as had happened in 1922, or going completely independent. Attempts to mediate between the extremes of those Regional Councillors who wished to do away with the boarding and travelling element, bus in pupils from outwith the parish, and even change the name of the school, and those Governors determined on complete independence, failed. The Region withdrew its support and the school was thrown on its own resources. A new Trust Scheme was drawn up in 1981. Under Ian Hendry the Swimming Pool and Dining Hall complex was completed and opened by Princess Anne in 1979, and the modernisation of the Boarding Houses was implemented. Corporal punishment ceased completely in 1981 and the famous "Lochgelly", made by a firm there from the shoulder hide of Spanish bulls, became a museum piece. Ian Hendry retired in 1984 and under his successor, Lloyd Harrison, a new Music Block was added and, on account of its style and substitute stone work, immediately christened "Tesco's".

An FP Register, now listing over five and a half thousand former pupils, and *Newsletter* were started, prompting a series of reunions. The then Deputy Rector, John Robertson, succeeded as Rector in 1994 and a new Business, Maths and Computer Centre was opened.

The most successful, aesthetically, of the new buildings has been the transmogrification of the little cement barrack block, built originally as a kitchen for an unrealised dining hall and which for years did duty as the Music Block, into a happy hostelry for Home Economics. Additional classrooms have also been carefully blended onto the freshly painted Prep School. One hopes the addition of a storey on top of the 1950s Science buildings now taking place will prove as successful. Hopefully someone will also replace the glazing bars on the Rowand Anderson building of 1910.

Nevertheless, inevitably, a gulf has opened between the Academy and the town of Dollar, with many local pupils now being bussed to Alva Academy instead of attending their own Academy. The break between the Local Authority and School provides a notable example of political petty mindedness as at the time the Academy was educating children more cheaply than the Region with the Region only having to pay half the cost.

SPORT

When organised games commenced at school is not known. Former pupils writing about the mid-1800s recollect only informal games – scratch games of football (Dr Mylne banned it in the grounds in 1827 as it broke fences and disturbed the sheep!); foot 'n a half, a form of leap frog; burniebaes or rounders; peeries or tops; button spinning; bools or marbles; hye spye; French and English; and hares and hounds. Girls would have added peevers or hopscotch, skipping, and ball bouncing. Some of these were played in the "trances" or entrances which in those days were not plastered inside. Nearly all of these have gone, although the Juniors can still be seen playing "Kingsball", a form of ball tig, and rounders in the summer.

The first gym teacher appears to have been "Daddy" Hand towards the end of the 19th century, followed by "Geach" McGeachan, both ex-army. Gym was very much Swedish exercises, the "Horse" or "Cuddy", and parallel bars. It is not known whether either coached Rugby or Cricket, although "Geach" coached the girls at hockey.

Some form of Rugby seems to have been played possibly as early as the 1850s and 60s, certainly being recognised in the 70s. Colonel H. H. Johnstone, who played in the 1877 Internationals – they commenced in 1871 – and played Rugby for the school in 1870 to 1873,

Institution First XV 1889-90
Captain: JW Simpson - DAA

stated: "We played in ordinary clothes, but removed caps, coats, collars and ties and placed them on the Academy window-sills. For matches some of us had jerseys." Teams consisted of twenty-a-side and new rules were being introduced, not to everyone's satisfaction. "Hacking" – presumably kicking each other – had just been outlawed as had "crying down" – twisting one's arm around an opponent's neck till he cried for mercy. "Tripping" was still dubious, a Perth team insisting on playing without it and being thought "great cowards". According to early reports one "chucked" the ball to team mates and "got behind" when one scored a try, the score being claimed by one's captain and its authenticity being agreed between the captains. There is no mention in the earliest reports of dubious decisions by such as "referees". "Tussling", in which two opponents struggled for the ball, often for several minutes, was allowed. Games seem to have consisted of endless scrums. Later, teams were reduced to three halves, two quarters and nine forwards. Astley Piggot remembered a game against a Tillicoultry Mills team in which a fight broke out between two spectators, much encouraged by the teachers, with the Dollar spectators stoning the Tillyites on their way home. In one game the tries could not be turned into goals because of "a defect in the ball". By the First War, however, the excesses had been tamed and the game had become highly regarded, the teams of Cross, Heyworth, and Myers all being famed for their performances. Over the years some excellent teams have been produced

although not until 1991-92 was there a completely undefeated team. Known internationalists are: H.H. Johnston (2), W.H. Masters (3), E.N. Ewart (3), D.W. Smeaton (3), F. Hunter (1), J.W. Simpson (13), J.A. Bell (6), H.G. Wilson (Ireland 18), I.M. Moffat Pender (1), E. Myers (England 18), C.H.C. Brown (1), A.W. Wilson (3), A.K. Fulton (2), H.J. Keith (2), A.W. Black (6), W.L. Renwick (1), C. Glasgow (1). The only one to be capped directly from Dollar Academicals was Kelso Fulton. As an antidote to our modern competitive spirit, Colonel Johnstone RAMC, the first cap, played at half-back but the Scottish selectors insisted he play at full-back, a position which he hated. He, thereupon, started playing forward so he wouldn't be chosen again! Simpson, Wilson and J. McGill became Presidents of the S.R.U. while Eddie Myers captained Yorkshire and England. Moffat Pender was wounded in WW1 but compensated by becoming Bard of the Gaelic Mod. Among teachers, Ron Glasgow and Adam Robson gained caps, the latter also becoming President of the SRU.

Richard Bell, who farmed at Castle O'er, reckoned he started Cricket:

Cricket was unknown at Dollar when I first went there – indeed it was in its infancy in Edinburgh, from whence I came. I knew very little of the game myself, but that little I thought I would like to teach my school companions. A difficulty, however, arose. I had no bat, and I considered it no use to ask either of my parents to give me one. I had,

Early Hockey XI with Sgt. McGeachan - DAA

however, a taste for drawing, so I made a very fair sketch of a bat and took it to Mr Stalker, cabinet-maker, to have it built to pattern.

My sketch was sufficiently good for Mr Stalker to copy, but the question of material arose. I had no idea myself that bats were made of willow, and on the suggestion of Mr Stalker walnut was agreed upon as "it would look so nice". When it was French-polished it was a splendid weapon, but oh, the weight of it!

Much less well recorded than Rugby, four former pupils were known to have played for Scotland by 1952: H.L. Stewart, G.W. Morris, I.M. Anderson and D. Mitchinson while Bryn Lockie is, at present, amassing a creditable number of runs and caps. There may well be more. Feminists can note that a Girls' cricket team is first recorded in 1920.

Hockey seems to have commenced in 1903 when a determined group of young ladies, under the leadership of Alison Wingate, interviewed a new headmaster on the subject. They were tutored by that invaluable jack-of-all-trades, Sergeant McGeachan. The neglected Ladies Pond and ornamental garden was levelled and turned into a pitch and a wooden hut known as the "Hen-coop" erected for their benefit.

Again there have been some excellent teams – as early as 1907 the team was reckoned as the best in Scotland – but again *The Magazine* records the results poorly over the years.

Much better recorded are the Athletic Sports which in the early days were for boys only, the "ladies" being expected only to admire. A ticket is known for "Academy Sports" from 1872 and a report occurs for one in the 1880s *Magazines*. They took place towards the end of April until 1938 when they changed to June and were run by the Former Pupils. As a whole they were taken slightly less seriously than now and had novelty races and FP and Band races, although competition for those counting towards the Edina Cup – presented by the Edinburgh FP Club – was always intense. Originally for nine events, these have been added to and changed over the years. Two events no longer counting are the Place Kick

– a pair of engraved silver napkin rings once being presented outright as the prize for this event, and Throwing the Cricket Ball which lapsed in 1939 – the record for this, a stupendous 327 feet 5 ins by the Argentinian Val Johnston in 1902 was never bettered or even approached. Young Mr Johnston was also, apparently, a dab hand at bolas throwing and cattle wrestling, abilities less appreciated by the local livestock and visiting circuses than by his compatriots. The first Athletic contest was with Atalanta in 1933.

The first notice of Girls' Athletic Sports occurs in 1919 but mentions an earlier one in 1918. The Girls' Sports were held in the more clement climate of June. On the Boys' being later dated also to June the Girls' Sports were from 1938 to 1948 held on the Thursday before the Boys and then reverted to a separate Saturday. Combined Sports did not take place until 1965. The Boys' Cross Country was inaugurated in 1924 with a Junior event in 1929 and Intermediate introduced in 1939. The Girls' competition was not introduced until 1974.

The relatively new sport of Orienteering was introduced in 1964 by the enthusiasm of a young teacher Elspeth Young, who presented a competition trophy the following year.

Tennis for both sexes was played well before 1900 although it was only invented in the 1870s. In the early days emphasis seems to have been placed on the girls playing it – no doubt as an alternative to Cricket for the boys – as in 1902 the grass courts were put at the disposal of the girls earlier than usual and no boys were allowed near, courts being provided for them later behind their changing rooms.

Swimming was only a leisure activity, various pools in the Devon being used over the years. The first Swimming Gala was held in 1936 and these were held in Alloa until the school was gifted its own baths with an instructor, since when Swimming has increased enormously in popularity.

Games records disclose many outstanding single records and all round athletes over the years. One constantly mentioned in memoirs for both Rugby and Athletics was a Chinese boy from mainland China, J. "Ching" Tong, around 1905, whose fate remains a mystery. A Manchu, he was reported assassinated in the 1920s but Sam Murray, whose own family suffered imprisonment during World War II, reported meeting him around 1934. Among other FP's the name of Hugh Neilson should also not be forgotten as he gained International caps in Hockey, Tennis and Badminton. He died in 1930.

SUMMARY ACADEMY HISTORY

RECTORS

Rev Andrew Mylne DD (Mill)	1818 - 1849	Retired
Rev Thomas Burbidge LLD DD	1850 - 1851	Resigned Leamington
Rev John Milne LLD	1851 - 1868	Retired
Rev William Barrack LLD	1868 - 1878	Resigned Kelvinside
George Thom MA LLD	1878 - 1902	Retired
Charles S Dougall MA JP	1902 - 1922	Retired
Hugh F Martin MA	1922 - 1936	Resigned Daniel Stewarts
Harry Bell MA BA BEd OBE	1936 - 1960	Dismissed d.1985
Graham E Richardson MA	1962 - 1975	Retired d.1992
Ian M Hendry MA	1975 - 1984	Retired d.1986
Lloyd Harrison MA	1984 - 1994	Retired
John S Robertson MA	1994 -	

DATES

1732 May 14	Baptism John McNabb. Dollar
1799	McNabb visits Dollar
1802 Jan 12	Death of John McNabb
	Will: Legacy of £60,000 to Dollar Parish
	Rev. John Watson's Plan. Architect Robert Burn.
1808	Meetings of Heritors and Parishioners. Petitions of objection
1812	Further Meeting of Parishioners
1815	Death of John Watson.
	Andrew Mylne (Mill) appointed Parish Minister and Superintendent of school
1818	Mylne Plan legally approved
	First Meetings of Trustees. Architect William Playfair. Teaching commences at New Inn
1821	Playfair Block completed. Institution Place Teachers' Houses building.
1826	Kirk Session (Trustee) numbers increased.
1828	First edition Statutes and Rules.
1830	Infant School commences at 6 Institution Place.
1838	Infant School built. Children 3 to 5.
1847	Act of Parliament & New Board of Trustees.
1850	Rev Thomas Burbidge appointed Rector
1851	Resignation of Thos. Burbidge and appointment of John Milne as Rector.
	Roll 1851: 344
1854	Small school established on Sheardale Ridge.
1857	Roll 1857: 479 (118 Boarders)
1863	First Indian connections. Results from Indian Civil Service Exam.
	10 vacancies. Academy pupils 3, 4, 7, 8.
1866	West Approach created.
1868	William Barrack appointed Rector. Hall added to rear of Playfair Block.

1870	Founding Dollar Academy Club by Dr John Strachan Jnr. (General membership)
1871	Founding Cooper's Hill Indian Civil Service Training College.
	(23 FP graduates – 7 top diplomas)
1872	Education Act Scotland. Compulsory education.
	School roll rises to 1014 in 1876 then declines. George Thom appointed Rector.
1876	London FP Club founded. (First FP Club) Roll 1882: 845
1881-84	First attempt at a *Dollar Magazine* (12 Editions)
1883	First half-yearly Reports
1887	Endowed Schools Act. Academy not allowed to provide free education for under 10s. Infant school & Sheardale school handed over to County. New Governing Body appointed by Scotch Education Dept. Ground provided at Cairnpark for Board School. Music introduced to curriculum full time. Grounds to be grassed and to be cut twice yearly. Large pond filled in. Apprenticeships terminated.
1891	Inscription on pediment of Playfair Block. Technical Building constructed.
	First school badge design suggested by Trustees
1898	*Our Home Journal* – mss attempt at *Dollar Magazine*.
1899	First School Flag.
1900	*Dollar Institution Magazine*. (1 copy – flippant!)
1902	Charles Dougall appointed Rector. *Dollar Magazine* founded (Dr John Strachan Jnr editor). Girls' Hockey Team established by Alison Wingate. South boundary wall reduced and railings erected. Staff meetings formalised and minuted. Pupils' Council under Rector inaugurated.
1903	Cadet Corps officially formed. Hockey Pavilion "The Hencoop" erected.
1904-12	Open Shooting Range created at Hillfoot.
1906	Horse drawn cutter and roller for grounds.
	Grace Livingstone wins British Empire Handwriting Competition.
1907	Stone gateway erected Cairnpark Street. South wall lowered and railings erected.
1908	Boys' Sports Pavilion built.
1910	Science and Domestic Block. Architect Rowand Anderson.
1911	Quints (boys' houses for sport, etc.) established (or 1915)
1912	Two school songs written. No copies extant.
1913	Pipe Band established. Boys' Golf Club
1914-18	First World War. 166 FPs dead. Over 60 MCs or equivalent awarded.
1918	Application for official change of name to "Academy".
	Official Coat of Arms (present badge) granted by Lyon Office.
1919	Girls' Athletic Sports
1920	Sports Pitch (Bowfold Park) bought for school to mark centenary. (£750)
1921	War Memorial by George Paulin FP erected. Girls' Sports Houses inaugurated.
	School apparently bankrupt. Taken over by Clackmannan County Council. 1st June 1921 New Board of Trustees appointed. Hugh F. Martin appointed Rector.
1926	New Hockey Pitch. Miniature Range
1927	Dollar Academy Boarding House Association formed. McNabb & Tait taken over.
	FPs begin to raise money to re-endow school. Endowment Appeal launched.
1929	School Song (W.K. Holmes/Mark Anthony)
1930	Westview (1 Harviestoun Road) bought and named Dewar.
1931	John McNabb's burial place found. Remains cremated and placed above main doors
1932	Argyll House Prep school bought.
1933	Dollar Academy Trust Scheme. School handed back to new Board of Trustees.
	County agree to pay half fees of parish pupils.
	New School Flag designed. Mylne House opened.
1934	Official handing back ceremony. 15/16 May.
1936	Harry Bell appointed Rector. Janitor's House built Cairnpark St.
1936	First Tractor and grasscutter. First Bisley Team, Swimming Gala, Prep School Sports.

1937	New fee-paying Preparatory school building opened. Argyll Boarding House opened. New Girls' Tennis Courts (3). Roll: 448 Seniors. 89 Prep school.
1939	Aberdona Villa bought and renamed Dewar. 1 Harviestoun Road named Playfair.
1939-45	Second World War. 70 FPs killed. Town and School broadcast 1942. Air Section founded in Corps. Iron railings removed. Roll 1944: 699.
1945	Victory Pirrick Cairn rebuilt Dollar Hill. Commemoration Fund established.
1946-54	Hill Pitch, Thornbank bought and added.
	Kitchen built for new refectory at rear of school – used as music classrooms.
	Old Manor House purchased and demolished. Parkfield House bought.
	Demolition of old Trees and replanting. New Miniature Rifle Range.
	Major Repairs to Main Buildings (£25,000) .
1954	Addition to Science Block. Boys' Pavilion extended. Girls' Pavilion built.
	Legion Hall purchased. Brookside ceases boarding.
1958	Second addition to Science Block. Boys' Pavilion extended. Newfield bought.
	Dollar Academy Trust Scheme 1958 (based on that of 1933) .
1960	Harry Bell dismissed. Consequent Court Cases.
1961 31 Jan	Playfair Building gutted by Fire. 0745 hrs. Appeal for Funds for rebuilding.
	Harviestoun Castle used for Prep School. Rosemount (1 Muckhart Road) bought by DABHA.
1961-65	Reconstruction of Playfair Block, Hall and Gym.
	Board School acquired as Junior School.
1962	Graham Richardson appointed Rector.
1963	Fire in Preparatory School. Visit by Queen Elizabeth and Duke of Edinburgh.
1965	Playfair Block reopened by Lord Heyworth. First combined sports. Rathmore (3 Muckhart Road) bought by DABHA and amalgamated with Rosemount (girls). 1 Harviestoun Road (boys) renamed Rathmore.
1968	Many park trees uprooted by storm.
1969	First Sponsored Walk. ("Shelter" £2,240).
1970	Games Hall built.
1971	Rosemount and Parkfield swap, becoming Heyworth (girls) and Playfair (boys).
1973	Girls' Corps Section formed.
1975	Ian Hendry appointed Rector. Appeal for Swimming Pool and Dining Hall.
1976	School Fete.
1977	Silver Jubilee celebrations. Pirrick Cairn rebuilt by school.
1979	Swimming Pool and Refectory opened by Princess Anne.
	Boarding Houses modernisation proceeding.
1981	Dollar Academy Trust Scheme 1981. (Region reneges on 1958 Scheme and refuses to pay parish fees.)
1984	Lloyd Harrison appointed Rector.
1991	New Music block opened by Sir Alexander Gibson.
1993	FP Register and *Newsletter* instituted
1994	John Robertson appointed Rector. New Corps building opened.
1995	New Business Studies, Computer and Maths building opened by Lord Younger
	Medical Centre opened Mylne House.
1996	New Home Economics building opened by Iona, Duchess of Argyll.
	Redecoration of Library and Assembly Hall. External painting of Prep School.
1997	Prep School 60th Anniversary Sports. Extension of Prep School building – two classrooms to east. Dewar boarding house sold. Saturday Film Club ceases.
1998	Extra classroom added to Prep School. Third storey on 1950s Science block
	Princess Royal inspects Corps. Main Rugby pitch moved to Pavilion side.
	New Cricket square. Junior School railings replaced.

ROUND AND ABOUT

ALDIE CASTLE
"Stream or rock?"

Built in the 16th century it belonged to the Murrays, William Mercer of Meiklour acquiring it as a dowry on his marriage to Aldia Murray, daughter of the Baron of Tullibardine. A curse that for nineteen generations there should be no male heir was said to have been uttered against a Baron of Aldie on his passing a death sentence against a man for stealing a cupful of corn.

ALLOA
"Rocky place or plain"

The lands of Alloa and a tower there were bestowed on Sir Robert Erskine, Chamberlain of Scotland, by David II. A descendant, John, the sixth Lord Erskine, was given the ancient lapsed title of Mar by Queen Mary in 1565. The title and lands were forfeited in 1716 by "Bobbing John", who led the 1715 uprising but were bought by his brother, Lord Grange. The title was restored in 1824 and married with that of the Earldom of Kellie in 1828. Lord Grange was the gentleman who had his wife kidnapped and kept exiled in the Highlands – seven years on St Kilda – till she died, a mock funeral being carried out, presumably in Alloa, to fool the authorities. His brother, the Earl, who had laid out magnificent gardens around the tower and the mansion that had been added to it, spent his exile producing plans, not only for his own possessions, but for an Edinburgh new town and a Forth and Clyde Canal. It was he who had Gartmorn Dam created to provide power for his coalpits at Alloa. The mansion attached to the tower was destroyed by fire in 1800. The tower, one of the most massive in Scotland, has been recently restored.

The old much-decayed town centre of Alloa was completely destroyed last century when Younger's Brewery and Patons' Mill were built on the site – the former now demolished and the latter semi-derelict – a new town being created around Mar and Forth Streets.

A port is first mentioned at Alloa in 1502. At first one of fourteen "creeks" of Bo'ness it had the Customs Post for upper harbours from 1710 and was created a full port in 1840. At its height it handled about 2,000 vessels a year and was a main port of call for the Forth Steamers. Shipbuilding commenced in 1790 and it possessed a dry dock. Its main imports were grain, timber, iron ore, and hides, while its exports were coal, ale, whisky, pig iron, glass, pottery, bricks, leather, copperware, and flour – all products of the town and surrounding area. The docks were filled in, somewhat prematurely perhaps, in 1951.

The town had the products of three main distilleries at Carsebridge, Cambus and Glenochil, all of which, with three others, in 1877 formed part of the original Distillers Company Ltd. Of the town's numerous breweries – it ranked second to Edinburgh – only the independent Maclay's Thistle Brewery is left.

The town possesses many fine buildings, the oldest being the ruins of the Old Kirk (1680) by Thomas Bauchop and his own fine town house (1695). A number of the large mansions are connected with the Paton family. Originally from the Muckhart area, two brothers, James and Andrew, came from there in 1760 to set up a weaving and dyeing business in Alloa. James's son, John (1768-1848), founded the Kilncraigs factory, while John's two sons, James and David, founded their own mill at Tillicoultry. Another son, Alexander (dwelling Cowdenpark), died without issue and the Alloa business passed to John's daughters and to their children. John Thomson Paton (Norwood), who gave money for the Town Hall and the old Public Baths, and David Thomson Paton (Greenfield) were sons of his elder daughter, while the younger, Mary, founded the Forrester-Paton family (Inglewood). The Gean was built as a wedding present for her son, Alexander. St Mungo's Church is by Gillespie Graham, St John's Episcopal by Rowand Anderson, but some of the finest buildings are by local architects such as Thomas Frame, William Kerr, George Kerr, John Melvin and Arthur Bracewell. The two fine War memorials to the South African and World Wars were designed by Sir Robert Lorimer, the first sculpted by Birnie Rhind and the second by Pilkington Jackson.

ALVA
"Rocky plain"

A small hamlet until the early 1800s, an attempt was made to plan a village round a square by the then Lord Alva, only two sides of which were completed. In 1801 there was only one mill. By 1886 there were nine spinning mills at work employing some 1500 people. The most imposing building is the magnificent Strude or Boll Mill, now converted into flats, which was only part of a complex owned by William Archibald and Son until 1976. Built around 1820, it has six storeys, each with twenty-five windows, each window originally intended to give light to a handloom. The estate seems to have anciently been held from Cambuskenneth by the Stirlings of Calder passing down through the Menteiths to the Erskines of Mar, the Erskines of Alva being descended from them. The Erskines held it from 1620 to 1775 when the then Lord Alva sold it to the Johnstones of Westerhall. Sir John Erskine is remembered for the discovery of silver in the Silver Glen around 1710 and the profligate way he used it for improvements. John Johnstone had made a large fortune serving in India under Clive and subsequently bought estates in Selkirk and Dumfries as well as Alva. In 1636 Sir Charles Erskine developed a mansion around an ancient tower and this was further developed in a large manner by the Johnstones about 1820. The last of the Johnstones, Miss Carrie, died in debt in 1929, and the house was left derelict to be used for target practice during the Second World War. The Stable Block serves as a Woodland Centre.

BLAIRINGONE
"The field of the smith"

The village was chiefly built to house the colliers of the Duke of Atholl, head of the Murray family, who provided a school for the children. Two of the pits were called Ladyhall and the Nunnery, an indication that a nunnery attached to Culross at one time existed in the vicinity, possibly being taken over and later known as Tullibardine House after one of the Atholl titles. No trace of the house is now evident on the ground though old names such as Kings Seat, Palace Brae, and the Ball Green indicate its existence. A Blairingone story that the McNabb legacy was first offered to their minister at his manse in Fossoway beyond the Yetts of Muckhart and that he refused it when he learned of the connection with slave trading is more than highly doubtful.

BLAIRLOGIE
"Field or clearing of the hollow"

The original tower of the house named The Blair dates from 1546 and was built by an Alexander Spittal. The centre of the tiny village forms a pleasant square. Blairlogie House Hotel was at one time the country cottage of Archbishop Tait after Harviestoun was given up. The large house Redcar high up the hillside was built for Sheriff T. B. Johnstone in 1880.

BRIDGE OF ALLAN

Originally an inn at the river crossing and a row of miners' cottages the village rapidly expanded, when the water from the mine workings was found to be medicinal, into a spa town with villas being built for retirement and holidays. Louis Stevenson came to know it well when his father came to recuperate and Madeleine Smith was sent here to cool off from her affair with the penniless clerk, Emile L'Angelier, whom she was later accused of murdering, the case being found "not proven".

CAULDRON LINN
see Rumbling Bridge

CLACKMANNAN
"The stone of Mannannan or Manau"

The county town of Clackmannanshire, it has long lost its central importance to Alloa. The lands were gifted in 1195 to Cambuskenneth Abbey and, later, by Bruce's son, David, to another descendant of Bruce in 1359. It was created a Royal Burgh between 1153-64. The older tower of Clackmannan Tower dates from the 14th century and the later taller one from the 15th. A mansion was added in the 16th. The last occupant of the house, Mrs Catherine Bruce (1701-96), a zealous Jacobite, knighted Robert Burns with the two-handled claymore of Robert the Bruce in 1787. Bruce's helmet was also apparently preserved, both being inherited by the Earl of Elgin.

While many of the old buildings have been replaced, the centre of the town still retains the outlines of its former layout. The old Market Cross has the arms of the Bruce family on it. Beside the tower of the 17th century Tolbooth, the small stone which was mounted on top of a later larger one in 1833 is the Stone of Mannan, said to have been moved here from the brae called Look-aboot-ye and possibly before that from the Inch of Ferryton. It may have marked a rallying or judgement point. The parish church, 1815, is by Gillespie Graham.

CLACKMANNAN POW

A former small harbour of which little remains at the emergence of the Black Devon into the Forth.

DEVIL'S MILL

see Rumbling Bridge

DEVON IRON WORKS

see Sauchie

FORESTMILL

A small hamlet on the Black Devon near which an imposing lade allows the cut-off that feeds the Gartmorn Dam. The local poet, Michael Bruce of Kinnesswood (1746-67), his father

Cauldron Linn - DMus

being a weaver there, taught here in 1766. His best-known works, often miscredited, are the paraphrases "O God of Bethel" and "Behold! The mountain of the Lord".

GARTWHINZEAN
"Field, enclosure + ?"

Also called Gibson's Craig, it belonged to the Murrays of Tullibardine, owners of Blairingone. They also owned Pitfar which is said to have been burnt at one time by a hostile clan. The Murrays in pursuing them found them celebrating in a local church and promptly burnt it around their heads. For this they were excommunicated and the Pitfar lands in penance granted to the Abbey of Culross. This led eventually to a boundary dispute between the Murrays and Culross and an enquiry was held on the disputed spot, a monk swearing on oath that the ground he stood on was the property of the Abbey. An irate Murray promptly slew him and on his boots being removed it was found he had covered the soles inside with a layer of earth from within the Abbey. Thus, of course, the spot known as the "Monk's Grave" at the south end of the Craig.

GLENDEVON

The lands are said to have belonged in the 17th Century to the Douglas family by whom the castle was originally built, it being enlarged to a Z plan when it passed to the Rutherfords. The 1792 *Account*, however, by the Rev. John Brown states that there was one house built for defence which was erected by the Crawfords, who owned the two farms of East Glensherup and Whitehills. In 1792 there were five heritors, two of whom farmed their own lands. The 1841 *Account* by the same minister gives the owners as Lord Camperdown, J.S. Hepburn, Robert Haig, William Low, and Miss Jane Rutherford. By this date a Turnpike Road had been driven through the Glen and a woollen spinning mill established at Burnfoot. The church is old and the manse dates from 1747. Glendevon House, possibly by Gillespie Graham, dates to 1830. The Castle is now a hostelry with a caravan site, and the old coaching inn, "The Tormaukin" (Hill of the Hare), has of recent years been updated to a popular hotel and eating house. Its close neighbour, the Castle Hotel, was burnt in the 1970s and

Glendevon - DM 1905

the surviving part is now a private house. The recently completed Castlehill Reservoir drowned the old and ruined St. Serf's Bridge, built in 1740, noted for the variety of masonic marks on its stones.

The Glen in the 17th Century became notorious as a centre of witchcraft, commencing with the trial in 1643 of a John Brughe accused of curing diseases in both humans and animals by means of enchanted stones and other sorceries. He was said to have obtained the knowledge from a witch by the name of Neane Nikclerith "a widow woman of thriescoir yearis of age, quha was sister dochter to Nik Niveing, that notorious infamous witch in Monzie, quha for her sorcerie and witchcraft was burnt foirscoir of yeir since or thairby", probably the "notabill sorceress callit Nicniven, condemnit to the death and burnt at St Andrews in the year 1569." Amongst the other charges was that he and others thrice met Satan in the "kirk-yeard of Glendovan, at quhilkis tymes there was taine up thrie several dead corps, ane of thame being of a servand man named Johne Chrystiesone; the other corps tane up at the Kirk of Mukhart, the flesch of the quhilk corps was put abone the byre and stable-dure headis" of individuals to destroy their cattle. A Katherine Mitchell, executed at Culross some time before, had affirmed that Brughe had been with the devil at "Rumbling Brigs" before her execution. He was sentenced to be strangled and burnt.

Nineteen years later a further "covin" of witches was discovered in the same locality and in 1662 an Assize Court of Justiciary was held at

Crook of Devon under the Justice-General Depute, Alexander Colville of Blair. The tribunal consisted of a jury of fifteen persons chosen from the proprietors in the district and other suitable residents. The court had five separate diets between April and October necessitating partial change of jurors. Among the jurors were David Carmichael in Linnbanks, Robert Hutton in Wester Ballilisk (Westerhall), James Alexander of Balruddrie, Edmund Mercer there, Henry Mercer in Aldie, Gavin Alexander, portioner of Blairhill, Adam Fult in Easter Downhill, Robert Quhyte in Gartwhynean, Robert Brown in Meadowhead, Patrick Hutton in West Blair, and William Flockhart in Annacroich.

Thirteen people were arraigned before the tribunal, one warlock, Robert Wilson, "indweller in Crook of Devon", and twelve witches: Agnes Murie and Margaret Litster at Kilduff; Bessie Henderson at Pitfar; Janet Paton (60) and Isabel Rutherford at Crook of Devon; Bessie Neil at Gelvine; Agnes Brugh at Gooselands; Margaret Huggon (79) at Gelvine, "relict of Robert Henderson"; another Janet Paton at Kilduff, "relique of umquhill David Kirk"; Janet Brugh (50), "spouse of James Moreis at Crook of Devon; Christian Grieve, "spouse to Andrew Beverage in Quhorlawhill; and Agnes Pittendreich. The Brughs were presumably related to John Brughe. The accused named others: Giles Hutton, spouse to Peter Coventrie in Garthwynean; Margaret Duncan in Broome in the parish of Dollar; Agnes Allene, Crook of Devon; yet another Janet Paton, spouse to James Sinclair at the new Mill of Glendovan; Agnes Sharp, Peatrighead; Janet Hird and Isabel Condie, Meikletoun of Aldie; and Margaret McNish in Tilyochie. None of these named were brought to trial.

Evidence against the accused had been obtained beforehand by a self-constituted body of locals, all of whom seem to have fervently believed in the witchcraft. They were led by the principal proprietor, William Halliday of Tullibole, his bailie Robert Alexander, and the minister of Fossoway, Alexander Ireland, with his Kirk Session. Assisting ministers were the Rev. James Forsyth of Muckhart, George Golden of Kinross, and James Halkerston of Cleish. Other inquisitors among many were: William

Hutson, schoolmaster; Robert Mailer, Crook of Devon; William Dempster, Bankhead; James Rutherford, Earnyside; Andrew Kirk, Carnbo; James Alexander, Wester Downhill; William Christie, Pitfar; James Hird and James Donalson in Lamhill; William Livingstone of Cruick Milne; John Hutton of Easter Ballilisk; John Drummond of Wester Pitgober (Westerton); and William Blackburn, bailie of Campbell. No details are given of the methods used to make the accused confess. Common practice involved the use of needles, the witch's bridle, starvation, sleeplessness, whipping, tearing off nails, burning, leg and thumb crushing, taking the skin off by means of a hair shirt soaked in vinegar, and torturing spouses and children. All the accused admitted frequent meetings with the devil, the main rendezvous being at Gibson's Craig near Powmill, "Turfhills aboon Kinross", the "Stanriegate bewest the Cruick of Devon", "the Heathery Know bewest the Cruick of Devon where the gallows stands", and the "Bents of Balruddrie". The meetings seem to have consisted of dancing and playing, with the Devil giving them new names and promising them riches. They bound themselves by "putting one of their hands on the crown of their heads, and the other under the sole of their foot and delivering all betwixt them over to him". Most described him as like a man with a blue bonnet in either black or grey clothes so there may have been someone duping them. The only real evidence against them were their own confessions. All but two were found unanimously guilty and sentenced to be "taken away to the place called the Lamblaires bewest the Cruick Miln, the place of their execution, and there to be strangled to death by the hand of the hangman, thereafter their bodies to be burnt to ashes for their trespass, and all their moveable goods and gear to be escheat and inbrought to His Majesty's use for the causes aforesaid". The sentences were carried out on the same day or that following sentencing. Only Margaret Huggan and Agnes Pittendreich escaped, the former because she died during the proceedings and the latter because she was pregnant and reprieved till her child was born. There is no evidence that the sentence upon her was ultimately carried out.

The prime mover in the proceedings seems to have been the minister at the Crook, Alexander Ireland. The son of the minister of Kinclaven in Dunkeld, he became a convert to prelacy when it was restored in 1660 and a fervent opponent of the Covenanters. He died in Ireland in 1698 having been deposed of his charge by the Privy Council after 1688 "for gross immorality and oppression".

The incident was only one of many in the mania that sporadically swept across Scotland in the years between 1563, when the first civil enactment against sorcery was passed and 1722 when the last witch was burnt, supposedly at Dornoch. The worst phase was after the restoration of 1660. 150 are calculated to have been burnt throughout the country in 1662 and somewhere between four to eight thousand altogether in the years of persecution.

KENNET
"Fair", or ken "headland"

Formerly a small line of colliery houses built in the late 18th century by the Bruce family for workers at Kennet Colliery. Kennet House, built for Alexander Bruce by Thomas Harrison around 1795 no longer exists although Brucefield, 1724, sold to James Abercromby in 1758, and later restored by Shearer of Dunfermline is still extant.

KENNETPANS

Originally the site of saltpans as the name implies. Later a distillery run by John Stein. See Kilbagie.

KILBAGIE
"Kil" = church or wood or ridge + ?

Before 1770 the Stein brothers, James and John, farmers on the Kennet estate, established distilleries at Kilbagie and Kennetpans, which quickly grew to be the largest distillery complex in Britain. Kilbagie alone used 60,000 bolls of corn annually to produce some 3,000 tons of whisky and gin spirit, the left-over mash being used to feed 7,000 black cattle and 2,000 pigs inside its four walled acres. The Kennetpans distillery produced about three fifths as much. They employed about 300 workers. Much of the machinery was worked by a small rivulet and the barrels were floated from Kilbagie down to the free port at Kennetpans along a narrow canal, now a mere burn. Kennetpans had the first engine of Bolton and Watt construction in Scotland. Between them they produced more excise duty than the whole of the land tax of Scotland. Pressure by English distillers led eventually to an iniquitous tax of £9 sterling per gallon being levied in Scotland as compared with 2s 6d in England and output declined. In 1841 they were feeding around 700 cattle. Kilbagie was sold to become a fertiliser plant in the mid 19th century and then bought by J.A.Weir Ltd. and developed as a paper works. James Stein's Kilbagie House still exists. Kennetpans, after ironically doing duty as a home for "those of intemperate habits", has been demolished, only the walled kitchen garden remaining. The shells of the great malting and storage barns are still to be seen as is the wreck of the little harbour and its attendant tree-crowned flat hillock composed of the ballast dumped by the ships as they came in to load. It was for Stein of Kilbagie that George Meikle, its inventor, erected the first threshing mill.

KINCARDINE
"At the head of the Wood."

In the past known as West Pans from the salt pans it once possessed, its name changed as it grew in importance, the "wood" presumably being the once great wood of Clackmannan. Kincardine was a grand ferry point and port on the Forth. In 1793 the ferry passage was only possible within the two hours before and after flood water that they could pass with a horse, foot passengers being often obliged to wade through forty yards of mud. Piers were built in 1826/7 and by 1840 two steamers were providing a five minute service. The roadstead could contain 100 ships and it was a regular port of call for Forth steamers and ships from abroad with iron ore, flax and linseed being imported from the Continent, and coal being exported. In the early 1800s it was also important for shipbuilding, up to fifteen vessels being built at a time. Besides saltworks it also possessed a distillery, brewery, rope and sail works, and collieries. The old Market cross bears the arms of the Elgin family. The nearby quarry of Longannet provided excellent sandstone and was

used for the Register House and Royal Exchange (now the City Chambers) in Edinburgh. Land was reclaimed on either side by the building of two extensive embankments to the east and west. The nearby Tulliallan Castle was owned by the Blackadders, the estate being purchased by Admiral Sir George Keith-Elphinstone who built the mansion house now used as a Police College. The building of the Road Bridge in 1936 has had the unfortunate consequence of slicing the town in two. Its centre swivelling span ceased operating in 1992.

KINROSS
"Head of the promontory"

Kinross is mentioned as early as 1195, a church being built by 1240. The original village lay on the promontory where Kinross House and the old graveyard are situated. Kinross became a county in 1426 and a burgh of barony in 1540. Kinross-shire was further enlarged in 1685. The same year saw the completion of Kinross House by its owner and architect, Sir William Bruce, apparently conceived as a possible residence for James VII. It replaced a house known as New House, a seat of the Douglas Earls of Morton, which, from the name, presumably replaced an older one. The house was sold in 1777 to a George Graham.

LOCH LEVEN
Possibly Gaelic leamhan "elm tree"

A natural loch of some 4,300 acres its surface area was reduced between 1826 and 1836, under a scheme proposed by Thomas Graham of Kinross House and carried out by a John Bell, to some 3,400 acres by means of a New Cut or drainage ditch with sluices, the water level being lowered from between 5 to 9 feet, the difference being used to supply flax mills and bleachfields on the river. The original four islands – Castle Island, Inch or St Serf's, Alice's Bower or possibly Reed Bower, and Paddock Bower – were much enlarged, Paddock Bower merging with the mainland. Scart Island, Roy's Folly, Reed (or Alice's) Bower, and Green Island were created. Castle Island, a seat of the Douglas family, – a "castle" may have existed here as early as A.D. 500 – was noted for the imprisonment of Mary, Queen of Scots in 1567 and her consequent escape. It was here that she was forced to abdicate in favour of her son and possibly gave birth to still-born twins. Inch Island, which contains a cell possibly that of St Serf, was occupied by Culdee monks by A.D. 600 or 700, their possessions – including seventeen valuable manuscript books – being confiscated by Bishop Robert of St Andrews in 1146 and handed over to Augustinian Canons. Franciscan monks may have remained on the island until after the Reformation. One of its priors, Andrew Wyntoun, wrote *The Oryginale Cronykil of Scotland* around 1420. Two skeletons were unearthed in an amateur excavation in 1880. The farm of Portmoak on the mainland, also the site of an ancient church, would appear to have been the landing place. A curious connection seems to have existed with the monks till recent times, the Birrell family of Kinnesswood only ceasing the production of parchment and vellum in the 1930s. The neighbouring hamlet of Scotlandwell may contain the curative well referred to as Fons Scotiae by Tacitus in his account of Agricola's campaign in A.D. 84 Robert the Bruce is said to have bathed in it as a cure for leprosy. Loch Leven was for many years the premier fishing loch in Scotland, noted for its red-fleshed native trout.

LOGIE
"Hollow"

Originally a small village around the ruins of the old church which lay on the road to Sheriffmuir under the yellow cliff known as the Carlin Craig, the inhabitants were removed to "The Heid o' the Causey" under "improvements" to Airthrey by the Haldane family. The old church dates back to at least 1380 and was dedicated like most of others in the Hillfoots to St Serf. A notable minister was Alexander Hume, died 1609, author of the poem *The Day of Estival*. The present Logie Kirk dates from 1805.

MENSTRIE
"Plain house"

The lands seem to have been feued from the Earl of Argyll by the Alexander family, one of whom, William (c.1580-1640), tutor to the young Prince Henry, was knighted by James VI and created Earl of Stirling by Charles I in 1633.

Charles also granted him some 40,000 square miles in Canada with the right of a grant of money and 30,000 acres of land along with a baronetcy to anyone willing to send out settlers. The ancient ceremony of handing over a handful of earth from the gifted lands was accomplished by creating a portion of earth at Edinburgh Castle part of Nova Scotia. William was also an accomplished poet but such accomplishments were of little use to him for he died in debt in London in 1640 and his creditors refused to allow burial of his lead coffin in the High Kirk at Stirling, it apparently lying outside for a hundred years. It was, presumably, his father who, in the 16th century, built the large mansion house known as Menstrie Castle which was only saved from demolition in recent years through a campaign led by the actor, Moultrie Kelsall. The Alexanders sold the estate to General James Holborne in 1649 and his descendants sold it to the Abercromby family in 1719. It was more probably in Menstrie than Tullibody that Sir Ralph Abercrombie, hero of the Battle of Aboukir in Egypt, was born. The last member of the Holborne family, Miss Mary Holborne, who died in 1882, left money to endow Menstrie Parish Church and to found the Holborne of Menstrie Museum and Art Gallery in Bath. One of the earliest of the Ochil woollen mills was built here in 1800 by the three Archibald brothers of Tullibody. The large Elmbank Mill was built in 1865 for a George Drummond who was succeeded by James Johnstone. Johnstone built the imposing baronial mansion of Broomhall. Burnt in 1940 when in use as a boarding school, it was long an imposing ruin until recently restored as a nursing home, although it is presently being sold.

MILNATHORT
"Mill of ?"

Originally a small hamlet at the loch side, the present town dates from around 1700, Orwell church dating to 1709. The main proprietors were William Bruce of Kinross House and Lord Burleigh. Burleigh Castle, a seat of the Balfour family, was traditionally founded in 1434. A Robert Burleigh in 1709, thwarted in love, shot his rival, Henry Stenhouse, the schoolmaster at Inverkeithing, and was sentenced to be beheaded but escaped and joined the Jacobites in 1715 only to be attainted.

MUCKHART MILL

The site of a mill here dates back to at least the 14th century. At one time owned by the monks of Loch Leven at the Restoration it came under the control of the Douglases and then James Paton, minister of Muckhart. A tithe in the form of oatmeal was paid to the Duke of Argyll. The mill wheel has a diameter of twenty-one feet and is one of the largest in Scotland but the interior workings have long been removed. Both the mill and the adjacent lime-kiln are listed buildings. The bridge has an eye on it, possibly to protect it from the ravages of floods. Now private houses, the mill was recently run as a guest-house for children by Richard and Morna Elmhirst, the former the brother of the founder of Dartington Hall, and the latter the first woman assistant stage manager in London and widow of the actor and poet Stephen Haggard, a great-nephew of the novelist Rider Haggard.

PITGOBER

There seem to have been at least four Pitgobers – Easter Pitgober (the present Pitgober), Wester Pitgober (Westerton Farm), Middleton of Pitgober (Middleton Farm), and a Hilton of Pitgober. "Pit" is taken to be an indication of a Pictish settlement with usually a personal name attached. These were all originally farmtouns – small settlements with the land farmed in common – and the present Pitgober, despite its updating, suggests what such a toun looked like. A large modern house has recently been built on the site of an old cottage named on maps as "Greenhead". Westerton and Middleton represent "improved" versions where the toun has been turned into one farm with its farmhouse and attendant steading. Westerton is also interesting as probably representing two stages in this process with at first a small farmhouse facing an L-shaped steading having a larger two-storeyed house, facing south, later added to it. The larger house bears an unidentified coat-of-arms above the door possibly transferred from another building. Westerton had a round horse-driven threshing mill which has been demolished. Middleton appears to have had a mill worked by water power.

Muckhart Mill - DM 1905

A charter by David, Cardinal and Archbishop of St Andrews, dated the 16th January 1542/3, grants the lands of Balrudry, "Pitgoger", and Blairhill in the barony of Muckhart and regality of St Andrews to Archibald, Earl of Argyll. He in turn, of course, feued these to minor tenants. That such a tenant, even of the old touns, was by no means a poor man is illustrated by a charter given at Stirling on the 3rd June 1569 by Argyll to John Sharp:

John Scharp in feu farm an 1/8 of Eistertoun of Pitgober = 1/32 of the lands of Pitgober with 1/32 of the hill of Pitgober called Cornehill, with common pasture at the furthest hill called the Utterhill of Pitgober or the Grisehill beginning at the first part at the head of Gregesburn and following that to the Quoy, hence to the foot of Roughcleuchburne and up that to source; there by the marsh called the moss to source of Aachlinskyburne where a cross stood, then west to Clatteryfurd at the source of Graneburne, and down that to the march of Castleton (a wall or dyke) in barony of Mukcart regality of St Andrews and shire of Perth. To be held in feu farm in capite of the earl for yearly payment to his superiors, the bishops of St Andrews of 19/- Scots, and to the Earl and his successors 2 bolls 1$\frac{1}{2}$ pecks of barley. 2 firlots and a $\frac{1}{4}$ peck oatmeal between Christmas and Candlemas, delivering in granary in Dollar in same of feu duty with

3 suits in the court of the barony of Mukcart; also 40/- Scots for whatever herezeld shall fall due, and 5 marks as duplication on entry of said heir. Also to carry pro rata with other tenants in Mukcart from the Pow of Alloa to Castle Campbell 1/8 of the wine to be drunk there and also pro rata furnish 8 horsemen with lances and 4 baggage horses for war when necessary. Witnesses Mr John Hutoun, John Wood etc . . .

The area can be easily worked out on a large-scale map, bearing in mind that Gregesburn will run by Greig's Grave. Why a cross should be at the source of the Achlinskyburn is not known unless this was Upper Achlinsky. If wood it will have perished, if stone it may have been toppled by Reformers.

RUMBLING BRIDGE, THE DEVIL'S MILL AND THE CAULDRON LINN

The bridge takes its name from the cataract of the River Devon, forming part of the Falls of the Devon, commencing at the Devil's Mill, some three hundred yards further up. The Mill is said to emit a clacking sound like that of a grinding mill while below the bridge it was said to resemble the rumbling of wagons. Both sounds have been much muted by the building of reservoirs. The bridge is about 120 feet above the river and was constructed in 1816 above an earlier one of some 22-foot span constructed by William Gray, a native of Saline, in 1713 to replace a wooden bridge. The 1713 bridge apparently had no parapets and coaches were led over while the passengers followed on foot. It is still visible below the later one and on completion of the 1816 bridge a celebration meal was held below it on the old bridge. A riverside walk has recently been restored. The Pigeon Cave near the bridge is also known as McEachern's Cave after Hector McEachern, a captured Jacobite, who after 1745 was imprisoned in Castle Campbell. Helped by Hannah Haig of Blairhill and a castle guard, named Allan Cameron, McEachern escaped and was hidden in the cave. Later recaptured and tried at Carlisle, McEachern was sentenced to death and Hannah, who had travelled down to be with him, fell ill. He was, however, reprieved on a technicality, and returned north to marry Hannah. The story has never been validated but the names bear the semblance of truth.

The river now flows through the Blairhill estate which belonged to a branch of the Haig family, being sold in 1953. The house, destroyed by fire in 1955, had done service to Dr Barnardo's and the Polish Army during World War II. The river narrows here to about twelve feet before plunging some forty feet into the Cauldron Linn, a series of four circular cavities (in the first and largest of which the water appears to boil) before finally ejecting in another forty-foot fall into the river. The falls were used to provide hydro-electric power to Blairhill House – a replacement for a private gasometer – and till recently large rusting iron pipes spouting water through their leaks were fastened to the left hand cliff. Their remains and that of the concrete generating station were visible but have now been replaced by a modern hydro-electric scheme supplying power to the Grid. Accordingly much of the strange fascination of the place has been lost. At present the Linn remains difficult and somewhat dangerous to approach. Stepping stones apparently once crossed the river above the Linn and a Mr Harrower of Inzievar is reputed to have missed his footing and been swept into the cauldrons. He survived and was rescued. *Gibson*, however, reports that an uncle of his was drowned attempting a similar crossing.

SAUCHIE
"Place of willows"

The present "New Sauchie" was a small mining village, little of which remains. Old Sauchie lay by Sauchie Tower, 1430, erected by the Schaws who took possession about that date, the earliest known grant being by Robert the Bruce to Henri de Annand in 1321. The land passed by marriage to the Cathcart family in 1752. The first Earl of Cathcart was ambassador to Russia during the Napoleonic Wars. The Schaws built a mansion house by the tower in 1631 but around 1700 they moved to a new mansion at Schawpark. There are plans to reconstruct the tower, but the mansions were demolished in the 1950s. The nearby Devon Iron Works were founded by Dr John Roebuck of Kinneil House and Mr Eddison of Bo'ness in 1792, much of the structure being quarried out of the rock of the bank into which the works were set. Local iron ore and coal were used, limestone being brought from South Queensferry. At its height three furnaces were in operation producing from 6,000-10,000 tons of pig iron annually, much of it being converted to pipes and shot and shell in the foundry. The works closed in 1856. The large spoil heap from the nearby Devon Colliery has recently been removed and the land reclaimed but the Beam Engine House with its cast-iron beam and pump of 1865 has been preserved.

Rumbling Bridge - DMus

TILLICOULTRY
"Hillock in the back land"

A tiny village mentioned in the chartulary of Cambuskenneth as being known for its woollen products in the 16th century, it remained small until a John Christie erected the first woollen mill in 1792. Eighteen factories, large and small, are mentioned as being in production in 1886, the parish population in 1881 being 5,344. At first producing the noted Tillicoultry serges and blankets, tartans and shawls were introduced in 1824, to be followed later by tweeds and silks. J & D Patons' mill, which has still survived, was once the most productive in Scotland. J & R Archibalds' Devonvale Mill, used as a barracks during World War I, was bought in 1920 by Samuel Jones as a papercoating plant, and of recent years has been run by the Knowles family as an enormous furniture retail store. Tillicoultry Quarry has demolished the eminence known as Castle Craig which was topped by a hillfort and, apparently, had the remains of an ancient castle at the foot. A stone circle and another sandy eminence known as the Cunninghar to the east were also demolished. The estate seems to have been granted to the Mar family by Alexander III but was in the Colville family from 1483 to 1634, after which it passed through many hands. Of Tillicoultry House, built in 1829 and demolished in 1938, only the converted stable block remains. The Tillicoultry Mains Farm steading has recently been restored as the Harviestoun Inn. St Serf's Parish Church, 1827, replaced an older church, the site of which is to be found in the old kirkyard on the hill opposite. A stone circle lay opposite the present church.

TULLIALLAN
"Hillock of Allan" see Kincardine.

TULLIBODY
"Hillock of the hut"

Formerly a small village, it had claims to be founded by Kenneth McAlpine who fought a battle here against the Picts in 844. The church was founded by David I in 1149 along with Cambuskenneth Abbey. In 1559 French troops in the employ of the Royalist forces removed the roof to use as a replacement for the bridge across the Devon destroyed by Kirkcaldy of Grange and the Reformers. The church was later re-roofed and used as a mausoleum by the Abercromby family. The Maiden Stone reputedly marks an ill-fated romance between a priest, Peter Beaton, and Martha Wishart of Myreton, who instructed that her stone coffin lie outside the church door to remind him of his deceit. Sir Ralph Abercromby, hero of the Battle of Aboukir in Egypt, may have been born at Tullibody House, an attractive large 18th century mansion house demolished in the 1960s, rather than at Menstrie.

TULLIBOLE
"Hillock + ?"

The castle appears to have been owned in 1473 by James Hering of Glascune, being sold in 1598 to John Halliday, an advocate, whose son, also John, seems to have built or rebuilt the castle, marking the event with the initials of himself and his wife, Margaret Oliphant. It was bought by a Henry Wellwood in 1749 who conveyed it to the son of his niece, Sir Henry Moncreiff Wellwood on condition he adopted the Wellwood name. It is still in the same family although the Wellwood has been dropped. It is said that on a visit by a king a drinking match took place here between a Royal Trooper and a vassal of the Laird, named Keltie. On the trooper falling prostrate Keltie took another draught and joined him. Keltie survived but the trooper died leading to the local phrase "Keltie's Mends" being applied to rejected or hurtful drink. The trooper was buried near a subsequently haunted pool named the "Trooper's Dub".

VICAR'S BRIDGE

This bridge was reputedly ordered built by Thomas Forrest, the Vicar of Dollar burnt as a heretic around 1540, as a replacement for stepping stones on the Devon further down-stream to assist his parishioners' attendance at church in times of spate. Originally of wood, it was later replaced by one of stone only nine feet broad without parapets, like the lower arch at Rumbling Bridge. It was widened by about six feet in 1765 by the then owner of Devonshaw who had a stone tablet – preserved near the present bridge – inserted on the western face reading: "Sacred to the Memory of Thomas Forrest the Worthy Vicar of Dollar who among other acts of benevolence built this bridge. He died a martyr A.D. 1538." The widened bridge was still without sufficient parapets, the Dollar Register of Burials recording: "19th November 1787, John Kirk of Balzeman, thrown from a

Horse over Vicker's Bridge into the Water of Dovan on 15th November and drowned." In 1830 Mr Colville of Barnhill was also thrown from his horse over the parapet but was rescued by a noted poacher, Auld Rab of Blairingone (*Dollar Magazine* No.60). After this two-foot parapets were added but still proved inadequate for in 1876, when four men were returning in a two-horse trap from a funeral at Blairingone, the horses swerved and one of them with the driver fell into the river, the driver being drowned. The parapets were then raised another foot. It is little wonder that about the middle of the 19th century a local doctor by the name of McQueen travelling that way on horseback swore he saw a ghost and refused to cross the bridge ever after. Strangely, around 1860, halfway up the hill to Blairingone, a local carter by the name of McQueen was shot and robbed by a Joseph Bell who later gave himself away by spending the scanty proceeds of the robbery. A small oak tree – it hardly seems large enough – on the banking up near the railway bridge bears the initials JB carved at the base and was reputedly the tree behind which Bell hid. Although only a sordid little murder, Bell's execution at Perth was long believed to be the last public hanging in Scotland. It has recently has been replaced by the discovery of a later one at Dumfries. It aroused sufficient local interest apparently for one noted Dollar worthy to spend his honeymoon attending the trial. It may be his annotated copy of the proceedings that is filed in the Academy archives.

Dollar's oldest living inhabitant?

INDEX

148

Index